THE JAIDYN LESKIE MURDER

THE JAIDYN LESKIE MURDER

michael gleeson

HarperCollins*Publishers*

HarperCollinsPublishers

First published in Australia in 1999
This revised edition published in 2007
by HarperCollinsPublishers Australia Pty Limited
ABN 36 009 913 517
www.harpercollins.com.au

Copyright © Michael Gleeson 1999, 2007

The right of Michael Gleeson to be identified as the author of this work has been asserted by him under the Copyright Amendment (Moral Rights) Act 2000.

This work is copyright.
Apart from any use as permitted under the Copyright Act 1968, no part may be reproduced, copied, scanned, stored in a retrieval system, recorded, or transmitted, in any form or by any means, without the prior written permission of the publisher.

HarperCollinsPublishers
25 Ryde Road, Pymble, Sydney, NSW 2073, Australia
31 View Road, Glenfield, Auckland 10, New Zealand
77-85 Fulham Palace Road, London W6 8JB, United Kingdom
2 Bloor Street East, 20th floor, Toronto, Ontario M4W 1A8, Canada
10 East 53rd Street, New York NY 10022, USA

National Library of Australia Cataloguing-in-Publication data:

Gleeson, Michael, 1969– .
    The Jaidyn Leskie murder.
    ISBN 13: 978 0 7322 8087 1.
    ISBN 10: 0 7322 8087 7.
    1. Leskie, Jaidyn. 2. Murder – Investigation – Australia
    3. Murder – Australia – Case studies. I. Title.
364.1523

Cover photographs courtesy of Newspix
Typeset in Bembo 10/13pt

Preface

Sunday, 15 June 1997 was a bleak morning. Drizzling and cold. *Herald Sun* photographer Darryl Gregory and I were driving around Lakes Entrance in eastern Victoria desperately searching for police drug raids. We'd had a tip the raids were going on that morning and, sure enough, they were – we just couldn't find them. We were facing the embarrassing prospect of returning to the office empty-handed, when we learnt from local police that a child was missing in nearby Moe. Details were sketchy, as is the way with these things, but what was known was both disturbing and compelling. A little boy was missing, apparently abducted. He'd been staying with his mum's boyfriend while she was at the pub. However, there was also an extraordinary twist in the tale: a severed pig's head was found at the house.

Soon the name of the little boy was revealed as police appealed to the public for help in finding the missing toddler. Jaidyn Raymond Leskie, 13 months and two weeks old, became a familiar name throughout Australia as the child's short, troubled history came under the spotlight and the events leading up to his disappearance became apparent.

As details emerged over days and weeks the story saddened and enthralled people nationwide. Little Jaidyn was missing, and the story behind his disappearance seemed too bizarre to be true. A pig's head was found along with smashed windows at the house from which the boy went missing, where he had been left home alone by the babysitter. What was its significance? Why would a mother leave her tiny toddler alone while she went out and got drunk in the first place? Why would that babysitter go out and leave the child on its own in a house? And how could the police insist the pig's head and the child's disappearance were not connected? But more than anything, the most important question remained: where was Jaidyn?

For the next month Darryl and I lived in Moe covering the story for the *Herald Sun*. The level of public interest escalated rapidly as the police hunt for Jaidyn became the largest hunt the state had undertaken since former Prime Minister Harold Holt disappeared 30 years earlier. The subculture of drugs, unemployment, incestuous relationships, violence and crime that was uncovered was shocking and raised questions of national conscience.

It soon became apparent the Victoria Police homicide squad's prime suspect was the babysitter, Greg Domaszewicz. But everyone had their own opinion. In the first instance, Jaidyn's uncle felt, quite understandably, that the pig's head was an occult symbol. That idea was soon scotched. Many felt the pig's head gang simply had to be involved. Others felt Bilynda, Jaidyn's mother, must have had some knowledge of who was behind it. Everyone developed their own theory and seemed to have their own bit of inside knowledge. Rumours abounded and urban myths quickly evolved. When Greg Domaszewicz was charged and subsequently tried, the lies, rumours and false assertions did not let up, indeed fuel was added to the fire.

It was in this environment I felt the full story of the case needed to be told and I decided to write a book setting out the context as well as the details of Jaidyn's death.

When on New Year's Day Jaidyn's body was discovered in Blue Rock Dam, it only answered the question of Jaidyn's whereabouts. The equally vexing question was left: who killed Jaidyn?

Greg Domaszewicz stood trial for the murder in October–December 1998. It is often said by those with a passing

Preface

knowledge of the case that the police didn't have sufficient evidence for a conviction. This is patently correct. It is also said at times the police botched the investigation, or that they had it in for Greg from the start.

This book chronicles the evidence against Greg, it puts the case against him and helps explain both why he was charged and why he was acquitted. It also explains how it was that the Coroner could subsequently conclude that Greg had disposed of Jaidyn's body without concluding that Greg had killed him. When the courts are unable to be definitive about what happened to Jaidyn, we cannot hope to explain who killed the boy. What we can do is unravel the tangled threads and present the facts; then it is for you to make up your own mind.

Michael Gleeson

Acknowledgments

I would like to thank a great number of people for their help, cooperation and encouragement in writing this book.

Firstly, a debt of gratitude is owed to the Leskie and Murphy families for their assistance throughout the entire ordeal. In particular Bilynda Murphy and Brett Leskie for their cooperation and help when they just wanted the whole nightmare to go away.

Also, enormous thanks to the Victoria Police Force for agreeing to cooperate and for their professionalism throughout the investigation. I would especially like to thank Detective Senior Sergeant Rowland Legg, who led the Homicide investigation, for his role in helping with research, sacrificing his own personal time. I also want to thank the other members of the Homicide crew, Detective Sergeants Steve Fyffe and Mick Roberts, Senior Detectives Paul Cripps and Russell Sheather, and Senior Detective Geoff Rumble of the Morwell CIB. Special thanks also to Nicole Hughes and James Tonkin of the police media unit, the head of the homicide squad Detective Chief Inspector Rod Collins, Trevor Evans of the forensic unit and Senior Constable Oscar Aertson who coordinated the search in and around Moe.

Thanks also to Noel and Karlene Huggins of the Moe Motor Inn for their unfailing hospitality during my lengthy stays in Moe, and to Henrietta Katz for her help.

I especially want to thank the staff of the *Herald Sun* newspaper for the help and encouragement I have been given.

Firstly, thanks to Nick Richardson for his editing, advice and enthusiasm throughout. Similarly, thanks to photographer Darryl Gregory for his great work in Moe and his help in compiling the photo spread. Thanks also to *Herald Sun* editor Peter Blunden for his support, to Laurie Nowell for giving me time to work on the book, and to Wayne Ludbey in helping with the photo spread. Sincere thanks also to *Herald Sun* Supreme Court Reporter Norrie Ross and to Nicole Garmston.

Thanks to my family, to Jeff Gleeson for his legal and literary advice and finally an enormous debt of gratitude is owed to my patient wife Michelle Edmunds for her love and support.

Since the first edition of the book was printed we have had two boys, Joseph and Rafferty, who have given a new personal perspective on the terrible, sad story of Jaidyn's life and death.

The Main Players

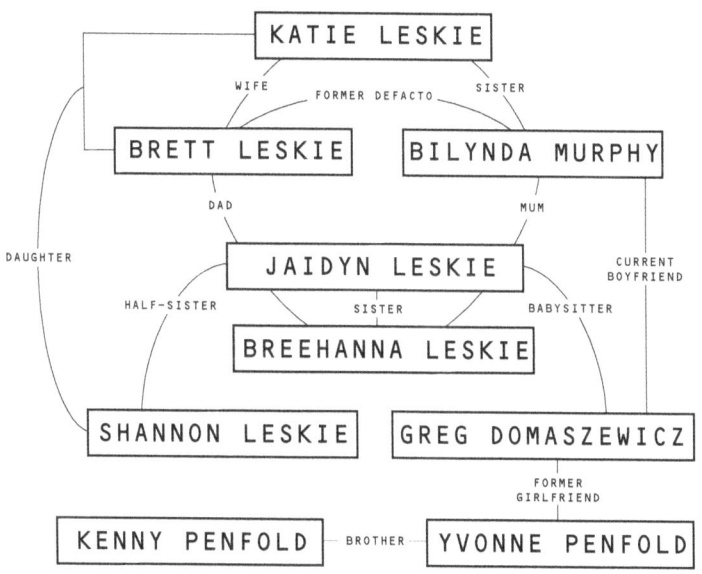

CHAPTER

Bilynda Murphy was sprawled across the floor of her lounge room in front of the heater, snoring. Her matted bottle-blonde hair was strewn across her face as she lay in the deep, heavy sleep of the recently passed-out drunk.

She was roused from the thick fog by several hard slaps across the face. She opened her eyes and tried to focus. Greg Domaszewicz was leaning over her, imploring her to wake up. Pale and crying, his straggly mouse-brown hair, bald at the front, was hanging in his face as he frantically yelled at her, "I've lied to ya, I've lied to ya, Jaidyn's not in hospital, he's missing."

Bilynda struggled to her feet, collecting her thoughts and trying to remember how she had come to be asleep on the floor. The two of them hugged, Bilynda not quite sure what had upset Greg but hugging him anyway. He said they'd better go to the police station.

The couple left the Lincoln Street house and drove quickly to Moe police station in Greg's old Ford Falcon. It was some time around 5.00 a.m. when the pair pushed through the door of the station and approached the counter.

Senior Constable Farnham Molesworth saw Mr Domaszewicz fidgeting nervously, his face pallid and anxious. Ms Murphy by his side was lolling about, obviously drunk.

Greg Domaszewicz was flustered as he stumbled through

telling the police that a 14-month-old boy had gone. Disappeared. Abducted. The police asked which boy. Greg pointed to Bilynda Murphy and said, "Hers."

Senior Constable Molesworth asked Greg to explain what had happened.

"I went to pick up my girlfriend," he said. "When I got back, someone had smashed all the windows and there is a pig's head outside the window."

The police asked Greg when all this had occurred and he replied, "about five minutes ago". He had only left the baby for "about five minutes" while he went to collect his girlfriend, he added.

Bilynda stood in the cramped foyer of the police station, overwhelmed by the surreal sensation of being a bystander in her own drama. She had heard her lover tell the copper her little boy was missing. "Don't worry about him, he's just a dickhead, Jaidyn's in hospital. I don't know why we're here," was all she could say.

Greg was sobbing while he pleaded that he was serious and kept repeating that there was a boy missing.

The young senior constable called his superior, Sergeant Max Hill, who emerged from a back room to speak with the couple. Hill was immediately worried that their stories didn't tally. Had the boy been abducted, or was he in hospital?

"Why did you take so long to report it?" he asked.

"I don't know, I don't know," Greg cried.

Sergeant Hill decided to act, sending two officers straight to Greg's house. The couple were brought through the station into a room, where they were sat down together for a matter of moments before being separated. Hill did not want to give them time to discuss the case.

Bilynda found herself in a cold interview room, still drunk. The whole thing was making no sense. Her child wasn't missing. No way. It was only Grishka, her mad boyfriend,

Chapter One

playing another prank. Jaidyn was okay; he just had a burnt bum. What was this copper on about, saying her little boy was dead and that Grishka had killed him? How could they know?

Outside, Sunday morning was cold and drab. The police station was no place to be; Bilynda just wanted to be warm and asleep, shut off from these crazy coppers whirling past her making claims she couldn't understand and didn't want to. She didn't even know what homicide meant; she thought it was some kind of special police.

A large policeman in a suit came into the room and challenged Bilynda, slamming his hand on the bench.

"I haven't done anything wrong," she protested.

"That maggot in the next room has killed your kid and smashed the windows to make it look like somebody else has done it," he seethed and left.

Bilynda was dumbfounded; she didn't know if Greg had confessed or not. She was becoming claustrophobic and restless. If Jaidyn really was missing, she wanted to be doing something to help find him.

The day dragged on; her hangover was slowly replaced by a gnawing fear. By the time she left the police station at 10.00 p.m., Bilynda didn't know what to believe.

"I didn't even believe it until that night when I saw Jaidyn's picture on the news and I thought 'maybe this is real'."

CHAPTER

The small industrial town of Moe nestles in the rich Latrobe Valley of south-eastern Victoria, some 140 kilometres from Melbourne. The descent into the valley from the lush farming districts of South-East Gippsland is barely perceptible, and it's not really until you pass Moe and ascend the Haunted Hills that the differences become apparent. Grazing cattle are replaced by power stations, their smokestacks prodding the sky, and the air of the farming districts is permanently powdered with steam clouds billowing from giant chimneys.

The social contrast is equally stark. Moe is not a service provider for the local farming districts; it is an industrial town. The people don't speak with the weary drawl of the farmer looking upward for rains or wondering about the drop in wool prices. Instead, conversations are littered with adenoidal concern for generators, turbines and night shifts.

Opportunity shops are common in Moe; they collect around the train and police stations and are among the most thriving businesses in town. But the main street looks much like any shopping strip in the working-class suburbs of an Australian city.

White-collar workers hustle between shops and cars, elderly people struggle for their groceries and a chat, while tracksuited young women push baby-strollers through the mall. Others, not

Chapter Two

at school and not at work, sit chatting with friends. There is no work. Or what work there is, they can't get or don't want.

The highway to Melbourne has long since bypassed the town and so do most people. Moe, derived from the aboriginal word 'Moia' or 'Mouay', meaning muddy or swamp, lies isolated in its valley. With food and petrol available from stores on the highway, there is little to draw traffic into town.

But the train still comes. The line that links the town with Melbourne to the west, and the rest of the valley to the east, cuts through the centre of Moe. A railway bridge straddles a huge roundabout in the heart of town, but it's a heart that has been broken by the twin effects of privatisation and unemployment.

Until the early part of the decade, Moe was almost recession-proof: sedate, socially balanced, and affluent. Parts of the town still are, where proud weatherboard homes with manicured gardens line the streets.

In better times, the valley's open-cut brown coal mines and the State Electricity Corporation's power stations employed the bulk of workers in town. And while the state owned the power company, Moe prospered.

With privatisation, however, came redundancy and with redundancy, recession. While some argue that massive redundancy payouts created a cash injection for the town and that, in any case, many workers were re-employed as contractors, unemployment in Moe remains high. Employment for contractors can be irregular, and one of the few growth industries in town has been gambling, particularly poker machines.

Post-privatisation, an exodus of workers meant a drop in housing prices in some areas; houses built for power station workers were vacated and for a long time stayed that way. Complete homes could be bought for just $10,000 in areas known locally as 'The Bronx' where, like its New York counterpart, police are regular visitors. This part of town is not far from where Bilynda Murphy and Katie Leskie lived.

Better quality homes in better areas of town – and it is not to overstate the situation, there *are* better areas of Moe – sell for more than $200,000. But the majority of homes for sale are in the lower bracket, which can start at as little as $25,000.

It was in this environment that the government developed a policy of assisting the relocation of single mothers to the town. The idea was that with the low cost of living, welfare payments would go further. If a mortgage could be serviced on less than $100 a week, it was feasible to be on welfare and still pay off a home.

The consequences on the social fabric of the area were profound and unpredictable. Pockets of socially dislocated groups emerged and grew. Some conventions of modern life went by the wayside. For many, the concept of work was foreign, that marriage would end in divorce was a natural assumption, and drug use was endemic, feeding a sense of persecution and helplessness.

The point is not to identify Moe as an exception, for it is not. It is no different in that regard to many other places in Australia – the industrial towns of Queensland and Tasmania, for example, differ in climate only.

Scratch the surface of any society, or group in society, and disenfranchised people will be found. We generally choose not to scratch, so it is only when there is an itch that it is uncovered. In Moe, Jaidyn Leskie became that itch.

CHAPTER THREE

Bilynda Robynne Murphy was born on 22 September 1975 in the large town of Bairnsdale, eastern Victoria. Her mother was the teenaged daughter of a policeman, her father a timber mill worker. The unusual spelling of her name arose because her mum had always wanted a boy that she could call Billy; she sort of got her way.

Bilynda was the second child. She had a sister three years older, Katie Ellen Murphy, who later, in an act of rebellion against a high school teacher, but in keeping with the family's penchant for unorthodox spellings, changed her name to Kadee.

Bilynda's family life was turbulent. Her father was often drunk and more often violent. They shifted to Myrtleford in 1977 where her younger brother Glenn was born. Pam would regularly throw her husband out of the home, but it would not be long before he would be back and she would take him in and the revolving door kept spinning. Eventually, Pam gathered up her brood and fled to Lakes Entrance, getting rid of her husband for good.

But it wasn't all sweetness and light once Pam, Glenn, Bilynda and Katie were free of Mr Murphy's drunken rages. The family stayed on the move through central and eastern Victoria before Katie, at fourteen, ran away for the first time.

Given her family's continual moving and difficulties in the home, Katie was anxious to grab her first opportunity to get out. While many teenagers take off for a night or two to provoke their parents into a demonstration of love, Katie doesn't seem to have been so motivated. Most kids return for a home-cooked meal and the warmth of their own bed; Katie eventually came home because her mum would buy her smokes when no one else would.

At sixteen, she ran away again, this time to visit a girlfriend in Moe. It was on this jaunt, while drunk at a party, that she met Brett Leskie. She gave him a poor 'score' out of ten when he walked in, deeming him too rough around the edges, but Brett was soon able to chat her up. They spent all of the next day in bed together.

Later, they headed to Pam's place for a few days so Katie could show off her new boyfriend. It was here that Brett Leskie and the very young Bilynda Murphy met for the first time.

The relationship between the Murphy sisters, known by some as Niff and Naff, is like that of many sisters; there is a love there, but not one that tolerates them spending much time together.

A strong rivalry between the two created tension. Bilynda, the younger, prettier girl, resented her elder sister's freedom and independence. At a time when Katie was out drinking and partying, Bilynda was at home caring for their sick mother. Katie, for her part, had always struggled with her sister's looks and temper.

Katie's relationship with Brett stumbled along, before they eventually moved into Brett's parents' house, on a dairy share-farm, where they helped to milk the cows and paid board while drawing welfare benefits.

It is difficult to imagine a more uncomfortable arrangement. Brett's parents, Ray and Elizabeth Leskie, were extremely devout churchgoing Baptists and it was just five months before Katie moved out.

She rejoined Pam and Bilynda, and they shifted to Moruya

Chapter Three

in New South Wales. They lived there for four years, the longest time Bilynda had spent in one place.

While living in Moruya, Pam had a stroke that paralysed her down one side and put her in hospital for several months. Bilynda was just sixteen when she began looking after her mother. Adulthood, or a form of it, was thrust upon her.

Katie became anxious within weeks of the move to Moruya and headed back to Victoria where she again bumped into Brett Leskie, this time at the drag races at Lakes Entrance. They spent a couple of days together in a caravan park.

Katie returned to Moruya pregnant, but not to Brett, and soon after, the Murphys were on their way back to Victoria to live with friends in Sale. It was here that Katie again met up with Brett Leskie. Brett saw that she was an expecting mother and presumed the baby was his. Katie didn't say otherwise and when he proposed marriage, to 'do the right thing', Katie accepted.

Bilynda always believed that Katie had tricked Brett into thinking the child was his. But she also believes that Brett had his own motives. He was facing jail after allegedly stealing some cheques from his boss. In court, he pleaded that he had a new young family to support and the magistrate acted leniently.

The wedding was a modest affair, Katie dressed in a second-hand debutante gown, their rings bought from a pawn shop in Morwell. A Baptist minister married the couple in the front yard of Ray and Elizabeth Leskie's farmhouse before a small gathering of friends and family.

While all of Katie's family had originally said they would not attend the wedding, only Bilynda kept her nerve and declined the invitation. They wanted her to wear a dress but Bilynda could not bring herself to look so girlish.

Elizabeth Leskie, however, thought otherwise about Bilynda's absence; she twigged that Bilynda wanted Brett for herself. Mrs Leskie had seen up close the unusual way in which the Murphy family operated: an argument would be followed by a filthy letter or an abusive phone call, but the following day, all would be friends again.

Brett Leskie's father, Ray, is a reserved man, typical of many that work the land. He is sparse with praise and offers criticism of people as often as he does optimistic weather forecasts. But he takes a dim view of Katie. The brevity of his view on his daughter-in-law belies his feeling. However he didn't say much at the time because, after all, Katie was his son's wife.

He probably wasn't entirely surprised then, that Brett and Katie stayed together for less than a year, maybe eight months. No one can be certain when it all ended. They had spent the first few weeks of married life living with Brett's parents, before they were booted off the farm after Brett had done 'burnouts' in his car on the front lawn.

They lived briefly with Brett's sister, Louise, before renting a house in Yallourn North. The arrangement lasted just long enough for Katie to become pregnant again, this time with Brett's child, a girl who would be called Shannan. However, it was too much for Brett and he suffered a sudden nervous breakdown. While Katie was expecting her second child, Brett could only lie around the house.

It came to a head at their joint twenty-first birthday party in June 1993, with Brett and Katie arguing fiercely. They managed to patch things up during a trip to Lakes Entrance but their relationship soon deteriorated again. Their problems were not helped by the fact that by now Bilynda was living with them.

Katie suspected an affair. And when Bilynda and Brett came back to get some things from the house at Yallourn North, Katie told them they needn't bother coming back.

Elizabeth Leskie wasn't so sure. She thought Bilynda was showing her son a kindness that Katie would not. Brett and Bilynda sought sanctuary with Brett's sister, Louise, however nothing happened between the two at that stage. Katie remained

Chapter Three

bitter about her break-up with Brett and the idea of his relationship with her sister, and things between them soured for a long time.

The Murphy sisters are of above-average height and solid – Bilynda slightly taller, Katie heavier and more powerfully built. The older sister wears a perennial scowl on her face and a mood as black as the mascara around her eyes. A string of earrings ropes down each of her ears.

Bilynda's hair is bleached and partially washed out leaving a dark streak through the roots. She is fond of wearing a silver thumb ring and chunky thick-soled shoes or, when at home, moccasins. Tight jeans and white shirts or crocheted tops complete the look.

Bilynda's relationship with Brett Leskie started a couple of months after her sister's marriage fell apart. A year later the couple had a child, Breehanna, who was named after a checkout girl from the Jewel supermarket in Moe. Although the girl spelt her name Briana, Bilynda wanted to blend it with her grandmother's middle name, Hannah, hence 'Breehanna', keeping alive the family tradition of distinctive names.

At this time, Brett was still married to Katie, so Bilynda was technically both mother and aunt to her own daughter. Brett, with children to both sisters, was father and uncle to both women's children.

In the week of the Port Arthur massacre in Tasmania, a second child was born to Brett and Bilynda, this time a son.

Jaidyn Raymond Leskie was born on 30 April 1996 in Moe hospital. His unusual name was drawn from a good-looking black man that Bilynda had seen on the *Rikki Lake* show.

Brett held his son up to the window and proudly predicted that he was going to be a mechanic as he pointed out a caryard. "See them cars, look," Brett said.

Jaidyn was a cherubic boy who loved to eat and he put on weight easily. He was known as a crier, a 'mummy's boy' who only seemed happy when Bilynda was around. She remembered coming home to Brett and finding Jaidyn crying but, on her arrival, Jaidyn's tears would dry up. Jaidyn's grandparents disagreed that Jaidyn was a crier, suggesting it was just teething or loneliness that made him cry.

Breehanna and Jaidyn were close and got up to the sort of mischief brothers and sisters do: like the occasion when Bilynda rose late and found Breehanna and Jaidyn helping themselves to a packet of Doritos corn chips. Bored with eating, they'd decided to stick the chips to the walls with honey.

The family was used to picking everything up off the floor when Jaidyn was around; otherwise, it would all go into his mouth, food or not. Even the scraps in the chook food bin weren't safe.

Like most children, Jaidyn loved to play with the telephone. He used to try to wrap the cord around his neck. One night, Brett had put him to bed at the farmhouse and when the family checked on him hours later, he had taken some material from the sewing pile in the room and wrapped it around his neck like a scarf. He liked having things wrapped around his neck and preferred to play with junk rather than traditional toys; empty cereal boxes or cordial bottles were more interesting to him than the latest tip truck.

It was at the farmhouse that Jaidyn took his first steps.

Brett Leskie, Bilynda and their two children lived together in Parkin Street, Moe, for several months until just before Jaidyn's first birthday when their relationship deteriorated. Katie, again, was to play a part.

No single event triggered their difficulties. A bitter Bilynda had come to believe that Katie was still in love with Brett, the man that Bilynda now wanted to marry.

"I wanted to marry Brett and Katie is still in love with him to this day. And I wanted a wedding; you know how some girls just go like that Muriel in Muriel's Wedding, a bit overboard

Chapter Three

about it and go out and get the dress, I was a bit like that," Bilynda said.

"I said to Katie, 'He won't marry me' and she was just filling my head with shit saying like, 'It's because he loves me more, because he married me' and all that sort of shit. And she said to me, 'Send him to Western Australia, he has always wanted to go there and if he loves you he will come back'. So I did, but then he didn't come back. He told me he was going over there and he was going to come back. But we did break up before he went."

Not only had they broken up, Bilynda had become involved with another man.

Before leaving for Western Australia, Brett had worked out of a shed-cum-factory in Della Torre Road, Moe; it belonged to a not-so-close friend, Greg Domaszewicz. Brett knew Greg from around town and they had mutual friends.

Greg had been using the shed for a while, almost as a hobby, and was struggling with the rent, so Brett decided to try his hand at small business and volunteered to take half the space. He anxiously points out, however, that the pair were not business partners, and they did not work together, they simply shared a residence. Brett felt that Greg was too lazy to work with and reckoned he'd done just three months work in the last eighteen months at the shed.

All the while, Bilynda and Greg were growing closer. Bilynda liked the fact that Greg took an interest in her son, playing with him and teaching him a few things here and there.

Another force had also been straining the relationship between Brett and Bylinda. Katie had told a number of people that she was going to break them up, and Brett's mum knew it. Brett also knew that if Katie couldn't have him, she would do her best to destroy him and she had told him so.

Given the events that followed, it's difficult now to disentangle fact from the bitterness Bilynda felt toward Brett.

Bilynda alleges Brett had his little princess in Breehanna and cared little for Jaidyn, showing him neither attention nor love. Perhaps it is easier for Bilynda to rationalise things if she recalls that Brett was not a great father to Jaidyn, and that another man wanted to provide a father figure. Either way, her version of events differs greatly to Brett's.

Bilynda believed that Brett had never taught Jaidyn anything, claiming he was "always too busy". Greg, on the other hand, "just took an interest in Jaidyn and me. He took Jaidyn off my hands," Bilynda said.

Greg would frequently offer to look after Jaidyn, not Breehanna, just Jaidyn. His only problem, Bilynda felt, was his reluctance to change nappies. On one occasion, he sent his mate Matthew Walsh home with Jaidyn to Bilynda's house because neither of them knew how to change Jaidyn's nappy, or couldn't face the stench.

Jaidyn's crying made Bilynda glad of the break she got when Greg looked after the boy. She always found it odd that for days after Jaidyn came back from visiting Greg, he wouldn't cry at all. Instead, he'd sleep most of the day and night and even his notorious appetite was gone. She didn't know what Greg did to him; later she said she didn't want to know.

Bylinda's attitude is perhaps partly explained by her own difficulties. Driven to despair by Jaidyn's incessant crying, she had taken him to the Moe Medical Centre more than once. On 2 April he was examined by Dr Kathryn Lesnie-Noakes who could find nothing to justify his incessant crying, and concluded that Jaidyn was a healthy, cheerful boy.

But the grizzling continued and on 21 April Bilynda returned to the centre, where another doctor examined him and took a urine sample. This doctor also found nothing wrong with him. Bilynda began to feel that the problem may have been her own, telling Brett that she thought she was suffering from postnatal depression. Yet this turned out to be a ruse to convince

Chapter Three

him to leave for Western Australia, so that she could begin seeing Greg.

Elizabeth Leskie knew that Greg had started to look after her grandson, and it never sat comfortably with her. She always felt it was strange that a single young man wanted to look after a baby on his own. But like so many things she didn't like about her son's relationships and the way her grandchildren were being raised, there was little she could do about it.

Jaidyn's first birthday came soon after Brett and Bilynda had separated, but the celebrations became yet another source of aggravation. Brett had telephoned Bilynda about the birthday arrangements. She told him: "Oh, we're going to McDonalds with Katie and her kids."

"Well I'd like to be there for my son's birthday," Brett said.

"Oh, no, no, no, it's not a good idea," Bilynda replied.

In the end, they didn't go to McDonalds; Jaidyn and Bilynda spent the day with Greg instead.

Brett managed to see Jaidyn on the weekend before he moved to Western Australia. It was the last time he saw him.

CHAPTER FOUR

Among the rusting car parts, broken concrete and weeds at the back of Greg Domaszewicz's house was a tall, white bucket with a thick plastic lid that sealed tight. It was the type of bucket in which chlorine for swimming pools is stored, but it wasn't full of chlorine. Greg kept this bucket three-quarters full of fish heads and guts; he kept it for his enemies.

When Greg wanted to take revenge on someone, he would take a large syringe full of his foul fish cocktail and inject it into, say, the air conditioning hose outside their house. The stench would be unbearable, and extremely difficult to get rid of.

It seems an extraordinary length to go to for an adolescent prank, but as the pranks got bigger, the consequences became more serious.

Greg Domaszewicz was born in Moe on 26 September 1968 to first generation Russian immigrant parents. He went to the local high school in the suburb of Newborough but dropped out in 1986 before finishing his HSC (now VCE). Greg rarely strayed beyond the Latrobe Valley, only occasionally travelling to Melbourne to visit a cousin.

Moe was Greg's world and he felt uncomfortable outside the valley. He was a small-town guy, with a hankering for a big-town reputation, a tough guy, a little weird and a little wild.

Chapter Four

He was not impressed or intimidated by authority. Once in a senior policeman's office when Greg was being questioned over his breach of an intervention order, he started toying with photos of the officer's family sitting on the desk. Greg picked up the photo and looked at the copper. "Nice kids," he said.

Greg had a close relationship with his family, his brother Peter and his mother Helen Chervev.

His father had died suddenly of a heart attack while he was working at a neighbour's house. Greg had spent that day at home and was preparing for a fishing trip with his dad when the telephone rang.

"Is your Mum there?"

When Greg told her his mother was out, the neighbour said, "Tell her your dad's dead." Greg was fourteen.

The death came in the important final years of school, when distractions were easy to find. And at fifteen, Greg turned his back on school. Life was easier out of the classroom and with the relative wealth of the dole. Maybe it was his dad's death, but Greg fell in with a circle of heavy dope smokers in town.

Greg had always been keen on cars and engines, but his mechanical skills were self-taught; he had never completed a trade, nor had any formal training. With the aid of a Job-Start grant, he opened a shed to do some panel beating, spray painting and repair work. Grishka's Panels, he called it. But it wasn't serious regular work, at least he didn't treat it that way.

Greg's mates know him as a cunning and manipulative character, prone to violence and with an eccentric side to his personality. But he is also a fun, off-beat, impulsive man with a strong love of his animals and music. He has a passion for The Beatles, but also Jimmy Barnes, Sheryl Crow and Alanis Morissette. Like many devoted fans, he has little or no musical talent of his own.

Greg is known as a practical joker, the kind of guy who will tamper with things to take you by surprise. Like turning up the volume of your car stereo while it's off so that when you turn the car on, the radio gives you a start.

Another of his tricks is to borrow a friend's car, then ring and say that he has just crashed it and that it's a write-off. Then when he returns it in one piece, the friend will be relieved. The humour is in the shock and surprise, but also in the deception.

One night he had gone to Bilynda's place when she had a house full of people and set off a firecracker by the front door. The startled partygoers ran to the door and discovered Greg standing there, laughing maniacally.

Bilynda would get her own back though, playing little telephone jokes like "dropping a bomb", which involved ringing him up and then hanging up, hopefully just as Greg was about to answer. Other times Greg would go around to Bilynda's house and quietly turn her clocks back to confuse her.

Sometimes, however, the jokes were of a nastier style. One night someone broke into Bilynda Murphy's house and swapped her children in their beds.

"I went into Jaidyn's room and Breehanna was there, I went into Breehanna's room and Jaidyn was there. And I thought, 'Wow, I haven't drunk any alcohol last night, and I know where I put my kids'," Bilynda said.

Some say Greg was responsible, others think it may have been Greg's ex-girlfriend, Yvonne Penfold, with whom Bilynda had been feuding. Bilynda reckons it was probably Yvonne, but didn't care so much who was responsible. What was important to her was that someone had done it and, as far as jokes go, it wasn't funny. She rang Greg and abused him for the prank. He was adamant that it was not him and told her to call the police.

Greg was known for his fondness of what he and his friends called mind games. While practical jokes were popular among the clutch of people with whom Greg associated, even for them his jokes were slightly unnerving. It can be misleading to selectively quote instances from anyone's background to

Chapter Four

illustrate a character trait. For Greg though, the anecdotes are not so much selective as endemic.

A friend claims Greg killed the feral cats he caught by putting them in hessian bags and setting them alight. Other times, he would go around to his girlfriend's house with his mate Glenn, both wearing balaclavas. They would crouch in the bushes, then throw stones at the house and break in using a spare key. Inside, Bilynda would be quivering with fear. But the aim wasn't to upset her; her son was the target. Jaidyn was taken from his cot into the kitchen and force-fed peanut butter sandwiches until he was sick.

Bilynda hated Greg Domaszewicz the first time she met him. He had asked her at the time to drive him around to the milk bar so that he could buy an apple. She thought he was weird and wondered what kind of person drove to the shop just to buy an apple. The type of guy who buys fruit and vegetables for the refrigerator – to add colour – but in fact lives on nothing but junk food, mainly McDonalds but also KFC, perhaps.

Greg told Bilynda on that first day about his theory that ants don't fight; he also talked a lot about aliens. Bilynda had no idea what he was on about.

Large posters of aliens adorned Greg's lounge room walls. He was obsessed with the concept of life in space, always talking about it with friends and people he met. He told friends that he had once met the little green men that he was so fond of.

When he walked down the street he could see people's auras and knew if they had been touched by aliens, at least that's what he told his friends. They could never be sure if he was serious; they doubted it, but he was so earnest that there was room for concern.

One of Greg's closest friends leading up to Jaidyn's disappearance was a local tow truck driver, Darren Farr. Darren had not long moved to Moe from Brisbane when he met Greg. Both were passionate about fast, hotted up cars and they got to talking one day in a service station about a Ford Falcon; the pair quickly developed a close friendship. Greg became a regular at Darren's place and would eat there at least once a week.

They are not friends now. Darren Farr became convinced of Greg's guilt soon after Jaidyn went missing. Later, Darren would say that he always had his doubts about Greg.

"He was big into aliens. He used to leave a Big M [a carton of flavoured milk] on the roof of his house so that when the aliens came down they'd get the Big M, but they wouldn't get him. He's weird," Darren said.

"He says he has to eat a sausage roll a day because aliens don't like sausage rolls, so if you eat them the aliens won't take you up. He'd make up these stories that he'd believe. He was doing community work at the hospital and he thought there was an agent that was undercover that he had to get out to America real fast. He had all these plans for underneath the hospital and, you ask him and he'll tell you, there's miles and miles and miles of tunnels underneath the Moe Hospital."

Greg had other superstitions. For instance, he wouldn't get in cars of a certain colour because he regarded it as bad luck.

Yet Greg also had a softer, more humanitarian, side. He loved strays and animals of any kind. Possibly the two most traumatic events in his life, after his dad's death, were the death of his pet pig, Stimpy, and the disappearance of a pup.

Greg's friends would laugh when he told them that he knew his animals so well, he could talk to them. His passion for takeaway food meant that his dogs ate a good deal of it too. He'd make his three bull terriers – Jack, Sam and Shepp – wait outside fast food restaurants, while he went in and bought food to share with them.

Friends also weren't sure how to take it when Greg would reprimand them for using environmentally damaging products, such as aerosols. They knew he was partly serious, although his idea of replacing wooden logs with plastic ones did seem a bit off beam.

Chapter Four

Greg was like a big kid when it came to toys and games. He just got older and more able to afford the games he wanted to play, from practical jokes like mucking around with cars, to playing with his Nintendo.

The jokes were a useful tool for Greg. They protected him from people knowing his business, and preserved an air of mystery. He would tell friends who rang him on his mobile phone that he was in different towns just to trick them and build a mystique.

But it was his kindness to animals and children that so impressed the women in Greg's life. It put them at ease. Here was a man who cared about what they cared about. He appeared to be gentle. Interested. Willing to spend time with them and their children. Yet this kindness didn't appear to extend to the times when he was in charge of the kids.

Greg had been involved in an earlier, tumultuous relationship with a girl called Yvonne Penfold, who had been very young when they met. When their relationship ended, he realised that he was not going to have a child of his own, at least in the short-term. He was convinced that Yvonne was the woman for him, the one to bear his children.

This romantic devotion, however, was limited by a concept of fidelity that meant he was prepared to carry on sexual relationships with Bilynda Murphy and Yvonne simultaneously. Like US President Bill Clinton, Greg did not believe that oral sex fell under the definition of sexual relations, and felt that he was only being unfaithful if he had full sexual intercourse with another woman.

Greg bragged to a friend, Paul "Lizard" Lietzau, that he would only let Bilynda perform oral sex on him; sleeping with her might stop him getting back with Yvonne. He had been pleading with Yvonne to have his baby and she claims he offered her $20,000 to do so.

When Greg eventually did consummate his relationship with Bilynda, he started to focus his paternal attentions and desire for a child onto Jaidyn. For a single mother of two, having a man interested not only in her but also in her child was a double blessing. Some suggest though that Greg was more interested in Jaidyn than Bilynda all along; he even encouraged Bilynda to let Brett Leskie take Jaidyn's sister.

Greg wanted to raise the boy, and to instil in him his own love of guns and of Arnold Schwarzenegger movies. His own father's death had created a void in Greg's life, and he may have been driven to become Jaidyn's adult figure to compensate for what he had missed as a teenager. "I told Jaidyn about war movies and such, as all blokes like guns and stuff," Greg said.

Greg certainly loved guns. Darren Farr said that he had a hole under the back steps of his house for storing guns. Darren also claims to have been with Greg one night when he paid $1500 for some guns because he wanted to do some unspecified "serious business".

Maybe some of Greg's eccentric behaviour had something to do with the fact that he was an extremely heavy marijuana smoker. While Bilynda claims she only ever knew him to use marijuana, others claim he was into much heavier drugs — pills and powders, not only for recreational use but also small-time dealing.

"I only knew him to do marijuana, he was a pretty heavy smoker. But if you speak to all the druggies, they'd say if you need anything he is the one to get it off," said Bilynda, who was not worried by his drug use. She drank heavily and was known to take soft drugs as well.

Greg was known to get his drugs — grass and a range of pills — from a local dealer called Dave Grios. In late 1998, Grios died in a car accident in Springvale in Melbourne's south-eastern suburbs.

Greg first looked after Jaidyn in April 1997. Bilynda and Brett had recently broken up and he took the toddler for only a couple of hours. This set the pattern for the next few visits but

Chapter Four

as the arrangement became more comfortable, the hours became longer. Soon, Greg was sending Bilynda away when she arrived to pick up Jaidyn because he wanted to spend more time with the boy.

Bilynda was glad of the respite, and Greg seemed genuinely interested in the child. However, Greg's temper was short and Jaidyn soon went from being an innocent playmate to a new form of amusement, something for Greg to control and tease.

Greg could not bear Jaidyn's crying and would take it out on the boy. Friends bridled when they saw him push Jaidyn over a few times onto his back, like an inflatable toy. Jaidyn would bounce on his nappy and topple onto his back, his head thudding onto the floor. He would look up startled and cry even harder.

It wasn't always a hard shove but neither was it a playful jostle. As Jaidyn lay there crying, Greg would leave the room to escape the noise.

Friends like Matthew Walsh, alias Spider, were troubled by episodes like this. He remembers that Greg once turned the stereo up loud to drown out the toddler's screams. Others said Greg would turn up the stereo and push Jaidyn close to the speakers.

Another friend, Terrence Carrodus, recalled seeing Greg often give Jaidyn a backhander during babysitting sessions. He also claimed that Greg goaded the dogs with Jaidyn, holding him by the arms and pushing him toward one of the dogs, while hissing to fire the dog up to attack. It didn't attack, but Jaidyn was terrified.

Terrence felt that Greg meant to be cruel when he pushed Jaidyn over – it was a half-push, half-hit, he told the court during the committal hearing, but when it came time to tell the Supreme Court, he refused to testify.

Ramen Le Mercier had similar memories, telling police that Greg had a peculiar way of caring for a child. But at the committal hearing, he seemed at pains to water down his original statement. He claimed that Jaidyn enjoyed playing with the dogs and that's why Greg had put the boy, at barely one year of age, in the backyard on his own with three aggressive bull terriers.

Greg was fond of fishing and took his mate Glenn Walker along with Jaidyn to Blue Rock Dam to fish. The dam is beyond the township of Willow Grove, north of Moe. It would not be Jaidyn's last visit to the dam.

As the two of them fished from the muddy bank, Jaidyn played with the dogs in the mud and grass. When they left, Greg carried Jaidyn under one arm, his fishing gear in the other and climbed over a fence to the car. As they approached the car, Jaidyn fell. Glenn didn't see the fall but saw Jaidyn on the ground a split second later. The boy's head cracked the ground, his lip bled and he was cut under the eye. Jaidyn returned home with half-a-dozen scratches on his face and a bump on his head. Glenn Walker still cannot be sure if Jaidyn wriggled free or Greg deliberately dropped him.

Glenn became accustomed to the treatment dished out to the little boy during his frequent visits to Greg's place – the backhanders, the verbal abuse. He often heard Greg call Jaidyn a "Mongoloid" or a "Mongoloid poofter cunt". He didn't explain why, it was some sort of joke. Glenn thought he should be in on the joke himself and joined in the name calling.

After Jaidyn disappeared, Bilynda gave police a crude drawing of her son, in which he was described as a "Mongoloid poofter cunt". She told police she'd found it on her fridge. Bilynda admits that she used to laugh at the names until she learnt what the term "Mongoloid" meant. Then she got angry, but still eventually laughed it off.

Katie agrees that Greg didn't handle Jaidyn's crying very well, telling the boy to "shut up". One day at her place, Jaidyn was crying so Greg picked him up and put him in the hallway with the light off and the door shut. Katie went and got Jaidyn.

Chapter Four

Greg wasn't the only one who was having trouble coping with Jaidyn's crying. One night, when Jaidyn had been crying for a couple of hours, it became too much for Bilynda. She had tried everything: fed him, carried him, sang to him, nothing worked. She was at her wit's end and lashed out, kicking the toddler in the arm. Jaidyn teetered but did not fall, but the episode shook Bilynda. She took him to the doctor, seeking help or comfort for herself as much as for Jaidyn.

Friends did not air their concerns about Greg's treatment of Jaidyn, and the babysitting visits became longer, until a month before Jaidyn disappeared when Greg was to mind him overnight. He'd already looked after him for the day, but Greg took Jaidyn home early, telling Bilynda that he had "lost it" with the boy. Bilynda didn't know exactly what had happened, but the toddler arrived home with a big bruise on his face.

Greg explained to Bilynda that he had gone to put Jaidyn in the car and had bumped the boy's head on the door. Jaidyn had started crying and Greg said he couldn't remember what happened after that because he "lost it".

The bruising did not stop at Jaidyn's face. There was a cut under his chin, he had a black eye and there was grazing from the left-hand side of his forehead down the right-hand side of his face, almost to his chin. Later that night, after Greg left, Bilynda bathed the toddler and was shocked again to find he had bruising to the inside of his left leg.

Bilynda felt sick when she saw the injuries. Greg had offered to tell the police or even welfare authorities that he had injured Jaidyn, but the offer came with a warning. If the social workers knew what had happened they might take Jaidyn away from her. Fearing that she would lose her son, Bilynda kept quiet and hid the boy for a few days until his injuries improved.

In later statements to police, Bilynda watered down what she'd said about the injuries. She said that Jaidyn had a bump on his head from the bang against the door, and a red hand-mark on his face with a small scratch under his eye.

Although Bilynda became slightly more wary of Greg, not letting him have Jaidyn for a few days, she still needed his support. She understood how easy it was to "lose it" with a child, hell she had lashed out at Jaidyn herself. And she certainly didn't want to dob him in when he had been doing her a favour looking after Jaidyn in the first place.

Just three weeks after the incident, Bilynda allowed Greg to look after Jaidyn for the day while she and Katie went shopping. It was only a couple of days before Jaidyn would disappear.

When she returned to pick up Jaidyn, she was perplexed to find that Greg had given him a haircut, but this was no ordinary haircut. Greg had shaved Jaidyn's head at the front and all that was left was stubble in a half-moon shape. There were two triangular shapes shaved into the back of his head. Katie said that she thought Greg wanted to make Jaidyn a clone of himself, giving him a haircut that resembled his own balding pate, and she said as much to Greg.

Greg's justification was that Bilynda had said she wished she had the money to get him a haircut, so he'd taken it upon himself. He admitted he did a pretty bad job, telling her he had slipped with the clippers over the front section of Jaidyn's fair hair.

Despite this, Bilynda again agreed to let Greg mind Jaidyn for the day. It was the last time he would mind the boy.

CHAPTER

Yvonne Penfold is a mousey girl; tall, thin and pale with a narrow face and lank blonde hair. She could be attractive and in other circumstances could even be described as a willowy blonde, but the life she has led has taken its toll. Still in her early twenties, Yvonne has a pre-adolescent maturity, a kind of trusting innocence, yet she is street-smart.

Yvonne left school young and fell in with Greg Domaszewicz too soon to avoid the stultifying influence of an intense relationship. He was an older man in his mid-twenties when they first started dating. They had met in a local nightclub where he quickly made an impression. He asked her if she wanted to come back to his place and she had agreed. She was barely 18 and soon worshipped the ground he walked on; he seemed to have his life together.

Greg was more base in his assessment of Yvonne; he was instantly attracted to her. When they got back to his place that first night, they had a few drinks and played around, but didn't have sex. That came the next morning after she had stayed over.

"Me and Yvonne just seemed to get on so well. She loved my dogs and I could feel she was a very sort of country girl. Old fashioned to some degree and slutty, which I really like in a woman," Greg said later. His vulgarity probably appealed to Yvonne.

Greg quickly became obsessed with her and demanded more of her time and attention. Despite encouraging Yvonne to get a job, Greg also pushed her to quit so she could spend more time with him. He was jealous of her other interests and fearful of something — work, other people, anything — coming between them.

Greg was forever vigilant. He would ring Yvonne at three or four in the morning and when she arrived for work at a curtain shop, there would sometimes be graffiti on the window.

If he got his own way he was happy but when he went off, it usually meant violence. Though a small man, Greg is strong and has a cruel temper. Men appear to have escaped his wrath. Women, however, have not been so lucky.

Yvonne regularly suffered bruises and red marks to her neck and body. She couldn't wear open-necked shirts after Greg had punched, pinched and slapped her, or put his hands around her throat.

Greg needed to know what Yvonne was doing and who she was with at all times.

"What did you do on your lunch break?" he'd ask.

"I saw a couple of girlfriends."

"You're lying."

"I'm not lying."

"Yes you are. Who were you with? Who'd you root?"

Yvonne found this increasingly difficult to deal with. Greg took to spying on her from the car park near her work at lunchtimes, a practice that continued during the couple's numerous separations.

They would live together in Greg's house for several months, then they would have a row and Yvonne would move back to her house in Austin Avenue. Intervention orders were taken out by both parties at various times, but they were routinely flouted, rarely enforced, and before long the pair would be living together again.

Chapter Five

Court orders were Yvonne's last resort. She still felt for Greg but didn't want the relationship to continue. When they finally broke up, he struggled to cope. Friends told Greg what the courts had already stated: leave Yvonne alone. But it made no difference.

Once Greg attacked Yvonne in front of Darren and Sheena Farr; he pinched her and Yvonne struck him. Greg raised his fist to hit her, before Darren jumped in and pulled the pair apart. He warned Greg not to threaten Yvonne in future.

"If you ever lay a hand on her and I find out about it, that will be the end of you," Darren cautioned his mate. It failed to stop Greg. He did lay a hand on Yvonne again, but Darren either didn't find out or didn't follow up his warning.

It was only after Darren saw Greg's violent streak first hand that he became aware of Greg's propensity for violence. Friends tried to resolve the deteriorating situation. They tried to convince Yvonne to leave Greg and not see him when she did move out, they told her to take out intervention orders and stick to them. They also tried to convince Greg that it was all over with Yvonne and to leave her alone to sort things out. Nothing worked.

Yvonne would stay home for weeks on end, rarely venturing out. Then Greg would come around in his car and do a "burnout" in her driveway. After one particularly bitter break-up, Yvonne had water, sand and dirt put in her petrol tank. When her car broke down in the middle of the road, she turned in desperation to a man she hardly knew, Darren Farr, who answered her call and got her car going again.

Darren was repaid for his trouble with an abusive phone call, followed by ten or so anonymous calls throughout the evening. Greg was the suspected culprit. After all, he and his mate, Glenn Walker, had seen Darren rescue Yvonne; the pair had been watching from a nearby service station.

Yvonne would regularly meet a friend, Cheryl Stubley, on a Wednesday night or a weekend for a drink and Greg began abusing her too, ringing her and allegedly threatening her. Eventually Cheryl contacted the police herself to have an intervention order taken out against Greg. After Jaidyn's disappearance Cheryl also made a complaint to police that Greg had again been harassing her. She made a statement to police claiming Greg had threatened to tie her up, weigh her body down and throw her in Blue Rock Dam. Little was thought of the claim at the time, but it was to have great significance for police later.

The litany of incidents between Greg and Yvonne when they were still together seemed to have no end. Greg cornered Yvonne in the backyard at one party and tried to force her to take some pills – uppers for depression. She didn't want to take them, but each time she tried to get past Greg he would block her way. Eventually, Darren saw the difficulty and intervened.

On another occasion, Greg became furious with Yvonne after she had spent most of an evening at the pub talking to her girlfriends. Eventually, Greg decided to leave and asked Yvonne gruffly if she wanted to come with him. He stormed out of the bar with her trailing along behind him. Other friends arrived at Greg's place that evening, but he was impervious to them, furious with Yvonne for not mingling and flirting with other men. The argument became heated and eventually Yvonne was pushed through the back window. Unfortunately the other people in the house were in a different room.

The couple had been going out for a year. Yet despite the public displays of violence, Yvonne stayed with Greg.

It didn't get any easier. They would argue to the point of mental exhaustion, Greg never allowing Yvonne to cut an argument short, always blocking her way to the door. After yet another wild fight, Greg locked his girlfriend in the bathroom. Enraged, she smashed the shower recess glass and badly cut her wrist.

Violence resulted from about two of these arguments every month, or so Yvonne claimed. Eventually, she resorted to a

Chapter Five

serious means of self-defence, using a kind of mace spray after he allegedly tried to strangle her.

Not surprisingly, Yvonne sought help for mental difficulties on and off for some time. She has seen doctors on an irregular basis for medication to help her deal with depression and has received prescriptions for Aurorix, an anti-depressant, and sleeping pills.

Two weeks before Jaidyn disappeared, the couple slept together for the last time. They had "broken up" some time earlier, but still spent the occasional night together. Greg had been seeing Bilynda Murphy during this time, although they had not yet fully consummated their relationship, and, while Yvonne had her suspicions about Greg and Bilynda, she was not certain.

She would soon discover the extent of their relationship.

CHAPTER

Greg Domaszewicz rose late on Saturday, 14 June. It might have been the weekend but for Greg, with no job, every day was the same.

He had filled in his week fixing the transmission of a car that belonged to his mate, Paul "Lizard" Lietzau. In exchange, Paul had agreed to knock down a small crumbling wall in Greg's backyard. It had taken each of them about three days work but by the Friday night Greg wasn't finished and Lizard needed his car for the weekend. He was taking a girl to a debutante ball.

Lizard's Valiant was driveable, but still needed some work so the pair planned that Lizard would return on Sunday morning for Greg to finish the job.

With no work to do, Greg eased his way into Saturday, finally surfacing at about 11.00 a.m. The weather was nothing to get up for. The sky was slate grey, with no hint of winter sun to leaven the gloom.

Greg skipped breakfast and went outside to work on one of his own cars. He had three: a green XC Ford Falcon bomb, a classier restored Ford of the same vintage, and his dad's old Valiant, which he kept in the shed. For no particular reason, Greg picked up his tools and headed for the old Falcon.

He had grown used to company while he worked, preferring it to the silence of his own labours. There was

Chapter Six

something about having someone else around, especially a kid, and as Greg set about work he started to miss his little playmate, Jaidyn.

Soon after Greg had started work on the old Ford, his mate Glenn Walker stopped by to drop off some tools he had borrowed. Around midday another friend, Clint McCarthy, called in to return the Nintendo controllers he'd borrowed the previous day. They chatted for a while, but Clint was on his way to work as a chef, so they arranged to meet that night. Clint said he'd pick Greg up after his shift at about 7.30 p.m. and they'd head over to another mate's place.

It was only in hindsight that Bilynda thought the day unusual. At the time, it was just another Saturday for her and Katie, except this time they had a big night out planned. They'd been invited to nearby Traralgon to a birthday party for a friend of Katie's boyfriend, Neville Hibbins. The party would start in the afternoon and kick on into the night.

The sisters decided that such a party demanded a bit of organisation. They arranged for a babysitter, Julie Brassington – a local girl who knew the children well – to care for Jaidyn and Breehanna, along with Katie's children Shannan and Harley.

She was not an ideal alternative. Julie was mildly intellectually disabled and, although she was becoming a regular sitter, there had been problems. For instance, she had called for an ambulance once after Jaidyn started crying when he got shampoo in his eyes.

Greg had his own plans. After his mates had left, and with some work to finish on the Ford, he drove over to Bilynda's house and told her that he wanted to look after Jaidyn for the afternoon. It took Bilynda by surprise. Greg usually rang ahead and asked to have the boy.

Bilynda was sitting near the open front door, talking on the phone to Brett in Western Australia when Greg came walking up the steps, smiling and nodding. He realised who she was talking to as soon as she cupped the receiver to her chest, so he kept it short, telling Bilynda that he was working on the car and wanted to have Jaidyn with him while he worked.

Bilynda had no trouble with the idea. She told Greg about the party in Traralgon and said she would be out for the afternoon and night. Greg said that he would go and put his Tattslotto on and come back to collect Jaidyn. The Tattslotto entry was Greg's Saturday ritual. He put his entry in every week on the same day with the same numbers and the same result. Before leaving, he told Bilynda to put some things together for Jaidyn, like an extra jumper in case he got wet.

Greg didn't like the idea that Bilynda was talking to Brett and the last thing he wanted was to hang around listening to the couple chat while he waited for her to get off the phone. It was probably just as well that he left. Bilynda spent more than an hour talking to Brett, but a few other people called while she was on the phone. The phone had a call waiting service and Bilynda was able to chat to Katie a couple of times about plans for the party.

After she hung up, Bilynda bathed Jaidyn and put a Huggies disposable nappy on him. She had run out of Jaidyn's nappies, so she used one of Breehanna's that was pink inside. Bilynda packed four more of the big disposable nappies into a blue plastic shopping bag along with some warm clothes, a clear plastic baby bottle, an apple, a lollipop and a muesli bar.

She dressed Jaidyn in his grey tracksuit pants with 'Baby Games' written on them, a green long-sleeved shirt, a blue-green windcheater with a hood, and a red jacket to go over the top. Even in the Moe drizzle he should be warm, she thought.

Greg returned early in the afternoon. Jaidyn was ready, but Bilynda asked him to drop her and Breehanna off at Katie's house in Hawker Street; the sisters could go on to the party from there. Both of the kids' car seats had been out on the veranda getting wet, so Greg grabbed the drier one of the two and put it

Chapter Six

in his car for Jaidyn. Bilynda strapped Jaidyn in while Breehanna was left to sit in the back with a seat belt on, like a big girl.

After the short run to Katie's place, Bilynda asked Greg for $50, telling him she wanted to pay some money off an overdue phone bill. She had no plans to drink that night, but Greg gave her the cash, along with an extra $20 so Bilynda could "have an extra special time" at the party. "You can't go to a party without drinking," Greg told her. And he offered her his camera. Why not come by and pick it up later in the day? Bilynda agreed. Sure. She'd drop by later.

Bilynda and Greg did not agree on how long he would look after Jaidyn. But there was an understanding that Greg would drop the toddler back at Katie's to join the babysitter later that day.

Bilynda leaned over to the back seat and kissed Jaidyn, climbed out of the car and waved goodbye to her son. Greg drove off. It was the last time Bilynda saw her son alive.

When Bilynda walked into Katie's place shortly before 1.30 p.m. on Saturday, Katie and her boyfriend Neville were still in bed, lying on a mattress on the lounge room floor.

Katie's car had broken down the previous night, so the girls and Neville had spent part of the day trying to get it started, without success.

When he arrived home, Greg unbundled Jaidyn from the back of the car and took him inside. He noticed that Jaidyn's pants were damp from the wet car seat and changed him, just as a dad would do. The pair sat down and played Star Wars on the Nintendo for a while, at least Greg played while the boy watched the screen dance into colours before him. Greg was pleased with this picture of domesticity.

When he tired of the game, he took Jaidyn outside and started throwing the ball and playing with the three dogs. But after a while Greg started to become anxious. He wanted to get back to the car before the rain came. He opened the shed door so that Jaidyn could shelter inside when it rained.

Greg wanted to fix his car heater. He crawled about in the front footwell searching for the problem, but eventually gave up to work on the holed exhaust. While he was welding, rain started to fall, becoming heavier and heavier. Greg took one look at the leaden skies and abandoned his repairs, taking Jaidyn inside.

The boy was hungry so Greg found a packet of potato chips and chocolate freckles and the two watched TV while waiting for the rain to ease. Greg worried about leaving Jaidyn alone in the house. There were detergents, sprays and poisons in the cupboards that the toddler could get into if he wasn't supervised. It was far safer to have Jaidyn on the couch: Greg's little friend sitting next to him, his right hand man and helper.

Around 3.00 p.m., the phone rang. It was Darren Farr, and he was angry. Darren and Greg's friendship had fallen apart a couple of months earlier over some minor car business, and Darren was upset about rumours that Greg was going to kill him by Christmas.

A direct man with a reputation for violence, Darren confronted Greg with the rumours. He wanted to know if they were true and he wanted them stopped. Greg denied ever having started such rubbish and the pair ended the conversation on amicable terms, even agreeing to have a few drinks the next day. Darren was going to call around in the afternoon with a few beers.

Darren might have been placated, but Greg was not. He was livid and at about 4.00 p.m., he rang Katie's house to blame her. Bilynda answered the phone. Greg still wanted to know what was going on – what Bilynda's sister had been saying about him – but he soon calmed down.

Bilynda checked that Jaidyn had enough clothes for the cold, and Greg reassured her that he was fine. He intended to finish working on his car, have a shower and then drop Jaidyn back. There was something else. Jaidyn had fallen over out the back with the dogs, but Greg would clean him up.

Chapter Six

When Bilynda got off the phone she asked Katie if what Greg had told her was true, and Katie admitted to having spread the story.

Bilynda erupted. "Youse are all rooting each other," she shrieked at Katie. She didn't know of any fight between Greg and Darren, and couldn't imagine why on earth Katie would spread such rumours. The party was off and Bilynda was going home. She grabbed Breehanna and walked home up the hill in the rain.

Greg had gone back outside to work on the car. He gave Jaidyn some greasy bolts to play with in the backyard so he'd get his hands dirty like a real working man. He always wanted Bilynda to call around and see her little working man in the backyard helping out. Helping dad.

Late in the afternoon, a neighbour heard Greg scream. It was not like a scream he had ever heard before. Greg was outside, in the rain, hosing down the driveway. Later, the neighbour said he could not work out whom Greg was screaming at.

Clint McCarthy rang Greg's place about three or four times that afternoon to make sure he'd be ready when Clint came around after work, but each time the phone rang out. At the end of his shift, Clint went around to Greg's place as arranged but did not stop because he couldn't see Greg's car in the driveway. It wasn't uncommon for Greg to change his plans, so Clint didn't think much of it.

No one heard from Greg until later in the evening when he rang Julie Brassington and asked where Bilynda was. She told him that Bilynda, Katie and Neville had already left for the party in Traralgon.

Bilynda tried to ring Greg twenty or thirty times at his house between about 5.30 p.m. and 7.45 p.m. to tell him not to drop Jaidyn off at Katie's place, but to bring him home. Every time the phone rang out, she pressed the redial button.

Bilynda explained later that she had not specifically told Greg to take Jaidyn to Katie's place. She just figured he would take him back to the babysitter or at least answer the phone. She expected him to be home when she rang; when he wasn't, like any mother, she started to worry.

Following Greg's phone call to Katie's place earlier that Saturday, Katie's boyfriend, Neville, had tried to make peace between the two sisters. He rang Bilynda soon after she left and apologised on behalf of his girlfriend, telling her he was really keen for her to come to the party. It would be a good night at his mate's place.

Bilynda wasn't sure. She didn't know where Jaidyn was and Greg wasn't answering the phone. Two hours had elapsed since she had first tried to contact him. Eventually, she rang Glenn Walker to see if he had seen Greg and Jaidyn that afternoon. He hadn't. She told him she was going to call the police if she hadn't heard from Greg within two hours.

Glenn assured her that they would be alright and, although there was precious little comfort in this, Bilynda started to think it might be alright to go to the party.

Katie and Neville arrived at Bilynda's soon after. The sisters did their make-up together in the bathroom before Bilynda was rushed reluctantly out of the house. She felt uneasy, but was mad at herself for being suspicious and knew she should just forget it and have a good time. She left Breehanna with Julie down at Katie's place and went on to the party.

Originally, Bilynda had intended to drive past Greg's place to collect his camera. However, Neville's car was unregistered and Katie, who was driving, didn't want to stop. Bilynda didn't have a driver's licence and had to rely on Katie for transport, and what Katie said, went. She had no intention of going anywhere near a main road if she could avoid it, because she was driving an illegal vehicle.

Bilynda had just started getting to know Neville's crowd, and was becoming excited about the party.

"We had just met a whole heap of people, they were guys

Chapter Six

actually, they weren't guys that you sleep with, they were just guys that were friends and they invited us over to the party," Bilynda said.

When she arrived at the party Bilynda tried Greg's place again, with no response. She still expected Greg to drop Jaidyn back with the babysitter, but she didn't ring Julie to check if Jaidyn was there yet.

At 8.11 p.m. Greg got a call from his neighbour, Mariann McKinnon, who had just arrived home with her husband and two friends from Ballarat. The "Plucka Duck" segment was on *Hey Hey It's Saturday* on TV at the time. Mariann asked Greg to come over and smoke a few "bongs" with them but he declined – he had Jaidyn with him.

Greg settled onto the couch with Jaidyn on his right-hand side again and they watched *Hey Hey It's Saturday*. The "Red Faces" segment was on and Greg giggled throughout, pointing out the silly people to Jaidyn. They flicked channels between a preview show to the new Batman movie and the old war film, *The Great Escape*, with Charles Bronson. Greg may have smoked a few "cones" of marijuana as he watched television with Jaidyn asleep on the couch next to him. He's not sure.

At about 10.00 p.m. he called Mariann next door and asked her if she had any nappies, or knew where he could get some because he was running out. Bilynda had packed four nappies with Jaidyn earlier in the day.

Although Greg certainly had changed Jaidyn's nappy in the past, he has a history of not changing the boy, leaving the nappy soiled until he returns him to Bilynda or gets someone else to drop him home. On Greg's reckoning – that he changed Jaidyn's nappy twice that night – there would still have been two clean nappies in the bag, provided Bilynda's memory was correct. Even if Greg ran out of nappies, he knew that there was a BP service station – a 24-hour mini-market – a few hundred metres down the road.

Mariann McKinnon didn't have any nappies but told Greg that the BP down the road would. Her husband, Michael, suggested that Greg use a folded towel instead and volunteered to go around and show him how to fold it. Greg declined the offer.

Mrs McKinnon said later that she thought she heard a child and a dog playing in the background, and that she thought the child was Jaidyn. She also thought she could identify which one of Greg's dogs she had heard from the tone of its bark and growl. It was the bitch, Sammy, because she's gentler.

Bilynda attacked the party with gusto, starting with a can of Sambuca and cola and two glasses of Cougar bourbon whisky and cola. Like her sister, Bilynda is a big drinker, though she claims not to take any drugs. She drinks more than her sister does on a day-to-day basis, but Katie is a binge drinker. She only drinks every few months but when she does it usually develops into a long session, involving plenty of different spirits and a fight or two. This night was to be no exception.

"I drink to get drunk, I don't drink socially," Katie says, matter-of-factly.

The party struggled to get going. In no time, only a handful of stragglers remained and they decided to go to the nightclub at Ryans Hotel in Traralgon. They called a cab at about 10:30 p.m. and it took only minutes to arrive.

Bilynda, Katie, Neville, a friend, Brett McGrath, and his girlfriend, and a few others got to Ryans just before 11.00 p.m. This meant they were able to escape the cover charge that was imposed after 11.00 p.m.

Ryans Hotel is no snug corner pub; it's more of a beer barn, a rough bloodhouse pub where there are usually fights on a Saturday night. Social drinkers searching for a quiet chat with a mate stay away. But for partygoers, people like Katie who were intent on getting drunk, or people just looking for a stoush, Ryans was the place to be. At least that's how Katie and Bilynda treated the place.

Chapter Six

When Bilynda arrived she went to the toilet. When she came out Katie was talking to someone, so Bilynda walked up and listened for a while before deciding she would ring Greg to check on Jaidyn. It was about 11.10 p.m.

This time, Greg was home and Bilynda immediately asked about Jaidyn.

"Shit's happened," Greg told her. Jaidyn had fallen against the heater and he had taken the toddler to casualty at Moe Hospital, Greg said. Jaidyn had had cream rubbed on his bottom but Greg thought the hospital hadn't done a good enough job so he drove Jaidyn to the new hospital, Maryvale.

Bilynda decided that she wanted to go home immediately, but Greg convinced her to stay at the pub. Jaidyn was okay, he said. There was nothing she could do. Greg told her to ring back later and he'd come to pick her up.

Bilynda went back to the bar and told Brett McGrath what had happened to Jaidyn. She was stressed and wanted to go home straight away. Brett offered her a lift, but Bilynda was confused and upset. Katie saw what was happening and decided to find out for herself what had gone on with Jaidyn. She rang Greg.

The public phone at Ryans Hotel is near the disco, where the music is throbbing and the crowd bustles past. At this time on a Saturday night, it's at its peak, thumping loud and packed with people.

"I can't hear you, you'll have to yell," Katie said to Greg, when she called.

"We've been to the hospital, he fell against the radiator and burnt his bum. They put some cream on it. He's fine now. Don't worry about it," Greg said.

"How bad is it?"

"They put cream on it, it'll be all right. There's no blisters or anything."

"Is everything all right, do you want us to come home?"

"No, you stay there, there's no need to come home, you stay there."

A few minutes later, Katie returned to the group. The burn was all a joke, she told Bilynda. Greg had said Jaidyn was alright, that there was nothing to worry about. Or that's what Bilynda remembers. Katie maintains she told her sister that Jaidyn had been burnt but that he had been treated. Greg had added that there was no need for her to rush home.

Katie says she would never have believed the burn story would be a practical joke. Although she and Bilynda regularly played practical jokes on Greg, and vice versa, "we never played sick jokes on him". She maintains she never said anything about Greg telling her he'd just been joking. In fact, he had stuck to the burn story. Bilynda's spirits immediately lifted when her sister told her the news that Jaidyn was fine and she could stay on partying.

Bilynda and Katie went back to the bar and attacked the drinks – and anyone that was around – for several more hours. Bilynda alternated between vodka, raspberry flavoured Sub Zero alcoholic lemonade and Jim Beam bourbon and cola. She lost count of the number of drinks she had, but spent at least $60.

After the two phone calls, Greg settled back on the couch to watch TV but quickly became bored. Jaidyn was asleep, there was no one to talk to and he was lonely. He had little idea what he was watching on TV, just pictures, and he played a little Nintendo.

At about 1.00 a.m. Mariann McKinnon was playing on the computer in her lounge room when she heard Greg's car start in the driveway. Mariann is familiar with cars. She knew the sound of Greg's car because it has a 250 cross-flow engine with a distinctive tone, not unlike her own car's, and given the vicinity, she knew it was Greg's. She heard it start, reverse and drive away from her house toward Moe.

Kim Wilson got up to go to the bathroom some time around 12.30 a.m. She had not been out of hospital long after

Chapter Six

having a stroke, so she was occasionally up during the night. As she walked back from the bathroom, she heard Greg's car in the street. She pulled the curtain aside and looked out the window. She saw his green XC Falcon pull up across the road and park outside Bilynda's house.

The sound of the car was distinctive and familiar to her as well. It always sounded like it needed something done to it – maybe the muffler, she thought – but she had no doubt it was Greg's car. The car was parked across the boundary between Bilynda's house at number 27 and a neighbour's place at number 25.

Brett McGrath was flirting with Bilynda in the pub. His girlfriend, who was nearby, wasn't impressed but Brett wasn't too fussed about that. He asked Bilynda to sleep with him in the back of his panel van, which was parked outside the pub.

Katie was keen for Bilynda to stay with her and Nev in Traralgon that night – maybe in the back of Brett's panel van, it seemed the only available accommodation. Those plans changed, however, as Bilynda became too drunk and loud by the end of the night. By then, everyone thought she should be sent home.

Late in the night, two women, one a friend of Katie's, got into a fight in the pub. Katie weighed in to help her friend and ended up kicking the woman in the head while she was on the ground.

It was the last straw for the management at Ryans. They had already stopped serving alcohol to Bilynda who, after keeping pace with Katie in her drinking, was far more drunk than her sister. And they soon stopped serving Katie because they knew she was buying drinks for her sister.

After the fight, Ryans shut down the music, kicked the crowd out into the street and closed the doors but it didn't stop more fights from erupting out on the street. Police "brawler" and "divvy" vans started to congregate outside for the regular Saturday night clean up.

Bilynda had had enough and, a couple of hours after hearing that her son had been burnt, she decided to go home. Katie was fed up with her sister, who was so drunk she was likely to get belted senseless by people she was annoying. At about 1.30 a.m., she ordered Bilynda to ring Greg and tell him to come and get her.

Greg was at home when Bilynda called at about 2.00 a.m. He agreed to pick her up and left the house at around 2.15, putting a plastic shopping bag in the green "wheelie" bin in front of his side gate. He got in his car moments later and left.

Greg drove to Traralgon, about twenty-five minutes away, in time to see the chaos outside Ryans Hotel.

Katie might have told her sister to go home, but she had also told Neville they couldn't leave until Greg turned up. Bilynda couldn't be left alone. She was abusing anybody who passed, including the police.

Katie managed to disentangle herself from the crowd long enough to be the first to greet Greg when he arrived. She put her head in the car and told him: "Take her home, she's giving me the shits". Katie noticed that Jaidyn wasn't in the car, but she wasn't surprised. Bilynda had said a friend called Jacqui had been at Greg's earlier that evening. She was probably keeping an eye on the boy, Katie thought.

Katie was heading back to Neville's place in Traralgon, so Bilynda got into the car alone with Greg for the drive back to Moe. She slumped in to the front seat and looked at Greg.

"Where's Jaidyn?"

"I told you, he's in hospital," Greg replied.

Bilynda grabbed for the small bottle of bourbon and cola that Greg had brought with him; she'd mentioned on the phone that they'd stopped serving her drinks, so he thought she might need another by the time he arrived.

Bilynda lolled about in the seat and asked again: "Where's my boy? Where's my boy?"

Chapter Six

Greg muttered "he's alright" and pointed to the new Maryvale Hospital being built outside Morwell. He told Bilynda that Jaidyn was in there. Bilynda had no idea that the hospital was not finished then and demanded he take her in there.

"You can't go in there 'cause you're drunk and you know, what are they going to think of ya? The mother goes in there and she's drunk?"

"But I want to go to him."

Greg was adamant, he would not take her in that condition, arguing that she should sleep it off and see Jaidyn the next morning. Bilynda didn't care what her condition was; she wanted to see her son, but some time before they got back to Moe, she agreed to go home.

They took the freeway from Traralgon and turned off the highway at the exit to Newborough and Moe. Greg pulled into the driveway of his house on Narracan Drive, and the headlights raked across the front of the house. In that moment, Greg saw that all of his front windows were smashed. He was stunned. What had gone on while he was away? There were big jagged holes in the windows and shards of glass were sprayed around the garden.

He parked diagonally across the driveway. The lights in the front porch and the kitchen were still on, and Greg could see smashed glass on the veranda. They bolted inside. Greg ran frantically through the house, looking in rooms and cupboards.

Bilynda's muddy thoughts immediately turned to Yvonne Penfold.

"Yvonne's done it," she told Greg.

For the past few weeks, Yvonne and Bilynda had been involved in a feud involving a series of tit for tat pranks, abusive phone calls and vandalism. When the women saw each other in the street, they would scream out "slut" among other abuse. Bilynda believed it was Yvonne who had swapped Jaidyn and Breehanna in their beds one night. And Bilynda's role in the pranks had been to spray-paint abuse on the front window of the curtain shop where Yvonne worked. The reason for the feud was simple enough: it stemmed from Yvonne discovering Bilynda's clandestine relationship with Greg.

"She was ringing me up at four in the morning saying 'check your kids' and I would get them up and bring them into bed with me because I didn't really know Greg and I never really knew," Bilynda said.

"Darren Farr once said to me, 'You don't know what you are messing with about Greg'."

Bilynda believed that Greg was still infatuated with Yvonne, and the pair maintained a stormy love-hate relationship, unable to sever ties with one another completely.

In one phone call to Bilynda's Lincoln Street house, Yvonne said, "Can I have an ambulance to Lincoln St? There's a dead bitch hanging from the ceiling."

Given the circumstances, it was not unreasonable for Bilynda to conclude that Yvonne Penfold was behind the attack on Greg's house. And in a way, she was right.

Greg's wild dash through the house showed he was looking for something, but he didn't tell Bilynda what it was. Bilynda went inside and straight through to the toilet; the drive from Traralgon is a long way with a full bladder. Not perturbed by Greg's frantic searching, Bilynda collapsed on the lounge room floor. The heater was still on. She curled up in front of the warmth and began playing a Star Wars game on Greg's Nintendo. She remembers the time on the video's digital display: it was 3.04 a.m.

Greg didn't tell Bilynda that the story about Jaidyn's burns was a lie. Nor did he raise the alarm about the boy he now knew was missing. Instead, he made an abusive phone call to Yvonne Penfold. He rang her mobile phone at 3.09 a.m. and in a seventeen-second conversation with her screamed, "Is this one of your sick games?" and hung up.

Chapter Six

Greg decided it was better to take Bilynda home and they had only been back at his place for ten minutes or so, when he started to hurry her along. Bilynda pleaded with Greg to let her stay, but he would have none of it.

Bilynda had not realised that Jaidyn was meant to be in the house; she believed Greg's story that her son was in hospital. She also hadn't realised that there may be some connection between the smashed windows and her son. She told Greg to call the police about the vandalism a few times and even picked up the phone once herself, but Greg said that he wasn't a rat or a dog and would handle it himself.

As they left for Bilynda's house, they noticed something in the gravel garden bed in the front yard: it was a severed pig's head. Neither Greg nor Bilynda had seen it on the way in, but there was no way of missing it now. Both were shocked, but decided to keep going.

Bilynda was angry, partly with Greg, but more generally about his relationship with Yvonne and how it had drawn her and her family into this stupid feud. Greg drove past Yvonne's house and, although her car was in the driveway and the lights were on, he didn't stop. He sounded the horn and drove on to Bilynda's house, where they arrived at about 3.20 a.m.

Once inside, Bilynda collapsed on the floor in the lounge room. Greg said he was going to try to find out who had damaged his house and left with the house keys.

Still drunk, Bilynda decided to ring a few people. She called Brett McGrath's house to see if he got home safely. He wasn't in yet. She also called Julie Brassington to check on Breehanna, to tell her about the damage to Greg's house, and to check if Jaidyn was at Katie's house after all and not in hospital. Julie, roused from sleep, told Bilynda that Jaidyn was with Greg and that she should go to bed.

Through the haze, Bilynda was starting to make some sense of what was going on. She rang Greg's house straight away. He answered and Bilynda asked what he was doing. He said he was trying to find out who had smashed his windows, but she urged him to come back to her place as soon as possible and not to stay at home because of the smashed windows.

While she waited for her lover to return, Bilynda fell asleep on the lounge room floor in front of the heater. About an hour and a half later, Greg was desperately trying to wake her. They had to go to the police station: Jaidyn was missing.

CHAPTER SEVEN

There was something about Greg Domaszewicz that Kenny Penfold instantly hated; it was probably the bruises he left on his sister's body.

Kenny Penfold is a large well-built man in his early twenties who has worked occasionally as a labourer, but more often than not has been on the dole or in prison. He has a long criminal record that includes almost any offence you care to mention, although most are assaults and petty crimes.

His little sister, Yvonne, had been living with her new boyfriend in his house in Newborough for some months when Kenny returned to Moe from Queensland. When he went around to visit, it took barely minutes for Kenny and Greg to be fighting in the backyard. Kenny didn't approve of the way Greg treated his sister.

Kenny's relationship with Greg never passed the stage of uneasy civility. For a while they called each other mates, but it wasn't mateship in the true sense of the word. There was no loyalty or genuine affection. Their friendship, for want of a better word, was short lived, like a marriage of convenience. Greg sold Kenny a car at one stage and they worked on the vehicle or smoked mull together. But Kenny remained dubious about his sister's relationship with Greg.

By 1997, Yvonne and Greg had broken up and re-established their relationship more times than either can recall. In June of that year, however, Yvonne and Greg had broken up for what was to be the last time. Greg was having trouble reconciling this to himself, despite his growing relationship with Bilynda Murphy.

Yvonne lives in a powder blue house in Austin Avenue, Moe. It is a neat kit style home, normally used as a beach holiday house, but able to be extended with new "stages" and rooms. Spotlessly clean and well decorated, the house is at the first stage, with high ceilings and a bedroom in the loft.

Yvonne was sitting with Kenny in the lounge, talking and watching television as they waited for a cousin to call around for a coffee. Kenny was wearing his favourite beanie.

A loud screech right outside the door broke their conversation; it was a car revving loudly, doing a "burnout". Yvonne and Kenny rushed to the door and looked out. Where Yvonne's car should have been was Greg Domaszewicz, quickly reversing his car out of the grassy driveway. Greg had rammed Yvonne's car, with his own vehicle, all the way to the back fence.

A furious Yvonne rang Greg the next day and demanded an explanation. He said that there were two four-wheel-drives parked on the nature strips of the empty blocks next to her house and across the road; he had presumed she had a couple of men inside.

Kenny also called Greg. He was less interested in why Greg had done it, and had a simple message: leave Yvonne alone or I'll belt you. Unconvinced that his threats of violence would have the desired effect, Kenny recalled Greg having painted a pentangle on his sister's car once before.

At about lunchtime on Saturday 14 June – the day of Jaidyn's disappearance – Yvonne finished work at the curtain shop in Morwell and called in to a girlfriend's house for a coffee on the way home.

As they sat at the kitchen table, Yvonne's mobile phone rang. It was Greg. He wanted to see her to discuss something. She was

Chapter Seven

immediately suspicious and, in any case, still angry after he had rammed her car in the driveway. She thought Greg probably wanted to know where she was and whom she was with, maybe he also wanted to try to talk her into having his baby again.

Yvonne didn't want to meet Greg, didn't want to talk to him and didn't want him knowing her business; after all, they were separated now.

"Where are ya?" he asked her.

"None of your business," Yvonne replied and refused to answer any of his questions. She told him she had nothing to say to him, until he fixed the damage he had done to her car.

Yvonne was surprised when Greg suddenly said, "Your arse is mine bitch," and hung up. Normally, he'd fight back, not surrender. Although Greg's calls were a regular event, Yvonne was always a little nervous afterwards. There were intervention orders out between the couple, and she didn't want to see Greg. But when he made that sort of threat, as idle as it was likely to be, it still unnerved her.

The route from the freeway to Yvonne's house takes her past Greg's front door, so she couldn't resist a glance on the way home at about 2.30 p.m.

Some time around 8.30 that evening, while Yvonne was getting ready to go to a party at the Haigh Street tennis courts, Greg rang again. This time, she left it for the answering machine; he simply said it was him, what the time was and asked her to please ring him.

It was not the last call she would receive from Greg Domaszewicz that night.

That afternoon, Darrin Wilson, a butcher and a mate of Kenny Penfold's, drove up from his home in San Remo, near Phillip Island. Darrin's parents still lived in Moe and he went to visit them. He then went with his parents to his cousin Karen Sultana's twenty-first birthday party at Jerralang, about twenty-five minutes from Moe, at 6.30 p.m. He stayed for about four hours and then left with his parents, who dropped him at the tennis court party where five rock bands would be playing.

Yvonne had arrived at the party with a girlfriend at about 9.00 p.m. There was a bonfire and a fairly large crowd, for Moe. Yvonne and her friend Becky ducked out soon after arriving to buy some cans of Jim Beam and Coke, before calling around to collect Kenny and return to the concert. When Darrin arrived, he quickly found Kenny and the pair spent most of their time drinking heavily.

Kenny had been brooding over the problems between Yvonne and Greg. He was angry and frustrated. Darrin had been Yvonne's boyfriend for several years, before she went out with Greg and, for a while, Darrin and Yvonne had even been engaged.

When Darrin heard what had been going on, he could understand Kenny's anger and frustration and his desire to get back at Greg, and as they talked further, it was decided that they needed to mete out some retribution.

Darrin approached Yvonne at the party and asked her if what Kenny had said was true.

"Why didn't you tell me sooner that this sort of shit was happening? I would have helped you out," he said.

Kenny had been thinking for a while about an appropriate attack on Greg and, when his thoughts turned to retribution, they also turned to a pet pig.

Using a pig's head would have a double effect. Kenny reasoned that a pig's head was borrowed from horror movies, where sacrificing animals is often a part of a religious sect or the occult. If Greg opted for pentangles, Kenny opted for pigs.

Lobbing a pig's head through someone's front window was a bit more frightening than a sign painted on your car and Kenny knew his symbolism. He had seen The Godfather and other Mafia films. Those blokes knew how to get a message across, and Kenny's message was simple enough: stop bothering my sister.

Chapter Seven

There was, of course, another reason for using a pig's head. When Yvonne and Greg were living together, Greg had owned a pet pig called Stimpy. The problem was that Stimpy kept growing, eventually dwarfing Greg's three dogs. Greg tried to find someone to take Stimpy, but in the end, they had no choice. The pig finished up at the knackery but Greg kept parts of him in his freezer as a memento. He was upset about the pig's death for years.

Greg believes Yvonne took the pig away to be slaughtered out of spite after one of their many fights. She returned with pork chops. Kenny knew how much Greg loved the pig, so he planned to convey his message to Greg by tossing a pig's head through his front window.

Kenny had kept a couple of pigs at his home that he reared for food. One had already been killed at the house but due to the mess and the loud squealing from the dying pig, Kenny decided he'd take the second pig out into the scrub to kill it.

The pig was something of a family pet for Kenny and his mates. Collingwood Football Club fans, they had even named the black and white pig after a former Collingwood champion, Darren Millane.

Perhaps in keeping with his desire to indulge the occult theme, Kenny killed the pig on Friday the 13th of June, the day before the attack on Greg's house. On that day he took an associate called Ken Boon, and his housemate Raymond "Tubby" Hopkinson, out to the Walhalla Road to kill the pig. They pinned the pig to the dirt road and cut its throat with a butcher's knife. As much as Kenny suggests the slaughter was prompted by ideas of revenge, it seems a greater motivation was hunger. Kenny gutted the pig and cut off its head before taking its body home and hanging it in the shower to bleed. They had to use Kenny's shower; Yvonne wouldn't let them use hers.

However, they left the pig's head in the scrub with the rest of its remains. Tubby, who was thinking of taking the head to a taxidermist to have it preserved and mounted, was dispatched to retrieve it. He rode his motorbike out to the site and collected the head – now covered in ants – brought it home and put it in a bucket of water to kill the ants. He left it on the doorstep.

That night Kenny, Yvonne, Darrin and Becky left the Haigh Street party in Becky's car. She drove them around to Darrin's parents' house, so they could collect his car. Although drunk, Darrin backed the brown Holden VH Commodore out of the driveway, so that his parents were not startled by the sound of a group of people stomping around the driveway. From there, Yvonne, who was more sober, took over and drove them around to her place for a few minutes.

They then moved on to the house in Gladstone Street, Moe, that Kenny shared with a couple of notorious characters. One of his housemates was Dean Ross, known as Dumb Dumb Deano; the other of course was Tubby, a drug user and alleged minor dealer with a reputation for violence and a string of convictions for assault, mainly against police.

They called at the house ostensibly to collect the pig's head. Kenny went inside with Darrin and Yvonne and they had a few drinks and a few "cones" of marijuana. Tubby was already asleep. He'd been drinking and smoking marijuana most of the night and had collapsed into bed. Kenny went into his room, giggling and laughing, and woke him up. As Tubby had been the one who had ridden his motorbike out to the Walhalla Road to retrieve the pig's head, Kenny believed it was Tub's severed head, so he asked his permission to take it. Tub wasn't pleased about giving it up but he was prepared to, as long as Kenny went through with his prank. Tub didn't want it wasted.

Deano said he'd come with Kenny because he wanted to get something to eat, but he didn't want any part of the attack. They collected the pig's head from the bucket at the front door and left.

Kenny and Yvonne were committed to the plan, and Darrin

Chapter Seven

also wanted in. He'd never really met Greg, but was still fond of Yvonne and he had nothing else to do.

The plan was simple. Yvonne would drop the group at Greg's house. They'd smash the windows of his car, hurl the pig's head through the front window of his house and run off. They had considered putting it in Greg's letterbox but realised it wouldn't fit. Yvonne would collect them ten or fifteen minutes later as they walked back along Narracan Drive toward the heart of Moe. Yvonne would satisfy her urge for revenge without really getting her hands dirty; big brother was used to this sort of thing, she wasn't.

Deano had precious little to do with what happened over the next few hours; his determination to stay in the car, to say and do nothing, was a smart move.

The third member of Kenny's house, Tubby Hopkinson, went back to bed, telling Kenny he was too wasted from the drug taking and beer drinking.

The four in the car – Kenny, Yvonne, Darrin and Deano – drove toward Newborough and passed the front of Greg's house in Narracan Drive. They drove into the Gunn's Gully BP Service Station a couple of hundred metres up the road. Yvonne wheeled the brown Commodore into the dirt lane behind the station and drove at a crawl down the track. She killed the headlights and brought the car to a stop near a railway siding. It was about 2.00 a.m.

Kenny tumbled out of the car, the pig's head in his hand. Darrin Wilson grabbed an axe handle from the floor in the back and joined Kenny, walking off toward the railway line. Kenny bent down and collected a fistful of ballast stones from the train lines and stuffed them in the tight pockets of his jeans. He grabbed some more and carried them in his free hand, the pig's head under his other arm, clutched to his side.

They scrambled down the train lines toward the house. Their courage, though, was fading with every bark of the dogs Greg kept in his backyard. A few minutes went by and late night traffic – probably people on their way home from nightclubs – straggled past.

They sat and watched the house, but Kenny's nerves got the better of him. The call of nature gripped his stomach and he responded by dropping his jeans and defecating on the train lines opposite Greg's house. With no toilet paper handy, Kenny improvised and ripped the breast pocket from his shirt. It would have to do.

He rejoined Darrin and they resumed their watch for about five more minutes from behind some bushes. Greg's dark green Ford Falcon was parked in the driveway pointing toward the road, its boot open.

A man emerged from the house and Kenny whispered to Darrin, "That's him there". Darrin had never seen Greg before that moment. Greg walked over to a large green council-issue garbage bin, opened the lid and put a white plastic bag inside before returning to the house. Kenny crossed the road and crept along the fence by a vacant block next to Greg's house until he was adjacent to the side gate.

Greg's car was on the other side of the fence and Kenny wanted to smash its windows. He stuck his head up over the fence. The dogs, loose in the backyard, pounced. Barking ferociously, they jumped at the fence as Kenny squatted against it, terrified. Greg came outside and Kenny held his breath while Greg looked around, before going back into the house.

Kenny ran back across the road to Darrin. They waited for their nerves to calm, and for a couple of cars to clear. Moments later, the pair were startled when Greg re-emerged from the house, got into his car and drove off.

They now had a free rein. Believing the house to be empty, they were free to hurl the stones and pig's head without fear of discovery, let alone confrontation. They crossed the road and climbed over the three-foot high fence that runs across the front

CHAPTER SEVEN

of the property, careful not to use the driveway because it was illuminated by a streetlight.

Kenny got to within a metre or two of the house and hurled the pig's head at the lounge room window, on the left-hand side. It bounced off. He picked it up and threw it again. Harder. This time, it had the desired effect. Darrin was sure it went sailing through the window into the house. Kenny also was adamant the pig's head went inside. Emboldened, Kenny threw the rocks from his pocket at the other window. Darrin didn't end up using the axe handle; after the noise of the window smashing, he had grown scared that the commotion would attract attention, so he fled from the noise.

Kenny jumped around near the front of the house, laughing. Bursting with adrenalin, he yelled and danced. Greg's dogs were barking madly and neighbours' lights were being turned on. But he did not hear a child's cry.

"I never heard no baby crying. Nothing. There were dog's barking and that, but there was no baby crying in that house. I would have definitely heard it. With all the glass smashing and that, it would have made some noise if it was in the lounge room and I would have heard it," he said.

"If there was a baby in there I would have heard it because I didn't just throw it and piss off, I hung around a bit and I was right there under the window. I'd have heard it if there was a baby in there and I'd have been straight in there. I mean if there was a kid in there that's different to smashing his windows to scare him. I'd have been right in there."

Kenny and Darrin were laughing as they ran off down the street toward Moe. They passed two houses before crossing the road over to the railway lines. As they ran along the lines, they saw two teenaged boys walking down Narracan Drive toward them. Kenny and Darrin, full of their success, hurled rocks at the two youths as they walked along the road. They stayed on that side of the road for a couple of hundred metres before crossing back to the footpath, where two other young teenagers were walking along toward them. Kenny couldn't resist challenging them. As they walked past, Kenny said "boo" in their faces. They kept walking.

As the pair neared a small bridge over Narracan Creek, Yvonne arrived and picked them up. She asked what had happened. Darrin replied: "His front window's gone". They drove to the BP Service Station where they bought a packet of Peter Jackson Extra Mild and a 1.25 litre bottle of Coke. The two youths they had just passed were in the store. One of them decided to get his own back on Kenny and walked up and said "Boo!". The boys remembered Kenny and Darrin quite clearly from their previous encounter on the road. They also remember that there was no baby with them.

When the group left the BP Service Station that night, they drove back to Yvonne's house. Kenny offered to stay the night in case Greg came around seeking retribution but it was decided that Darrin Wilson would stay with his former fiancée. They dropped off Kenny and Deano at their Gladstone Street house before returning to Yvonne's place.

It didn't take long for Greg to find his smashed house and ring Yvonne. At 3.09 a.m. she received the call. It was short and succinct, with Greg screaming and asking if it was another of her sick jokes. He didn't mention a missing child or that Jaidyn had been in the house.

Yvonne had been expecting Greg to come around that night; he could not let an incident like that pass without some form of comeback. Within half an hour of the phone call, he drove past and bipped his horn outside her place. She thought this was odd; normally he'd stop and have a good look, particularly as Darrin's car was in the driveway. This unnerved her and, as she cuddled into Darrin's arms, she feared that Greg was planning something.

CHAPTER EIGHT

Senior Constable Farnham Molesworth had clocked on at 11.00 p.m. on Saturday, 14 June. His shift in the divisional van with Senior Constable Matthew Georgeson was more than four hours old, when a car heading down Lloyd Street, Moe, in the opposite direction caught his attention.

The policemen did not recognise the green Ford Falcon by sight, although it was fairly well known to Moe police. Nor did they realise who was driving it, but any car out in Moe at that time of night is worthy of interest for two bored coppers.

They did a U-turn and followed the car, up and through the roundabout. The Ford began to speed up as it headed north along Anzac Street. They followed as it turned right at the next roundabout into Albert Street. Shortly after, it turned right into Bennett Street, where the police finally flashed their lights to stop the car.

Senior Constable Molesworth approached the Ford as his partner logged the time and location. He knew now whose car it was and who would be behind the wheel.

"Have you got your licence there Greg?," Senior Constable Molesworth asked.

"Yes," Greg said, and flicked through his wallet before handing over the licence.

"Where have you been tonight?"

"Nowhere."

"Are you heading home?"

"No."

The policeman gave Greg a breath test, which was negative, but Senior Constable Molesworth was puzzled. He detected a new caution in Greg's manner. He'd had numerous dealings with this bloke in the past. Usually, Greg Domaszewicz was cocky and self-assured. This time, he was subdued, even quiet, and unlike on previous occasions, he wasn't so presumptuous as to call the copper by his first name. The policeman couldn't explain it. There appeared to be nothing amiss, it was just a feeling he had and he couldn't detain Greg on that.

Senior Constable Molesworth had a brief look inside the car, but did not look in the Ford's back or in the boot. Satisfied, he sent Greg on his way.

Some time later a rumour emerged that Greg was saturated with water when police pulled him over. It wasn't so. In fact, it was clear to Senior Constable Molesworth that Greg's head and shoulders were dry.

The mystery of this episode is that Greg did not breathe a word about Jaidyn's disappearance. Nor did he mention that his windows had been smashed, or that a pig's head was in his front garden.

Soon after the police had stopped him, Greg arrived home. That was when Bilynda rang. She'd made a number of calls around the place, to Brett McGrath's house and to Julie Brassington, and she wanted to remind Greg not to stay at home, because of the smashed windows. Bilynda wanted him back with her. He promised her he'd come.

CHAPTER NINE

It was just before 8.00 a.m. on a cold, wet Sunday morning in Melbourne. Rowland Legg was about to leave his home in the city's suburbs for the homicide squad offices in St Kilda Road when his pager went off.

Legg was not surprised. He was head of the homicide squad crew on duty that weekend; of course his pager would go off.

He read the familiar message: call the Victoria Police Force's communications on-line supervisor. The Force has one detective inspector on duty for the state during weekends and after hours. Their job is not so much to turn up to crime scenes, but to act as advisers and to coordinate other detectives for more serious offences. The on-line supervisor asked Legg to call the detective inspector on duty, Detective Inspector Paul Hollowood.

Morwell detectives had called Detective Inspector Hollowood about a case that had started to puzzle them. On the face of it, a child was missing, apparently abducted. What concerned the detectives was that they were getting different stories from the people involved. Something didn't make sense.

Occasionally in these situations, the police call on the Special Response Squad, especially if it is feared that the child may be held to ransom. But there was no ransom in this case and Detective Inspector Hollowood thought the best option was to call homicide. Missing persons in suspicious circumstances were also homicide's domain.

When Legg phoned in that Saturday morning, Detective Inspector Hollowood told him that a child was missing. He also told Legg that the child had been left alone in a house which had been vandalised that night, and there was something else: someone had left a pig's head at the scene.

Detective Senior Sergeant Legg was not sure if it was a homicide squad job at first. But the more his superior told him about the case, the more convinced Legg became that it was. Besides, he was starting to feel that there was something distinctly odd about the whole case.

His first call was to Detective Sergeant Ian Riccardo, at Morwell CIB, who was in charge of the investigation at the scene. Although the Moe uniform branch had taken the complaint, the CIB had also been called in before the state crime squad.

Legg wanted a clearer picture of what was going on in Moe. The local police had the crime scene preserved and under guard, but Legg also wanted the two suspects separated and everything they said recorded.

Then Legg contacted his crew – the next in command, Detective Sergeant Steve Fyffe, Detective Sergeant Mick Roberts, Senior Detective Russell Sheather and Senior Detective Paul Cripps – to meet at the squad's office.

Detective Senior Sergeant Rowland Pelton Legg is not your average copper. His distinguished-sounding English name and his Carey Grammar education are badges worn almost as proudly as the gold lapel badge of the Victorian Police Force that he pins to his dark suits.

A former minder to Victorian Premier Jeff Kennett, Legg's politics would not be far removed from the Premier's, if only the Premier were a bit more conservative. His allegiance to Mr Kennett and his fondness for the lapel pin are a legacy of time

Chapter Nine

spent in the counter terrorist services, which looked after the Premier and other VIPs.

A man of average height, thin and with short-cropped hair, Legg has small, dark, squinting eyes. He looks remote and grim, sometimes foreboding, but there is something reassuring about the determined set of his jaw.

Legg would become the public face of the investigation, making regular appearances on television and in the newspapers, dispensing morsels of information to the media and trying to tease new leads from dead-ends. Legg had a strong team.

Detective Sergeant Steve Fyffe, a large affable man in his mid-thirties with boyish good looks, had been with the homicide squad for a number of years and had worked on a number of big cases, including that of serial killer Paul Charles Denyer.

Detective Sergeant Mick Roberts was a quietly spoken, diligent officer with a barrel chest, thick neck and a passion for boxing. He had recently been transferred from the Asian crime squad to homicide.

Russell Sheather and Paul Cripps, two extremely enthusiastic young detectives fresh to the crime squads from the suburban CIBs, completed the team.

They were joined by forensic and crime scene specialists, plus police photographic and video specialists. The crew gathered at the squad offices on the 9th floor of Melbourne's St Kilda Road Police Complex for a preliminary briefing.

Legg was given regular updates about the situation in Moe, and shortly after 11.00 a.m., four of the five detectives were on their way to the town. Legg followed shortly afterwards on his own. He wanted time to coordinate support services and to think. Different theories and possibilities crisscrossed his mind. Did those who broke the windows and left the pig's head take the child? Had this bloke, Greg Domaszewicz, done it? Maybe he broke the windows himself and threw the pig's head to make it appear like someone else had done it? Or had he concealed the child as a cover-up for a domestic dispute?

Legg's priority was the child's safety. He couldn't decide from what he knew whether Jaidyn was alive or not. Not even experience, or instinct, helped. Perhaps the boy had been secreted away somewhere by a family member, or a stranger. Maybe he was already dead. Then again, the pig's head incident could be unrelated. It would have to be an extraordinary coincidence, but it was possible and coincidences of its type were not unprecedented.

The detectives arrived at the Moe Police Station amid drizzle and lifting fog at about 2.00 p.m. Legg led the briefing; it was standard procedure for what was shaping up as a distinctly non-standard investigation.

The briefings touched on the volatile relationship between Greg Domaszewicz and Yvonne Penfold. The local police knew all about it, because of the regular breaches in the equally regular intervention orders. The Moe police were not even surprised at the vandalism at Greg Domaszewicz's house. There was a kind of weary acceptance that those sorts of things would occur at that house, and in that part of Moe.

It was soon clear that Legg could discount one line of questioning: Greg hadn't smashed his own windows. Nor had Bilynda been involved in the vandalism. But the police did want to talk to Yvonne Penfold.

When he had walked into the police station, Greg said he reckoned Yvonne or her family were behind the attack. However, the police had baulked at acting. There were other more pressing issues, and Greg was saying things that caused them greater alarm. Before going off on a tangent, the detectives wanted to be sure that Greg's complaint was true. There was no clear story about Jaidyn's whereabouts, so the investigation of Yvonne Penfold would have to wait.

Chapter Nine

Homicide detectives, local police and forensic scientists left the station and went to Bilynda Murphy's house first, and then on to Greg's house. The extent of the damage at Narracan Drive surprised the police. The size of the holes smashed in the windows of the house meant that it would have been almost impossible for someone to have entered through them, they figured on first glance.

Legg knew that the house was locked when Greg had driven to Traralgon to pick Bilynda up. Or so Greg claimed. The detectives checked the bolt on the back door and the locking arrangements of the house, however the police did not know whether Yvonne had a key. As it turned out, she did not and, in any case, the locks had been changed since the couple's last separation.

The police also noted immediately that, as well as having relatively small holes, the windows had not been "rimmed", whereby a person climbing in smashes out the remaining shards of glass in the frame for a safe entrance. There was no blood or soil inside either. Clearly, unless someone had a key, no one had got into Greg's place through the windows.

Other clues confirmed this theory. The blinds, curtains and furniture remained intact and none of the small items near the windows had been knocked over.

Meanwhile, Moe police officers collected Yvonne Penfold from her house in Austin Avenue. She was brought into the station by Sergeant Russell Fraser who knew Yvonne well, and had known her mum and stepfather for more than ten years.

Sergeant Fraser had recalled a conversation with Yvonne some weeks earlier when she had mentioned a pig's head but had not given it any thought at the time. He had passed this information on to Detective Sergeant Riccardo who, after checking with Paul Cripps from homicide, told Fraser to bring Yvonne in. It took little time for Yvonne to confess to her involvement in the vandalism at Greg's house.

But Sergeant Fraser had another concern. He was worried that there could be a perception of impropriety if he continued on the investigation, because of rumours that he was having a relationship with Yvonne. He asked to be given other duties and the officers agreed. At the time, Sergeant Fraser – a father of two – had been separated from his wife for about six years. Both he and Yvonne denied there was a sexual relationship, but rumours persisted.

Yvonne quickly explained her role in the raid on Greg's house. She told them how she had driven the car and identified the people she was with.

Police went after them. Darrin Wilson had left Moe and was home in San Remo. Police at Phillip Island were immediately alerted and sent to collect him, arriving just after Darrin heard of Jaidyn's disappearance on the evening news. Once in the police station at Phillip Island, Darrin made a full statement.

The other two accomplices followed suit. Quickly brought in, they gave police details that were remarkably similar to Darrin's version of events. But it was Yvonne's account that prised open the truth of the bizarre attack on her former boyfriend's house.

"None of them were automatically cooperative," Legg said, "but basically as a result of Yvonne being brought in and admitting the fact she was behind all of this, the others were all rounded up and, totally separately, gave corroborative accounts of each other's stories."

Legg knew that one part of the riddle was solved. The stories from the four were certainly much more consistent than those being told by Greg and Bilynda. The pair had been interviewed on and off during the day by police from Moe and detectives from Morwell. Early on, the interviews had taken the form of statements, rather than interrogations.

Sergeant Max Hill, who had dealt with Greg and Bilynda at the station when they came in that morning, interviewed Greg with Senior Detective Shelley Rees of Morwell CIB.

Chapter Nine

Legg first spoke to Greg at about 7.30 that evening. He ushered in Detective Sergeant Mick Roberts, introduced himself and sat down in the sparse interview room. It wasn't a formal interview, Legg simply wanted to explain to Greg what was going on and to gain an impression of his demeanour. Greg was going to have to stay at the station for a while. There were a few more inquiries to be made, more questions to be answered.

Legg watched Greg as he explained the situation and was struck by his manner. He fidgeted and seemed nervous and when they talked of Jaidyn's fate, Greg's concern appeared insincere.

Legg believed that Greg's demeanour in that first meeting did not help Greg's cause. But any suspicions were tempered by the lack of detailed information about what happened. All the police had were claims that Jaidyn had been burnt, Greg picking up Bilynda at Ryans, Greg being stopped by police and a few assorted clues. More would come, but what Legg had at that moment were contradictions between the stories told by Bilynda and Greg.

The investigators had their suspicions. Greg's story didn't appear to add up and, as fanciful as it first appeared, the police were beginning to consider that the vandalism incident was no more than an extraordinary coincidence.

By Monday morning, Yvonne and her accomplices' stories were looking more credible. It was a simple task for police to check what they had bought from the service station using the shop's cash register roll. The kids who Kenny had tried to spook were also found. The couple they had thrown rocks at were located. Their story held. Added to this was the fact the pig's head throwing prank had Kenny's name written all over it – would they commit the more serious crime and leave such a telltale sign behind?

Although still unable to rule the group out, Legg started to believe that the pig's head episode was not directly related to Jaidyn's disappearance.

"The picture we were building, as time went by, the actions of the pig's head group were not those of people involved in a baby's abduction," he said.

"Not only weren't they seen with a baby in their arms, they had no apparent concern of being identified – hardly the actions of someone who has just abducted a child."

Police did not get the key evidence provided by the cash register roll and the witnesses to Kenny and Darrin's stone throwing for several days. However, other factors convinced them that Yvonne's gang of four had, in fact, behaved exactly as they described. The houses of all those involved on the pig's head throwing expedition were searched and clothing confiscated. But the vital component in arriving at the view the group were not involved was Yvonne's brother, Kenny.

The local police had interviewed Kenny often enough to know how he conducted himself under the pressure of interrogation. Kenneth Stephen Penfold has an extensive criminal record, which runs to five pages. A few crimes had been committed in Queensland but most were in Victoria, and most of those at Moe. Local detectives knew that Kenny was a "soft" interview. Within minutes of starting an interview, the hard man exterior would disappear and he would tell all. Even his schoolteachers remembered Kenny as an extremely difficult student, always in trouble, but one who would always put his hand up to admit his misbehaviour.

After his interviews with police, Kenny was quickly found on the Monday following the raid by Channel 10 and the *Herald Sun*. His interviews were typically forthright. In a now notorious exchange with Channel Seven's police reporter, Peter Morris, on the Tuesday, Kenny was amusingly direct, admitting that as soon as he saw Greg leave his house that Saturday night he thought "Bingo!" and launched the pig's head. Kenny told Morris that when he returned the next day to inspect the reaction to his handiwork and saw all the police

Chapter Nine

around: "I thought, 'You're fuckin' joking, all this for a fuckin' pig's head!'"

Kenny's credibility was not the most scientific tool in the investigation, but it was important. In his roguish way, Kenny charmed the police and the media, with his disarming candour lending him sincerity.

Police training demands that detectives always keep their minds open to the prospect of the unexpected and the unusual. And by Monday morning, Legg knew that without new information it was appearing more and more unlikely that Kenny's group had been involved in Jaidyn's disappearance.

"The strongest considerations were whether it was just Greg, whether it was Bilynda and Greg or whether it was a third party we hadn't identified," Legg concluded.

The police asked Bilynda and Greg who they thought was responsible for the toddler's disappearance, now that the vandals were fading in their estimations.

Neither of them could think of another suspect. That was not unusual; if Jaidyn was a random victim, then Greg and Bilynda would not be likely to identify a possible suspect. However, nothing seemed to indicate that it was a random crime. The possibility of an unknown third party being involved was even more coincidental than the pig's head connection.

The investigators' view was slowly emerging, but they continued to chase down leads. Legg and his crew were still working on the basis, and the hope, that Jaidyn was alive. Finding him alive was their first goal, and although Legg already had grave doubts, the hunt maintained an urgency that a normal homicide investigation would not assume. They were working to prevent a homicide; they were trying to find a missing little boy.

Had they known at this point that Jaidyn was already dead, they may have done some things differently, such as the forensic testing of Greg's car and the time at which he was interviewed and by whom.

A local pig farmer had been contacted on the Sunday to find out if he'd had any pigs killed overnight. Was there a headless carcass lying around? Police were hoping to establish the origin of the pig's head. Any clue would help.

Inquiries were made at Ryans Hotel to confirm the Murphy girls' night there. Management remembered them alright.

All of the local hospitals were contacted to check Greg's story that Jaidyn had burnt his bottom when he fell against the heater. And although Greg said he had made up the story on the phone to Bilynda and Katie, police doggedly went through every detail.

After his brief chat with Greg, Legg went in to see Bilynda. It was Sunday evening, and a chilly, grim darkness had settled on Moe although the fluorescent lights were bright as Legg entered the interview room. Bilynda Murphy was sitting behind a laminex table with wood veneer in the sparse room. A policeman outside kept an eye on the room to make sure she didn't chat with her boyfriend next door. Legg felt there was still a chance that Bilynda Murphy could have been involved in her son's disappearance.

Legg sat down at the small table and introduced himself. He told Bilynda there were a lot of unanswered questions in the accounts that she and Greg had given them.

"Where do you think Jaidyn is?" Legg asked gently.

"No idea."

"Who do you think did it?"

"Well, it can only be Greg."

Bilynda was sober by this stage. She was also worn out and emotionally fragile. She had been up all night, except for the one to two hour gap between Greg dropping her home and collecting her again, and she hadn't had a drink for sixteen hours.

Bilynda Murphy was a constant challenge for the police, not just in the early stages of the investigation, but all the way

Chapter Nine

through. She was both the grieving mother of a missing child to be comforted and sympathised with, but also a suspect. When she left Moe police station later that night, Legg had no idea how to read her. He didn't know if she was involved or completely innocent. He leant towards the view that she wasn't involved, but could not stop himself wondering.

Bilynda's mood during the night swung from being a distraught mother to a woman more concerned about getting home to bed, having a long sleep and waking up the next day from a nasty nightmare. Legg was intrigued by her reactions during the interview.

"With the variety of inquiries we conduct and people we come across, you initially, instinctively judge a reaction or statement or demeanour on yourself and the way you have been brought up. You say to yourself, 'this has to be untrue because she should be crying or she should be nervous or she should be angry'," Legg said.

"Because automatically, your initial judgment of someone is whether they behave in the way you would expect, or you would behave, or your friends or family or whatever would react. And then you come across someone who has had a totally different upbringing to what you have, totally different background and the reaction they might have or what they might say might be totally innocent."

It posed some difficult challenges for the investigators. They could neither discount Bilynda's reactions, nor rely on them.

"So, again it's the situation with all our investigations, you remain as expansive as possible, not discounting anything and remain receptive to anything," Legg said.

"You don't discount what reaction you get, or someone's demeanour or what they say. You have to judge it based in relation to a whole conglomeration of all sorts of things. You can't rely totally on gut feeling, however with extensive experience of a broad array of individuals over many years, gut feeling and instinct can be very accurate. You must, however, consider a person's background, motives and so on. Physical evidence, information from other witnesses and contradictions between accounts all must be considered. There are so many elements and you have to use judgment in determining what you rely on or put weight on more so than something else."

Eventually, at about 10.30 p.m., Bilynda was allowed to leave and police took her to Katie's house.

It soon became apparent to police all would not be revealed and they were not going to be able to charge Greg Domaszewicz that evening. His story was changing, but he was not moving toward a confession. It was later revealed in court that as the night wore on, Legg telephoned his superiors in Melbourne and organised for the on-call surveillance unit to be sent to Moe immediately.

A handful of undercover officers drove to Moe that night in their nondescript, second-hand cars, arriving about 1.00 a.m.

Police needed Greg out of the station and mobile that night because they still didn't know where Jaidyn was, whether he was alive or dead. Legg believed it important to be aware of Greg's movements after he left the station. Would Greg go to the body to further dispose of it if Jaidyn was dead? Or was he alive and being kept somewhere where Greg would have to tend him? And if he did none of those things, what would it suggest of his involvement?

Police quickly examined Greg's car, which had been driven into the compound behind the police station earlier that day. Under a portable light, officers scrambled over the car searching for clues as best they could. While a thorough examination would have been preferable, it was not possible if police were to make the car available to Greg that night. Had police known Jaidyn was already dead, the car would have been impounded for proper forensic testing; as it was, they didn't know, and they needed Greg to have a vehicle.

Chapter Nine

Any hope police had that Greg would lead them straight to Jaidyn was wishful thinking, however. Greg Domaszewicz left the Moe Police Station at around 2.00 a.m. on Monday. He didn't go home, and he didn't go looking for Jaidyn.

He went to see Bilynda Murphy.

CHAPTER

Bilynda left the Moe police station in a daze.

She'd arrived drunk, with less than an hour's sleep between her and a marathon drinking binge. She had then spent about seventeen hours locked in a police station making two statements, one brief while still drunk, the other lengthier while rapidly sobering up. A string of suited and uniformed police had walked in and out of the room. Some had asked questions, others had given her things, some had screamed and others had made accusations.

She was in a spin. She'd been separated from the man she had walked in with and wasn't able to speak to him. Didn't want to speak to him. By late evening she was convinced he had taken, and possibly killed, her son.

She was driven home. But home wasn't how she'd left it. What was of significant interest to the investigators was that Jaidyn's room was now in turmoil. When Bilynda had arrived home at 3.30 that morning, knowing her kids weren't home, she hadn't bothered to go into their rooms. Jaidyn's bedroom, left tidy, his cot neatly made up, was now in disarray, his quilt drooping over the side of the cot. The mattress was on the floor and one end of the curtains was hanging off the rail.

And Jaidyn was not there.

About 10.00 p.m., Bilynda arrived at Katie's house. She

Chapter Ten

walked in and was hugged by her big sister, and her mum was there too. They didn't know what to say but they talked anyway.

She'd arrived back in time for the news, to find the story of Jaidyn's disappearance on television. That's when it hit her. It was only while watching her life suddenly turned into public property by the banality of a television news item that Bilynda started to feel it was all real. Television is often accused of desensitising its audience. But for Bilynda, it had the opposite effect: this was reality.

"By the time I left there that night, I was going to kill Greg. They [the police] took me up to my place and I walked in and there were like twenty people in the lounge room and I thought, 'What the hell's going on here?'" Bilynda recalled later.

Police wore gloves as they searched through bags and asked if there was anything illegal in the house. Bilynda remembered Greg's bong. A small stash of drugs suddenly had her worried. Would the police think she was a druggie now and not believe her any more?

When the search was over, Bilynda went back to Katie's house. The sisters sat and talked some more. Around midnight, Katie asked Bilynda if she thought Greg had killed Jaidyn. Bilynda, frustrated, said she didn't know. Of course she couldn't know, and she wasn't yet prepared to admit to thinking Greg did it. Not to Katie. Not even to herself.

But there were times when Bilynda did believe that Greg had killed Jaidyn. When she left the police station that night she was convinced of Greg's guilt, but in her heart she was wrestling with the notion. She didn't know what to believe; all she knew was that she wanted to torture Greg to get the truth out of him.

Bilynda told her mum that night that when she saw Greg she ought to shoot him in a kneecap and order him to tell her where Jaidyn was. Then she'd shoot him in the other knee if he didn't answer. She didn't know where she was going to get a gun, but she was desperate to find her son.

Greg turned up at about 2.00 a.m.

"But why would you go to the mother? I mean, that's just looking for a punch in the mouth," Bilynda said later of Greg's visit.

"I think he thought that convincing the mother that he didn't do it was going to be his best defence."

Greg's first words to Bilynda were: "I'm sorry".

She didn't punch him. She didn't even throw him out. She could not explain why later, but she let him in the door and within a short time, she was swayed back to believing he wasn't involved.

Maybe her own feelings of guilt by association had something to do with it. Perhaps she felt that if he was responsible, then she too was in some way guilty because she'd delivered her son to his killer, a man who had mistreated him in the past. Why had she stayed drinking that night after being told her son was injured? Better to believe in him – maybe he was innocent.

If Bilynda did not wish to confront those issues then, she certainly did not want to later. Plenty of people would rush to judge her. They would argue that, as a mother, she should have known better than to leave her son with someone who appeared to be erratic and violent. Of course, it is not that simple. Who would reasonably suggest that someone with whom they were having an affair could not be trusted to look after their child?

Bilynda's biggest desire in those days was for everything to be back the way it was. She may have been guilty of not wanting to believe her little boy was dead. Guilty even of hoping her boyfriend was not involved in Jaidyn's disappearance. But guilty of anything else? Not at all.

Bilynda didn't hug Greg when he arrived at her place that night, but she quickly became his strongest advocate. He was constantly upset in the days that followed his release and, like Jaidyn, cried regularly.

Chapter Ten

Bilynda too cried, her anguish endless. "I mean I just didn't believe it, this is just a dream I'm going to wake up from," she said.

Instead, Bilynda had to try to chart a course through a maze of half-truths, deceptions and pain.

"With Greg, everything you ask him he has got an answer for. Everything you check up on, and [you] find out he is telling the truth," Bilynda said.

"I didn't think Jaidyn was dead until the day I found him. Never ever once, didn't even enter my mind. But I just said Yvonne Penfold has done this but you don't really know. In those days afterwards, Greg was still making jokes and it didn't really mean anything."

CHAPTER ELEVEN

That Sunday morning in Moe, Bilynda Murphy wasn't the only person passed out drunk.

Darren Farr was sound asleep in his daughter's bed, having been carried home by friends from a party a few doors up the road. His wife, Sheena, has a simple rule. When Darren has a few drinks he snores. Loudly. And Sheena won't have it, or Darren, in her bed.

However Sheena happily puts up with the chattering and scratching of the radio scanner programmed to the emergency services frequencies that sits by her bedside. Darren was a tow truck driver for years and needed to listen to the scanner overnight in case of an accident. Sheena got used to it, so now the Farrs fall asleep to the chat of police, fire and ambulance officers.

Early that Sunday morning, Sheena was woken by an unusual amount of traffic on the scanner. It was clear something was wrong, but she couldn't work out what. She heard enough, however, to know that most of the activity was taking place in and around 150 Narracan Drive. Although still half asleep, Sheena realised that the address was Greg Domaszewicz's house. While the couple hadn't seen much of Greg for a while, he was still a friend.

She got up and roused Darren from his sleep. He took some shaking, but Darren eventually got up at about 8.00 a.m. and

CHAPTER ELEVEN

decided he'd try to find out what was happening. He went to the police station and asked if Greg was there. He was told that he was, but that he wasn't allowed to see him.

"Why, what's wrong with him?" Darren asked.

"What do you want to know?" the desk copper said.

"Why the fuck's Greg here, I'm his mate."

"Basically we can't tell you at the moment, we'd love to but we can't."

Darren left the station perplexed. He didn't know if Greg was in real trouble and wanted to speak to him, just to make sure. Uncertain what to do next, but thinking he should do something, Darren rang Greg's mum Helen Chervev and went to Spider's house. When he got there, he told Spider that Greg was in trouble.

"Oh God, what's he done? He had the kid last night," Spider said.

That was the first time the friends made any connection between Greg's appearance at the police station, and Jaidyn. Darren realised that Greg could be in serious trouble so he called his solicitor, Paul Vale, and left a message. When the solicitor called back soon after, Darren told him that his friend needed help. He didn't know why, he just knew he needed help.

On Monday morning, Greg was at his brother Peter's house in Newborough with his mum, when Bilynda and Katie arrived. Soon after Darren and Sheena Farr called in and offered Greg a place to stay during the turmoil. The media were gathering in town and his place was crawling with police.

When Darren saw Greg that day he was typically direct.

"What the fuck's going on?" he asked.

"They've taken the boy," Greg said.

"What are you talking about?" Darren asked, momentarily thinking Greg was talking about his dog Shepp, whom he also called "The Boy".

"They've taken Jaidyn."

"Who took Jaidyn?"

"Kenny and Yvonne Penfold have taken him."

"That's fucking bullshit," Darren said. Darren had seen Yvonne at the police station the day before. As soon as Yvonne had seen him, she'd burst into tears and said, "I'm sorry". Darren didn't know what Yvonne was apologising for at the time, though he later presumed it was for smashing Greg's windows. Yvonne was scared of Darren because he had been like a bodyguard to Greg during the previous couple of months when her troubles with Greg had reached their ugly peak.

Darren didn't consider the apology to be an admission of any sort about Jaidyn's disappearance. He just felt Yvonne was scared that he'd want revenge, but something about her expression and face instantly struck him, he didn't know why.

Darren repeated to Greg that he didn't think Kenny and Yvonne were involved.

"Well, who the fuck is? Somebody is," Greg said.

"Well I don't know, who've you been playing games with?"

The Farrs took Greg back to their place; it was Darren's birthday so he cooked eggs on toast for Greg and his mum and they sat around talking. About what the police were doing. About what they should be doing. About where Jaidyn was. And about the Penfolds and "that bitch Yvonne". Greg kept up a steady stream of vitriol about his former girlfriend, making it clear that he believed she had something to do with Jaidyn's disappearance. Greg was jumpy and vague, disjointed in his sentences and ideas.

He watched videos of the TV news reports and the scanner was on in the background, fixed on the police radio frequencies. While a lot of what the detectives were doing was relayed by mobile or landline telephone, there was still plenty of traffic on the scanner.

Chapter Eleven

Darren asked Greg if there was anything at his house that shouldn't be there. He knew Greg smoked a lot of marijuana, in fact there had barely been a day he had seen him without a "bong". But Darren considered Greg straight; all he wondered was if he had some grass stashed there.

Greg didn't mention the marijuana, but there was something he was worried about. He had a pair of jeans at the house with blood on them. Jaidyn's blood. The boy had an ulcer, or something, that was bleeding and Greg had used the jeans to wipe it up, he said. Later, Greg told Sheena the blood was from a cut on Jaidyn's lip.

The Farrs were supportive. Greg was their friend and they believed him, and until they could be convinced otherwise, Greg was rock-solid. Their falling out over the previous two months was forgotten. Darren and Greg had planned to patch up their differences with a few drinks the day before, and Darren was going to help as much as he could.

Sheena was more critical. Regardless of whether Greg had taken Jaidyn or not, she was disgusted with him for leaving the toddler alone while he went to pick up Bilynda. She confronted him in the kitchen early that Monday morning.

"Why did you leave him in the home? What were you thinking leaving a baby on the couch while you went all the way over to Traralgon and back again?" she asked.

"I don't know, I don't know why, I just don't know," Greg kept repeating. He said that he wished he hadn't left him alone, that he thought Jaidyn would be safe, and he talked about how he couldn't undo the past.

A strong woman with long curly hair pulled back off her face, Sheena had physically thrown Greg out once before when they argued. Now she stood against him, relentlessly questioning. Greg dropped his hands and said that he had no excuse.

His explanations had to do. Greg was the Farrs' friend and they offered him the run of their home to escape the insistent media. He couldn't go home – crime tape was criss-crossing his house, like some kind of sinister wrapping paper.

Around 8.00 p.m., Senior Detective Shelley Rees called around to Darren's place with another detective to take him down to the station. Police put the scenarios about what may have happened and who may have been involved to him. They also argued, based on the evidence, why they thought Greg was involved. Darren was unconvinced. They asked for details about Greg's background, what he was like with kids and if he had ever been violent before. Greg was his mate, he wasn't a child killer, Darren thought. He was standing by his friend.

The search for Jaidyn Leskie intensified. Thirty police and another twenty State Emergency Service volunteers were combing paddocks and bushland around Greg's house looking for clues.

Forensic experts examined the house, dusting for fingerprints and conducting a variety of other tests. They had found what they believed to be a crucial breakthrough. In the bin outside Greg's house they found a plastic bag with five tissues inside. The tissues had Jaidyn's blood on them, or so they believed. Subsequent tests would prove them right.

The investigators noticed that some of the tissues were twisted at the ends, suggesting that they had been used to pack a bleeding nose or ear.

Police were also surprised to find $600 in cash under Greg's mattress. The intriguing element to the discovery was that the money was wet. It had all been laid out flat, as though to dry. The wet money provided a compelling link with Greg's wallet, which the police had found in his green car, sopping wet. The wallet was so wet that the dye on the various business cards inside had run. It didn't look like it had been dropped in a puddle and quickly scooped out; it seemed to have been immersed in water.

The wet notes under the bed added weight to that theory.

Chapter Eleven

Police had already found Greg's wet jacket on the back seat of his green car. Legg started to wonder.

Why all these links to water? It had been wet the day before but not that wet.

CHAPTER TWELVE

The Moe Motor Inn and the pub next door, which surround the police station, became home for the next few weeks to an influx of media personnel; it started on Sunday, 15 June and soon the town was over-run with journalists. There wasn't a bed to be found for weeks. Police, photographers and cameramen added to the population boom. Some out-of-town police officers were forced to doss down on the floor of the police station or on friends' couches because they were unable to get a bed in a motel.

But while the influx of people injected money into the local economy, the trade-off was an instant unwanted notoriety. The locals believed that they were being maligned by association with what was considered a small pocket of people. They believed that the bizarre nature of this case had been extrapolated to suggest that the people of Moe were bizarre as well, or at least all working class, on the dole or drug smokers. The cruel jokes soon started and numerous locals complained about the media coverage; others lodged official complaints with the Press Council, which were eventually dismissed.

The town seemed to be fragmenting. Few people, it seemed, wanted to be known as being from Moe. They were from suburbs or regions around Moe, or visiting from neighbouring towns. But not all sections of the community were falling apart.

Chapter Twelve

And those people who were deservedly proud of their home town started to fight back.

After an article in the *Age* by Paul Heinrichs, which examined the social problems in the town, at least one newsagent refused to stock the newspaper. The ban, in protest at the perceived unfair treatment of the town, extended beyond sales of the newspaper. Police reporter Jason Koutsoukis was given a hostile reception in the shop and refused service. The ban on the paper prompted managers at the *Age* to send representatives down from Melbourne to help solve the problems.

Sensitivities were high in Moe. The journalists, who had been a novelty in the early stages, were soon resented. The reporters, not those involved in the case, were responsible for giving the town a bad name. The desire of newspapers and TV news services to give their readers or audiences a picture of where this was taking place, and to provide a context for what had happened, inevitably led to stories on Moe itself. These only served to inflame the situation.

Moe's Chamber of Commerce took matters into its own hands and spoke out strongly in defence of the town. A senior policeman for the Latrobe Valley region, Superintendent Adrian Fyffe, was also moved to defend Moe from what was considered an unfair attack.

However, the media role in Moe was significant from the start. The day after Jaidyn went missing, the media masses sought fresh pictures of the toddler and an interview with Bilynda. Brett's family had informed the media that Brett was in Western Australia.

Bilynda told police that she was too distraught to speak to the media. Police were keen for Bilynda to make a broad plea to the public for help. She was assured that, as her son was possibly still alive, it was extremely important she make an appeal for his safe return or for any information that could help police.

She was still reluctant.

Then police discovered that Bilynda had spent most of the day at Katie's and had already been interviewed exclusively by the television current affairs show *Today Tonight*. They also believed that she had been paid for the interview and were furious.

Rowland Legg had a stern word with Bilynda and she was finally convinced to speak to all the media. She appeared on the lawn of Katie's house in moccasins and skin-tight jeans, a chain of earrings in her ear, her dyed blonde hair growing out to expose the roots, and her eyes black from make-up and crying. She was clearly shaking with emotion. Sobbing and speaking in a whisper she confronted the journalists, with Katie at her side.

Bilynda's tear-streaked face was shown in almost every newspaper and on almost every television in the country, pleading for her son's return. Although the appearance was undoubtedly hard on Bilynda, it was essential for the message to get to as many people as possible.

Over the next few months, the case received coverage of an almost unprecedented level, both in Victoria and around the nation. Parallels were drawn with the Azaria Chamberlain case. It was an image which became a crucial motif in the final days of the mystery.

Inevitably, the mystery drew questions. What kind of life would Jaidyn have had? Would he have broken the cycle of domestic and financial problems that beset his family?

Whatever the answer, one thing Jaidyn did have was hope. Only a glimmer of it, but it was there. Yet after not quite 14 months, it was taken from him.

CHAPTER THIRTEEN

Greg slept late that Tuesday morning, before heading straight around to Katie's place to see Bilynda again. It was becoming more difficult for him to move about town and avoid the media. They still didn't know what he looked like, but they were getting closer.

About sixty police search-and-rescue officers and volunteers were now gathering in Moe to search Lake Narracan, eight kilometres to the north-east. Divers were scouring the Lake as well as Moondarra Dam, fifteen kilometres north of town. The investigation was increasingly focused on links to water.

For Greg, matters were getting serious. The police and media attention was not abating; it was intensifying. He rang Darren's lawyer, Paul Vale, and discussed the situation with him; they decided to meet.

Ian Riccardo and Rowland Legg called in to Darren Farr's house that day to talk to him about Greg. They stood in the lounge room, discussing the possibilities and asking questions about Greg. They put some of what they knew to Darren, who was starting to have doubts, but wasn't yet prepared to accept that his friend might be behind the child's disappearance.

Legg wanted Greg isolated from his friends and family, to help exert pressure on him.

Darren spoke with the detectives for a while but eventually got fed up and asked them to leave. They would be back. The Farrs were critical to the plan to isolate Greg; they were giving him shelter and comfort. They were questioned almost daily for the first week, with Legg continually revealing new information that fuelled doubt about Greg, hinting to Darren that he might be harbouring a killer. The conclusion was inescapable: Greg was the main suspect.

Bilynda wanted to talk to Paul Vale about another matter – custody of Breehanna – so she agreed to go to Melbourne with Greg to see the lawyer. Greg's mum would drive them.

Bilynda wanted to make a family court application to gain sole custody of her daughter. She feared Jaidyn's disappearance could prompt Brett Leskie to fight for custody of the three-year-old. She'd lost her son; she didn't want to lose her daughter as well.

Surveillance police followed the car to Melbourne and watched as the couple went shopping in Taylors Lakes. They were like young lovers again, Bilynda groping Greg on the backside as they laughed and joked in the shopping centre.

Rather than fleeing Moe, Brett Leskie was desperately fighting to get there. Stranded in Kalgoorlie, he didn't have the money to get home. The boss, where he had been working only a short time, agreed to cash his $500 pay cheque. But he was still well short of the airfare.

The manager of the local pub chipped in $100 from his own pocket, the staff donated $300 from their social fund and, after passing round the hat to the punters, he scraped together the balance.

With help from an airline, Brett arrived at Melbourne's Tullamarine airport at 7.00 p.m. on the Tuesday following Jaidyn's disappearance. He sobbed and shook as he walked off the plane. His brother, Glenn, wrapped an arm around his shoulder and walked with him from the arrival lounge. Brett

Chapter Thirteen

stopped and spoke to the media, pleading for Jaidyn's return. He cried out for anyone who knew anything about the case to contact police. To give them a hint. Let them know. Please. Brett was devastated.

Glenn took Brett to see family in Melbourne, where he tried to compose himself before the drive back to Moe. He stopped at Glenn's place to change his clothes and by 9.30 that night, Brett Leskie was being briefed by detectives at the Moe police station.

The following morning, Wednesday, 18 June, Rowland Legg revealed to the media that Greg and Bilynda had fled Moe without telling the homicide squad. They were not "wanted" by police, in the normal sense of the term, but detectives certainly would have preferred them to have stayed. Legg said police had not been told where the couple were, although he suspected they were in Melbourne. He was concerned that, if Jaidyn was found, they wouldn't know where to find the boy's mother and he told the media he would prefer it if they were in Moe.

Obviously, this was a tactic. Police no doubt knew exactly where Greg and Bilynda were. It was later revealed in court that Greg had been under surveillance from the moment he left the police station that first night. By using the media to let Greg and Bilynda know they wanted them back, they could avoid alerting Greg to the fact he was being followed.

The tactic also raised the level of intrigue. Greg was seen to be, if not on the run, at least on the move, fleeing to a lawyer for protection. If he was not a main suspect in the public's eyes before that, he certainly was now. Public sympathy for Bilynda was also waning. Many people questioned how the mother of a missing child could drive 140 kilometres from the place he had disappeared, only days after he went missing and in the midst of a police hunt.

Greg hired a car from Delta Car Rentals near his cousin's place at Melton, in Melbourne's west. His mum lived in Eltham and he needed his own transport. Late in the afternoon, Paul Vale contacted the police on the couple's behalf and told them he was acting for Greg and Bilynda. They would be back in Moe soon, he said. Legg said he wanted them back that night for blood samples.

Mr Vale said his clients were prepared to submit to a police request for blood tests. The police wanted to check the blood found on the tissues with that of Bilynda and Greg. At 7 o'clock that night, Greg Domaszewicz and Bilynda Murphy appeared at the Ringwood Police Station and provided blood samples to a forensic medicine officer in the presence of two other detectives from the homicide squad in Melbourne.

Later that night, Darren received a call from Greg on a mobile phone. Greg was in Warragul, on the drive back to Moe with Bilynda and Breehanna. He was worried about what to do next and told Darren that they wanted to flee to Brisbane to escape the turmoil. Could he help? Darren calmed Greg down and arranged to meet him in Trafalgar, midway between Moe and Warragul. They met in a side street and Darren talked Greg out of the plan; fleeing wouldn't make the problem go away, it would only make him look more guilty, he said.

Bilynda was also eager to escape the chaos but realised it would not be possible just yet. Greg's other worry was that he needed more clothes; he had been wearing the same ones since Sunday morning. Darren agreed to lend him some.

When they arrived back in Moe, Darren went in the front of his house to put a bag of clothes together, while Greg drove around the back. Darren passed the bag over the fence and Greg left, saying he was going to stay with friends in Dandenong.

At about 10.00 p.m., Darren heard over the scanner that there was a fire at Greg's house; Mariann McKinnon had reported the smoke. He rang Helen, who was staying with her other son in Newborough, a short distance away.

Minutes later, Greg phoned. He was back at his house and had smashed a side window to break in, while Bilynda waited in the car; he wanted to find out what the police had been up to.

Chapter Thirteen

Greg had cut himself climbing in, and asked Darren to clean some blood off the windows.

Homicide detectives, dining in a Newborough Chinese restaurant, were called to say there had been a break-in at Greg's place. Neighbours had heard glass smashing and Greg's hire car was parked at the back of the house.

Legg thought it may be a breakthrough. What was Greg checking in the house? Was there something there they had missed that Greg was going back for? Was he going to remove evidence or get something for the baby? What was he up to?

When Darren pulled into Greg's driveway minutes later, a police car pulled in behind him.

"What are you doing here?" one of the coppers asked.

"Checking the place."

Greg was sitting up on the Princes Highway watching the action from his car.

Surveillance crews were sitting further up the highway watching Greg.

Brett Leskie spoke out again. He was better informed now, having been briefed by police on the details of the case, and he was angry. How could anyone leave the boy alone at home in the first place? He pleaded for his son to be returned.

He accepted every interview request, speaking to anyone who would listen. He wanted the world to know that he wanted his little boy back.

At Darren's place that morning, Greg watched videos of the news bulletins. They showed footage of Brett Leskie sobbing openly and pleading for Jaidyn's return. Greg sat on the couch transfixed by the screen. Tears rolled down his cheeks as he muttered to himself and shook his head.

"I'm sorry. I'm sorry. Man I didn't mean to do it," Greg said.

When he realised what he'd said, he looked up at Darren and Sheena and asked them what he'd just said. They shook their heads.

"Nothing. Didn't hear nothing," they said.

They spoke about it later. Was he sorry because he had left the boy home alone and caused this trouble? What else could he be sorry for?

At 3.00 p.m. Greg arrived at Moe Police Station. As he stepped from the unmarked police Commodore the media mobbed him. It was the first time they had seen the babysitter, the last person known to have seen Jaidyn alive. Greg wore a green "Fosters Special Brew" cap and a stupid grin, as he weaved through the reporters and cameras and entered the station. Paul Vale followed soon after.

CHAPTER FOURTEEN

Greg was led through the police station to an interview room. He was wearing a padded, reddish-brown and white flannelette shirt, with a blue T-shirt underneath.

It was his second formal meeting with police. The first had been a statement, this was an interview. It was 3.38 p.m. on Thursday, 19 June when the video recording began. Greg took a sip from his can of Coke, while Paul Vale sat in an adjoining room listening.

Detective Sergeant Michael Roberts asked questions, while Detective Sergeant Stephen Fyffe took notes and Senior Constable Paul Edwards manned the video camera.

"How well do you know Jaidyn?" Mick asked.

"I have known him for a fair few months," Greg explained. "He is just over one [year-old]. He had his birthday a couple of months ago."

Greg explained how he knew Brett from school, and how the pair had worked together in Greg's car repair place. He had met Bilynda through Brett. They were all good friends, but when Brett left, Greg had started babysitting Jaidyn regularly.

Was Bilynda now his girlfriend then? "I guess."

He rambled vaguely about getting a run-on with babysitting at times, so that he was looking after the children virtually every day.

"The majority of the time I was looking after them at my place. Shopping. Took them to the shopping centre once," he said.

"At first [I looked after] Breehanna. She is just a cute little kid. You would be doing something on the car or something and she would be always passing the spanner and stuff."

He explained how he also began to babysit Jaidyn and had him "many times".

"I took him fishing just the once. He turned out to be a bit young ... he was a bit messy, dirty. I took the dogs with me ... you could imagine," he said with a reflective chuckle.

"I went with someone else that day anyway so it was not just like me and the dogs."

Glenn had been with them, Glenn Walker, a good mate of Greg's.

"Had you ever had any problems when you were babysitting Jaidyn?" Detective Sergeant Roberts asked.

"Oh, only like the first couple of times. To be honest he was a bit of a crier and I sort of thought well, if the kid's clean and he's not hungry and that, if he wants to sook, I just used to [let him]. The first times I really started looking after him actually I was doing a bit of painting at home ... he would be looking at me and have these looks. The best thing to do [was] just talk to them and painting the architrave. At the end he was amazing with the steps and that. You could just see him advance and advance and advance."

"You said he was a bit of a sook, and I suppose that's normal for kids that age, how did you cope if he started to cry?"

"You could generally stop him. I have got a Nintendo at home and just used to do that or used to let him and that. Ask him if he is hungry, he was never really that bad. I used to just leave him in the lounge room if I was painting in the kitchen or something. He would come and [be] more inquisitive or something.

"Bilynda used to practically just carry him if she was having to cook or clean."

Chapter Fourteen

"Would you describe him as a bit clingy to his mother?"

"Oh all kids are. You look at Breehanna, you know she is pretty tight with her mother."

"When he was crying would you like pick him up and give him a cuddle?"

"I used to pick him up ... he used to love the dogs at first, I suppose he hadn't seen dogs before that. At the end they were just excellent [to] muck around [with] and that. I used [to] get Jaidyn and throw the ball."

He explained that he wasn't sure what breed of dogs he had. One was a bull terrier bitch, he knew that, but he wasn't sure about the others.

Greg explained how he'd feed Jaidyn and give him a bottle when the boy came over. He wasn't so keen on changing his nappy though, in fact a couple of times he'd sent him home to mum to be changed because the stench was too much.

"What sort of sleeper is Jaidyn?"

"Depends on what sort of day he had. When he slept we just used to let him sleep."

"What I am getting at I suppose is, he was not upset about being at your house? He would sleep?"

"Oh yeah, me and him were pretty good friends I guess. That's how I wanted to keep it. He has got his family, whatever is happening there."

"Whereabouts would he sleep?"

"Out on the couch, I used to put me cushions around."

Greg explained the layout of his lounge room, with its two two-seater couches and an armchair, and asked if he should address his questions to the video camera, like a TV anchor person. No, just talk normally, he was assured.

"Did you ever hit him?"

"No. Oh he would get the odd little smack on the hand or something, if they are big they really know what's wrong, but when they're little they don't really know what's what."

"Would you pick him up and give him a shake?"

"Nah."

Police then asked Greg to talk them through the Saturday he was minding Jaidyn.

"The main thing I remember like on the Saturday is like a ritual of putting on Tattslotto on for years like, with my dad [and I] pick the numbers together and kept them tickets. I always got to put them on by Saturday, after the Wednesday or Thursday draw. I have to get to the Newborough Tattslotto agency by lunchtime on Saturday," Greg said.

He recalled that a friend had dropped around to return a large car jack he had borrowed, but couldn't recall whether it was before or after the Tattslotto visit. While he was at the Tatts agency, he had bought some lollies and headed around to Bilynda's house.

"Who was at Bilynda's house?"

"Her and the kid. I only sort of went there and she was in her pyjamas or something on the phone ... "

"Do you know who she was on the phone to?"

"Maybe her sister or Brett I suppose. I dunno. She sits on the phone a lot."

"What happened from there?"

"The majority of my mission was me Tattslotto sort of thing, other than that, whatever, sort of went there and then like if she was up would have stayed and talked a bit ... "

But Greg hadn't stayed for long at Bilynda's: she had clearly just got up, the kids were running riot and he got the hell out. He went for a drive and came back later.

"I sort of went home and that and that was so ... pretty much nothing on the telly until like in the afternoon there was superbikes on."

Greg went on to explain that he'd been working on his car in the backyard, with the gates closed. He kept them closed because of the dogs and Jaidyn and the busy road out the

Chapter Fourteen

front. He had neglected to mention at what time he collected Jaidyn.

"Was Jaidyn with you at this time?"

"Yeah."

"How did you come to pick him up?"

"When I got home probably, whether Bilynda rang me back up or when she finished on the phone or I rang her, I dunno. I didn't even know what she had done that day, I said I was going to work on the car that day. Like with Breehanna and like Jaidyn and with Brett and everything that it was good for the boy to sort of do stuff you know. I picked him up, yeah."

He thinks it was after putting his Tattslotto on and coming home again.

He drove Jaidyn to his house, the boy sitting in a damp car seat that he had collected off the front veranda. On the way, he had dropped Bilynda and Breehanna off at Katie's house.

Bilynda had packed some extra warm clothes for Jaidyn.

"She always used to pack spare clothes because, with the dogs and that, he would get wet and dirty and never want him to get cold so she always brought spare clothes," Greg said. He couldn't remember how many spare nappies Bilynda had packed but he always encouraged her to pack too many, rather than not enough.

Greg was asked if there was a specific arrangement for him to return Jaidyn to the babysitter.

"Yes and no, he should have probably really gone back with the others but he didn't really have to, the others knew where he was and everything," he said.

"At what stage were you supposed to take him back to be with his mum?" Detective Sergeant Roberts asked.

"Well I didn't really even know what time she was taking off or anything so . . ."

"So again nothing was really . . ."

"I . . . nothing really. Oh, maybe for tea really. I didn't really have anything on the go or anything. Maybe for tea yeah."

At Greg's place, they had spent the day working on the car, playing with the dogs and with the Nintendo. But they didn't eat. Greg hadn't eaten breakfast and wasn't hungry at lunch either. Neither was Jaidyn. Greg presumed that Bilynda had fed Jaidyn up before bringing him over because that's what normally happened. He explained how he had tried to feed the boy cereal once but it hadn't been a good idea. He'd hated it, or at least hadn't eaten it. Other days he seemed to have a huge appetite but then the remnants of a sandwich would be found later in pieces on the floor all around the chair.

Greg had explained to Jaidyn what he was doing as he fixed the exhaust on the Falcon.

"He would not even know what an exhaust system was but I would say, 'Oh this is the exhaust here Jaidyn', whatever," he said.

After working on the car, Jaidyn and Greg had gone back inside to get cleaned up. Jaidyn was showered and changed first and Greg had left him in front of the heater to warm up.

"I remember *The Great Escape* was on. I tried to teach him all man things and that ... I wanted to show him about man things, show him war movies, I dunno," Greg said.

Greg repeated how Jaidyn had stood in front of the heater to warm up after his shower, but he'd been there for too long and had burnt his backside. He seemed okay though, he "wasn't bawling or anything".

He explained how Bilynda had called during the night from Ryans Hotel and they had chatted about nothing in particular. Greg told her how Jaidyn had been carrying around greasy bolts while he worked on the car.

Katie had called soon after.

"What was the context of that conversation?" Sergeant Roberts asked.

"It was like all Jaidyn was in front of the heater and went a

Chapter Fourteen

bit red and would have panicked her and Katie just rang back and said of . . . 'nah that's it'."

"So when you spoke to Bilynda you told her Jaidyn had gone a bit red?"

"Yeah, well. Oh I am just an idiot with things like that. I will sit there and say, well if you let me borrow your fishing rod I will say 'Oh I snapped it I am sorry' you know? You know tackle box. You know, anything, borrow your car and say 'Oh I crashed it' and you get it back and it's alright. Katie rang back up again, I guess concerned, and I said 'nah it's nothing to worry about'. I was sort of expecting them all 'cause they are all from here [Moe] to come back past."

"Is that why you said it?"

"Is that why I said?"

"You know, said Jaidyn has gone a bit red, hoping they would come back?"

"Nah. Nah, it's nothing like . . . "

"So just a bit of a silly prank?"

"Very stupid, yeah," Greg said shaking his head.

Greg explained how he never left Jaidyn on his own. Even when he went to the video store, he'd ring ahead to make sure the movie was waiting; he'd dash to the counter and out again so that he didn't leave the boy alone for long. But on this occasion it was different.

"I guess probably because he was asleep and he was alright you know . . . I don't even know."

Greg explained how he grabbed a rag and wiped the condensation from his car's windscreen, threw the rag in the front console and drove out to Traralgon. The car had been pointing toward the road, backed into the driveway, so he could drive straight out. The house had been secure when he left; the front door was locked and the back door bolted. He'd collected Bilynda, who was drunk and driven her home. On the way back, they'd passed the new Maryvale hospital being built outside Morwell.

"Why didn't you tell her Jaidyn was at home?"

"Probably because I wanted her to get home and there is the boy and, I dunno, just to make her happy, I dunno, just stupid I guess."

When they arrived home to find the house had been vandalised, Greg was stunned.

"I just straight away thought someone 'molytoffed' it or something. You know you get, sometimes you get someone pissed walking from the pub and the dogs barking, they pick up all rocks from me front yard or whatever," Greg said.

He explained going to the front door, which was still locked, unlocking it and running inside to find the child missing. He said he then searched in cupboards and in every room for the boy, thinking that he may have woken up to find himself alone, been scared and crawled into a cupboard to sleep.

"When you went in there and saw he was missing, and you knew you had not taken him to the hospital, what were you thinking?"

"Just panic. I just thought that he is only a baby, I thought he might have got scared and gone behind, like I mean I don't even know, there's probably not enough room, he has never done it actually, crawled in behind the couch. I didn't want to panic Bilynda. I was going through enough," he said.

Greg fidgeted with his hands and frowned as he explained that he had taken Bilynda home and returned to his house. He realised that Jaidyn's nappy bag was also missing, and rang Yvonne Penfold because he had a feeling it all had something to do with her. He then explained that the phone call to Yvonne had actually occurred while Bilynda was still at his house, before he had taken her home.

He had called around to Yvonne's place and found the lights on. So he'd tiptoed up to the house and peeked through the window, under the curtains, but couldn't see Jaidyn or anyone else inside.

Chapter Fourteen

Detective Sergeant Roberts went back over Greg's movements, quizzing him on what he was doing that would have prevented him from hearing, or answering, the telephone when Bilynda rang up to twenty times between 4.45 p.m. and 8.30 p.m.

"Was she ringing the right number?" Greg asked.

Greg was also adamant that he never left his house that evening, apart from going to collect Bilynda from Traralgon. He said that his neighbours, and Bilynda's neighbour, must have been mistaken when they heard his car leave his place and arrive at Bilynda's at about 12.30 a.m. Greg detailed how he was pulled over by police but hadn't mentioned anything about Jaidyn being missing or his windows being smashed.

Detective Sergeant Fyffe, who had been meticulously taking notes all this time, began asking a few questions of his own. The change in style was evident almost from his first question. His tone was more forceful and he seemed more cynical about Greg's rambling answers.

"Did you feed him after the shower?" he asked.

"He didn't seem hungry."

"Didn't seem hungry."

"No."

"Had you fed him at all during the day?"

"No, well he didn't seem, to want to be, gave him some lollies or something a pack of chips, just like junky food ... maybe ... "

"Did you prepare a meal for yourself?"

"No."

Fyffe went over the period after Greg had discovered Jaidyn missing and dropped Bilynda home, and asked him to explain what he had done for the missing two hours.

"Went home, went around to Yvonne's and then back to Bilynda's," he said.

Finally, after hours of questioning, an accusation was put to Greg.

"What I am saying to you is that is it possible that he has had some form of accident and died and that in a panicked state you have thought of some way of covering it up?" Mick Roberts asked.

Greg shook his head silently, his hands crossed in his lap.

"You understand that this is a situation where, from an investigator's point of view, the last person to see Jaidyn alive is yourself to the best of our knowledge. We have got no indication one way or another if he is alive or dead at this stage. Now I am going to put a number of things to you, one of those things ... is it possible that he has had an accident that's resulted in death and you have tried to cover it up?"

"No."

"Is there some possibility that he has suffered from something along the lines of sudden infant death syndrome? Are you quite satisfied Jaidyn was alive when you left him that night?"

Greg nodded his head.

Greg denied he had taken any drugs that night.

Steve Fyffe resumed questioning Greg, and again the tone changed remarkably.

"Did you do anything else outside [when you left for Traralgon]?"

"No."

"Did you put anything in your rubbish bin, just prior to leaving to go to Traralgon?"

"Maybe rubbish bags or something, yeah."

"Do you remember, did you or did you not?"

"Going past ... the bin is there next to my car."

"Can you remember doing that?"

"Yeah, probably, I dunno. That's, I can't remember like, you know."

"We conducted a search of the rubbish bin."

"Yeah?"

Chapter Fourteen

"And we located a number of tissues with what we believe to be blood on them."

"Mm."

"Can you tell me whose blood was on those tissues?"

"Either be mine, me dog's or Jaid's. Jaid fell over and done something. I wiped his nose or lip or something."

"Right. Jaid fell over and hurt himself?"

"Not hurt himself, no."

"Well, you're saying he's bleeding?"

"Well, that's what I mean – like he – like with the dogs, like I remember the first time I seen him he had a scab on his nose and the dog licked it off."

"Okay."

"Like yeah, it was terrible, yeah."

"Terrible? Why didn't you mention this before?"

"What do you mean?"

"Well when I asked you all about what's been happening with Jaidyn, there's been no mention of Jaidyn being injured or has any blood coming from his nose."

"No not his nose. It was his lip, but Bilynda knew about it. You could ask Bilynda what time it occurred or whatever."

"Was Bilynda there?"

"No, it was when like you know, but claim she rang up in the afternoon. Was when she may have been. I dunno . . ."

"Did you tell Bilynda, 'Hey listen, Jaidyn has had a bit of blood on his lip and I have cleaned it up?'"

"Yeah well."

"Did you tell her that?"

"Would yeah."

"You would have or you did?"

"Did."

"How did Jaidyn have blood on his lip again? Can you tell me again from start to finish?"

"He was in the backyard when I was in the car."

"When you were taking good care of him, because there was no drama while you were working on the car?"

"Well it's like he's right, yeah."

"Well what happened?"

"It's like, it was nothing."

"Well you don't start bleeding from nothing, especially not from the lip. What happened?"

"Well he might have just ... I can't remember how it happened."

"You have a lot of problems remembering don't you?"

"Mmm."

"Why is that?"

"I dunno."

"We are talking about five days ago. Not a long time is it?"

"Mmm, not really."

"Didn't he have a cut on his lip?"

"You should ask Bilynda about it."

"Was Bilynda there? Are you saying Bilynda has seen the cut on his lip?"

"No well, I sort of told her he fell over and..." Greg started to lightly rub his nose and top lip area, pointing. "On his nose or his lip or something, I can't remember. I just had to wipe something."

Steve Fyffe went on: "Which adult helped him? He is 14-months-old, he can't fix a cut himself."

"Me."

"Where was it? Was it on his nose? Or was it on his lip? Where was it?"

"I can't remember."

"How come? Why can't you remember? You are the one who helped him. This is a 14-month-old child. Are you lying to me now?"

"No."

"Well why can't you remember where it was?"

Chapter Fourteen

"On his nose or chin or something maybe there. I dunno."

"Nose or chin, not his lip?"

"His lip. His tooth," Greg said rubbing at his upper lip pointing to the general area. "Went into his lip when he fell."

"His tooth went into his lip? Mr Roberts asked you before of any accidents or anything happening to Jaidyn. You didn't consider him bleeding, a 14-month-old child bleeding to be an accident?"

"It was not severe. Like I said he was not . . . was it on a tissue or something?"

Greg was asked about some drops of blood that were found in the house, in the bathroom.

"Have you used tissues to dab up blood off the dogs?"

"Yeah."

"When last . . ."

"I have not seen the dogs for a while."

"No no. You know when I am talking about."

"Yeah, well would have been a while."

"Some of the tissues looked as though they had been rolled up. Did Jaidyn have a bloody nose?"

"Mmm."

"This is a very easy question. Was Jaidyn's nose bleeding?"

"Yeah, possibly bleeding, yeah."

"What have you done to Jaidyn?"

"I have not done anything to Jaidyn . . ." and Greg rambled.

Steve Fyffe asked again: what happened to Jaidyn?

"Your excuses so far are that the lip was bleeding or the chin was bleeding and even initially that he had a scab that the dogs licked off."

"That was, that was some time ago," Greg said.

"Well why did you tell me that that happened Saturday? I asked you specifically about Saturday, not some time ago."

"I dunno, what do you mean?"

"Well why have you given me all of these excuses for Jaidyn's blood being on the tissues?"

"Well like I say, is there mucus or, say, spit?"

This line of questioning continued to go around in circles, with the detectives unable to get a satisfactory answer. Greg suggested that Jaidyn may have been knocked over by the dogs, or slipped over out the back when he arrived, but he couldn't be sure.

The detectives repeatedly offered Greg the chance to say something to clear his name.

"Has something happened at your place and you've struck Jaidyn?" Detective Sergeant Fyffe said.

"No, no," he said, shaking his head. "Yeah, Jaidyn's good, yeah."

"I know Jaidyn's good, but we all have tempers and we all have breaking points. Has there been something that's happened with Jaidyn that's caused you to lose your temper?"

"Jaidyn is me friend, that's what I mean like, you can ask people how I am with me animals and that you know, like, yeah, no."

"How is your temper normally?"

"I dunno, pretty ... I dunno really. I guess everyone has got some sort of temper, of ... I dunno."

Mick Roberts again asked what had caused Jaidyn to bleed, pointing out that if a child of that age had injured themselves enough to bleed, they'd probably have screamed. Surely Greg would remember that ... but still he couldn't.

Roberts also asked him how many nappies were left in Jaidyn's bag at 10 o'clock, reasoning that Greg would have checked before bothering to call his neighbour to ask where he could get more. Unless, of course, the phone call was a ruse.

"Would you tell us if Bilynda had killed Jaidyn?" Detective Sergeant Roberts asked.

"Mmm. She would not."

"See, we're left in a situation where we've got a missing 14-month-old boy and we are extremely concerned for his welfare."

Chapter Fourteen

"Mm."

"Now if it turns out that he's alive and well, we'll be the happiest men you've ever seen. But the situation is at the moment, it's ... you're the last person to see him alive. We've found certain things at the scene, at your house, that may indicate that something's happened to Jaidyn."

"Mm."

"Now if it has, as Mr Fyffe said before, this is your opportunity to tell us everything you know."

"I've told youse and told youse and told youse, that's all I know. That's it. I have told you what happened."

"Well, you've had the conversation with us tonight and you had a conversation with other police on Sunday. In fact, there was five audio tapes consisting of some hours. Why, until I mentioned tissues with blood on them, don't you tell anyone that Jaidyn's cut himself and had a fall?"

"Well, I didn't think of it. It's not like ... "

"This whole thing we are talking about is Jaidyn."

"I know, I know ... I thought what I mean like, maybe it could have been like a dog bumped, maybe he fell or something. I can't even remember like the, the, the occurrence, like nothing major like. Jaidyn is just a good little kid. What can I say? I've told you and told you."

Police told Greg that they had found the wet $600 in cash under his mattress.

He explained it was from a boat he had sold with Spider; he was hiding his share for safekeeping. He didn't know how it came to be wet, and said it hadn't been wet when he put it there. He said that his wallet, which was found in his car and was also wet, could have got wet from being on top of his car while he worked on it. Or it might have got wet while he was lying under the car on wet ground or maybe "my bum just sweats".

The detectives told Greg they had found a pair of surgical gloves in a drawer at the bottom of his bed. They were the type with fine powder inside and some of that powder had been found on the steering wheel of his car and on his cap.

Greg said he had grabbed a few pairs while he was at hospital so he could wear them if he had any dirty jobs. The only type of powder he wore was talcum powder.

The detectives returned to the missing tissues, asking how many he had used for Jaidyn's cut.

"Maybe one or two, if that, yeah," he said.

"Okay, there's five tissues there with blood on them."

"Well, yeah, well, if that's what's there, that's what's there, but I wouldn't think nothing like that, no."

"And the tissues would indicate that it was more than just a graze or a small type of injury that would require just a little bit of dabbing to get the blood off."

"Yeah, I think he's, well, Jaidyn did bleed a lot though too."

Greg remembered having cut himself on the Saturday as well, and wondered if maybe some of the blood on the tissues was his. He'd also had a bit of trouble with a bleeding cold sore ... maybe that was the blood.

The video operator zoomed in on the cold sore on his mouth, irritating Greg. All through the interview, Greg had been fidgeting with his hands and wearing a deep frown. He would look at his lap as he concentrated intently on what was being said.

The interview was completed at 10.37 p.m. and Greg was allowed to leave. Detectives told him it was likely he would be needed again.

CHAPTER FIFTEEN

When the police finished interviewing Greg they followed him back to his house. Greg had admitted in the interview that he'd changed his clothes after showering Jaidyn. This meant that the clothes he was wearing at the police station on Sunday morning were not the same ones he'd had on while working on his car the day before. Police hadn't examined the clothes and they wanted to see them.

Mick Roberts, Steve Fyffe and Rowland Legg followed Greg into the bedroom and laundry area; there were clothes all over the floor, as usual. Greg smelt different items, trying to ascertain which he'd been wearing, but he couldn't decide. The police left empty-handed.

Bilynda arrived at the police station after Greg left that night. She had been summoned by Rowland Legg, who felt it was time she was told a few home truths; he was annoyed with her mood swings and erratic behaviour.

After initially thinking Greg was involved in Jaidyn's disappearance, Bilynda had gone full circle and was now acting in full concert with Greg. She had travelled to Melbourne with him and was known to be spending the night with him again.

Legg knew what he had to do. If Bilynda was going to act like the collaborator of the suspect, rather than the mother of the victim, then she would be treated as such. Legg was brutally frank, launching into a carefully considered and measured tirade. He told Bilynda how she looked to the rest of the community: she had forsaken her child and was messing around with her son's suspected killer.

Legg knew this was a gamble. It could easily backfire and alienate Bilynda, but Bilynda had alienated herself already by sleeping with Greg Domaszewicz again. So he took the risk, hopeful that his intimidating performance would wake her up.

Bilynda left the station fifteen minutes later in tears. She drove off with Katie, both sisters angry, both wanting a drink. They met Greg at his house in Narracan Drive; police had pulled the crime tape down and Greg had been allowed back home.

A few other friends were at Greg's with a TV current affairs reporter and his camera crew, who had arrived with a large amount of alcohol, apparently paid for by their station. It infuriated police. Police were doing what they could to assist the media; they didn't want them making the suspect feel more comfortable.

The police continued to pressure Greg's friends. Detectives called again at Darren Farr's house, this time while Greg was being interviewed at Moe. Geoff Rumble of Morwell CIB sat in Farr's lounge room talking about the case for three hours. He implored the Farrs to distance themselves from their personal view of Greg and consider the facts. No matter how distasteful they found it, he said, those facts pointed inexorably to Greg's involvement in Jaidyn's disappearance: the bloody tissues, the long wait before telling police, the fact that no one could get into the house. Then there was Greg's behaviour since the disappearance and his previous behaviour in caring for Jaidyn. They had built a picture that pointed to Greg, Rumble told them.

"Put all your feelings aside, put all your emotions, everything, aside for Greg and have a look," he pleaded with them.

Chapter Fifteen

Rumble's pleas had an effect. The Farrs started to have grave doubts about Greg's innocence. It was the tissues that did it.

Greg stayed at the couple's house that night, after arriving at about midnight. The next morning when he got up, things had changed. Gone was the idle chatter. Now Darren and Sheena watched Greg, scouring his body language for any sign of deception. Greg, inevitably, sensed what was going on. He had just left the police where everything he said and did was scrutinised. Now his friends were doing the same thing. He didn't say much but was clearly uncomfortable.

The Farrs made little attempt to hide their suspicion. Sheena asked Greg about the tissues; he told her Jaidyn fell down in the garden and cut his lip. Darren asked the same question. Greg told him the dogs had knocked Jaidyn over, and that they had licked a scab from Jaidyn.

Greg told Darren that his wallet got wet when he was under the car working on the exhaust, also that it fell into a puddle. Later, he told Sheena that it got wet when he'd left it in the boot of the car.

Bilynda called that morning. She was going to the police station to be interviewed and wanted to know what she should say about the tissues. Greg wouldn't come to the phone. Darren told her that Greg had said to simply tell the truth.

Bilynda arrived at the station early, and was interviewed by homicide detectives on and off for the next eight hours. She was more cooperative this time, indicating that Rowland's stern words may have had some effect. She left at 4.30 p.m.

As the interview progressed, police divers were searching Lake Narracan and Moondarra Dam for clues to Jaidyn's whereabouts. Volunteers had flooded Moe to join the hunt and Legg was trying to cover every possibility. He confirmed that the police were considering partly draining Lake Narracan.

Steve Fyffe told Bilynda to get hold of Greg's video-taped interview, watch it and make up her own mind. Interview subjects are always given their own copy of an interview. When she saw that interview, the look on his face alone would be enough to convince her of his guilt, Fyffe said.

When Bilynda was released from the police station, she went straight to Greg's house. That night, she asked him for the tape but he made up a range of reasons why she couldn't have it.

"You'll get your fingerprints on it and police need it back," he said.

Bilynda believed him at first, but when Greg left the room, she searched for the video but couldn't find it. She was furious, and grabbed a carving knife from the kitchen. When she went into Greg's bedroom he was sitting on the end of his bed, his head down. Bilynda held the knife in her hand by her side. She tightened her grip on the handle but just then, Greg looked up. She slid the knife behind her back. Greg didn't see the blade and never knew how close he'd come to being stabbed.

Bilynda was deeply confused. The police had told her that Jaidyn could well be dead and her boyfriend had probably killed him. When she left the police station, Bilynda believed he had killed Jaidyn. Then she spoke to Greg and what he said seemed to make sense. On top of that, her friends, who were also Greg's mates, were telling her that he was innocent. She was in a spin.

The next day, a pile of rubbish was found in the hills south of Moe. Among the rubbish were some baby items. Legg thought it was a breakthrough, especially when the name Katie Leskie was found on documents. But it was a false alarm, some of Katie's garbage, inexplicably dumped in the hills.

On Monday, 23 June, Legg went ahead with his bold plan to drain Lake Narracan. About 3,000 megalitres of water was drained, lowering the shoreline across the mudflats by a metre or so. The swamp and marshes at the Edward Hunter Bush Reserve were also drained. The dam at the reserve is barely a kilometre from both Bilynda's and Greg's houses and is in a direct line between the two.

Chapter Fifteen

The move perplexed Greg. He told Darren Farr that he didn't know why the police were draining the Lake. They wouldn't find anything.

"They're wasting their time," he said.

Police stepped up the search for Jaidyn the next morning. The forensic evidence pointed to water, and Legg felt sure that the baby was hidden near water or had been dumped in it. Everywhere in the area was considered a potential burial ground, from the biggest lakes like Narracan – a kilometre wide at its broadest point, and eight kilometres long – to Moondarra and Blue Rock Dams, to Narracan Creek and the smaller swamps and dams in the Edward Hunter Bush Reserve.

Police in rubber dinghies and helicopters scoured the surface of the larger waterways. A body would be likely to pop out of the water and searching such a large area with divers would be next to futile.

Dive searches are notoriously slow and expensive. However, Legg and search coordinator Senior Constable Oscar Aertssen (a local expert) wanted to dive at Blue Rock Dam. Waterway officials had advised that the spillway area was a likely site for discarded items, such as stolen bikes, to turn up. Later it was revealed that trial finances prevented divers conducting such an expensive search. The detectives were frustrated, they wanted to dive the dam because of the connections to water and the fact that Blue Rock was Greg's favourite fishing spot.

About 140 police and SES volunteers combed the fifty-four hectares of scrub and bushland in the Edward Hunter Reserve, while police searched Lake Narracan and Moondarra Dam. It was time-consuming, labour-intensive and ultimately fruitless.

On the Tuesday ten days after Jaidyn's disappearance, the search was expanded. Thirteen police now had the unenviable task of raking through garbage at the Yallourn Tip. Legg was determined to exhaust every possibility and follow every lead, however small.

Greg was confused by the new search, but his comments worried Darren and Sheena Farr even more.

"He's not there, he's not there," Greg said as he watched the television, shaking his head and smiling.

"Bloody idiots, they won't find nothing there."

He was right. For thirteen days, local police, police from the Force Response Unit and hundreds of volunteers, from freemasons to the SES, searched the tip. It was a laborious and putrid task.

A number of people had told investigators that Greg regularly visited his father's grave in the Yallourn North cemetery, next to the tip on Haunted Hills Road. The informers thought Greg may have dumped the body there. Others told police that Jaidyn had disappeared on garbage collection day and, although Greg's bin had been thoroughly searched, the body may have had been left in someone else's rubbish bin, then dumped at the tip.

On Tuesday, 24 June, Darren and Sheena Farr took Greg and Bilynda to see Paul Vale, again at his Melbourne office. They were early so they went to the Eastland Shopping Centre to find a chemist; Greg wanted to buy cream for a cold sore or ulcer. As they walked around the shopping centre, Greg drank from a can of Jim Beam and Coke. He taunted uniformed police and security guards walking around the shopping centre, sticking a finger up at them.

That night, when Bilynda returned to Moe, she was met by homicide detectives again. Russell Sheather was struggling to contain his disgust. He spelt out to her the inconsistencies in Greg's story but Bilynda did not want to hear it, warning Sheather that it was the job of the police to prove Greg's guilt. Until then, she would continue to believe in his innocence.

Bilynda was struggling to cope with the strain. She told Sheather that she "needed someone to cuddle up to" at night.

Chapter Fifteen

Moments later, she broke down in tears before shouting at him to "fuck off" and storming out.

Bilynda's moves to keep custody of Breehanna failed. Social workers spoke to Bilynda and Brett on Thursday, 26 June and she agreed to surrender custody to Brett. Breehanna would be better off away from the chaos, it was reasoned; Brett and his parents would take care of her.

Later that day, Greg's green Ford Falcon XC was seized by police and taken to McLeod forensic science centre for further tests.

The following morning, Greg asked police if he could take a lie detector test. Legg declined Greg's offer. Polygraph tests, while popular on US television dramas, are not admissible as evidence in Victorian Courts.

The search for Jaidyn became progressively more sophisticated. Interest in the case was so intense that companies donated state-of-the-art technology to help with the hunt. Selby Bio Lab donated the use of a $100,000 thermal imaging camera, which looks like a video camera and can be attached to a helicopter. The chopper flew over the Yallourn Tip and surrounding areas during the weekend. All it found was a sick joke – two bags stuffed with chicken carcasses floating on Lake Narracan, tied together in the shape and size of a small child's body.

The next morning, the search of the Yallourn Tip was completed; nothing of value had been found.

Michael Korbut didn't think his cousin Greg had killed Jaidyn, or been involved in his disappearance, but he had his doubts. 'Mish', as Greg knew him, asked his cousin Grishka to come down to Melbourne to get away from the media and the pressure.

Secretly, Mish contacted police and convinced them that, although he was not overly close to Greg, if he was going to confess to anyone, it would be to him. He asked police to wire him with a listening device and to bug his house.

The Jaidyn Leskie Murder

On 1 July, Greg drove down to Mish's house in a car hired for Bilynda and Katie by Channel Seven, following Bilynda's interview with *Today Tonight*. He arrived and had a few drinks with Mish, then a few more. Mish got Greg quite drunk, but the plan fizzed. Greg said he didn't do it and Mish told him very early on that the conversation was being bugged. He needn't have bothered. Neither of the recording devices worked properly and nothing was taped.

In what by now appeared academic, on 1 July the homicide squad officially announced that the case was a murder investigation. Officially, police no longer believed that Jaidyn would be found alive. Detectives had aired their doubts within days of the disappearance.

Commander Peter Blick said it was likely that Jaidyn was dead and admitted that, while it would be difficult, they believed it was possible to secure a conviction against someone even if the body was never recovered.

The search extended to a number of disused mine shafts in the area. Legg had again received tip-offs, but was not optimistic. The searches were more about running a thorough investigation, and there was less and less faith that the information would lead to Jaidyn being found.

One large mine shaft near the town of Willow Grove on the banks of the Blue Rock Dam became the target for special attention. Greg had fished in the area and knew the dam and its surrounds well. Like all of the searches, it was a dead end.

Emotions were running high among the locals in Moe. On 1 July, vandals showed they had no doubt about who was responsible for Jaidyn's disappearance. Greg's prized blue Ford Falcon was spray painted with the words "Murderer", "Sinner" and "Killer".

Later that day, a cardboard cut-out dressed in baby clothes was found on the shore of Lake Narracan.

Chapter Fifteen

All this time, the media remained camped in town. Their presence inevitably kept up the public pressure on Greg. Crews would herd around the front door of the Moe police station, waiting for police to bring in witnesses and suspects. Others were permanently stationed opposite Greg's house, not far from where Kenny Penfold and Darrin Wilson had hidden before throwing the pig's head.

Both the police and the media attracted some criticism later that their relationship in Moe had been too close. While the police and media inevitably worked closely together, this did not impede or detrimentally affect the job either party was performing. A child was missing; the media were a key part of the story and indeed the investigation as a tool to appeal to the public for information to help find the child.

Furthermore, Moe is a small town and with only a couple of pubs it was inevitable journalists and police officers would bump into one another after hours.

Nicole Hughes of the police media unit was responsible for managing the media in Moe, fielding press and TV calls to free up detectives for the investigation. It was well handled, the police were open and forthright in doorstop interviews, often held twice daily. While it could be claimed this was giving the press too much information or seeking to sanction what went on air or in print, this would be a naive view. With the level of media interest the competition among reporters to get a story was intense. Also the number of people in town willing to talk about the case and the level of rumour and misinformation was high. The regular doorstops helped ensure the information the media was relaying was accurate.

"At the end of the day a child was missing and that was the key motivation for whatever was done through the media. Daily briefings were preferable for both parties to ensure information received and given was accurate," Nicole Hughes said.

Yet while Legg was happy to keep the media onside, he was furious when they became participants in what was now an extremely finely balanced investigation. His anger was directed at a Channel Nine cameraman who was going into Greg's house and playing with the dogs. Legg believed the cameraman was passing on information about the investigation and advising Greg on police methods.

The detectives warned him, and then the wider media, of the dangers of passing on information to someone they considered a suspect.

Greg could barely move from home without being filmed and followed. He resorted to climbing over the back fence to get in and out. Legg's strategy was to drip-feed stories to the media to sustain its interest. It proved an easy task, as stories seemed to generate themselves without a great deal of police effort.

By Friday, 4 July, however, Legg's search plans had failed and another approach had to be found. After twenty days and about $1 million, police called off the biggest search since the disappearance of Prime Minister Harold Holt thirty years earlier.

Police staged a media conference for the announcement, adding that the investigators would be returning to Melbourne the next day. It was a deliberately high profile decision to leave but this was another tactic. Detectives left Moe for Morwell, not Melbourne. They wanted to continue the investigation a bit more discreetly.

CHAPTER SIXTEEN

The detectives spent weeks compiling a picture of Greg's behaviour. It wasn't just a case of establishing what had happened that Saturday and finding Jaidyn's body, they were looking for a pattern. The police interviewed Greg's friends and family, often more than once.

"It was a background behavioural thing, but also building up as clearly as possible a picture of what he did do that night and the morning of the fifteenth," Legg said.

Eventually, the police reached a point where they didn't believe they could take the search any further. Nor did they believe they would get more information about either the night in question, or Greg's background. Rowland Legg spoke with his boss, Rod Collins, and they decided that the evidence should be put before Paul Coghlan Q.C., chief crown prosecutor and Deputy Director of Public Prosecutions.

On Tuesday, 15 July, Rowland Legg, Rod Collins and Steve Fyffe met Paul Coghlan in the Lonsdale Street offices of the O.P.P. The three detectives laid out the evidence they had against Greg Domaszewicz. Crime department analysts had prepared graphs, time lines and colour-coded charts, plotting the characters and their connection to each other.

The colour-coded charts showed Greg's explanations during different interviews and how they contradicted one another. It included evidence from other people's statements and interviews, and how that contradicted what Greg had said.

It was decision time. Could they charge or not? Was there enough evidence? Should they wait? If they did, how much more evidence were they likely to gather? Could they get a conviction without a body? How much harder was it going to be without a body?

Charge him, Coghlan said, with certainty. He was sure there was enough evidence to justify charging Greg Domaszewicz with murder and gave written advice to that effect.

Legg had been given the green light; now it was just a matter of timing. The previous day Legg had wanted one last issue cleared up before they moved. For the sake of completeness, he wanted the roof of Greg's house searched thoroughly. He was not satisfied that a proper search had been conducted. That afternoon, a search warrant was executed on Greg's house and the roof searched. Nothing was found.

The police surveillance team, known as "dogs", were following Greg again.

They told Legg that at 8.00 a.m. Greg was at his mum's home at Eltham. The court heard later his car was bugged, so they knew he was planning to drive to South Yarra to the offices of another lawyer, Michael Rafter. Greg was by this time consulting two lawyers and deciding which to hire.

It was perfect. The lawyer's office was just around the corner from the homicide squad's headquarters in St Kilda Road. Legg wouldn't have to go far.

Greg left his mum's place shortly after lunch. Just before 2.00 p.m., the homicide squad crew left the St Kilda Road Police Complex in two unmarked cars, heading north along Chapel Street until it became Church Street. They waited by the roadside as Greg drove past but failed to notice them. They pulled in to the traffic behind his green Ford Falcon and

Chapter Sixteen

followed him as Church Street once more became Chapel Street. It was raining heavily, so they waited for the downpour to ease.

At 2.13 p.m. on 16 July, Rowland Legg's car pulled in beside Greg's and hit the sirens. The officers approached Greg, who was sitting stunned behind the wheel.

"Hello Greg," Legg said.

Greg looked up, smiled and replied, "Hello Rowland".

"Greg, I'm arresting you for the murder of Jaidyn Leskie," Mick Roberts said and cautioned him, reading him his full rights. Greg was dumbfounded. He was taken from the car in front of a crowd of onlookers and handcuffed.

Greg wanted to ring his solicitor. He was put in the back of the unmarked car and driven to the St Kilda Road office, from where he was allowed to ring Mr Rafter. Mr Rafter, an experienced criminal lawyer, told Greg not to say anything or answer any questions until he got there.

Mick Roberts again interviewed Greg, although this session was considerably shorter than before. Other than to deny that he had murdered Jaidyn, Greg refused, on Mr Rafter's advice, to answer any questions and was formally charged.

By the time Greg left by the rear driveway of the St Kilda Road Police Complex, a crowd of photographers had gathered. The suspect sat in the back seat of an unmarked car between Mick Roberts and Steve Fyffe, looking small and wide-eyed. His green "Fosters Special Brew" cap had been taken off his head, and his hair was flattened forward. He made no effort to hide his face or cover his head with a blanket. Everyone knew what he looked like anyway.

In a packed out-of-sessions court hearing at the Melbourne Custody Centre in Lonsdale Street, Greg appeared before Bail Justice Alan Scott at 7.32 p.m. No summary of events was led against him and Mr Scott asked Greg why he should not be remanded in custody.

"I am not guilty of anything," he said.

Mr Scott followed procedure and Greg was remanded in custody to appear in Melbourne Magistrate's Court the next morning. The hearing lasted just thirteen minutes.

It is a bizarre requirement of the legal system that an accused person be brought before a court to be remanded at the soonest possible convenience. Regardless of the time of night, the accused must still appear before a bail justice to be remanded to court the next day. In serious cases, such as murder, the bail justice is not at liberty to release the person on bail in any case.

Greg spent the night behind bars in the custody centre. He had made a handwritten statement earlier that day pleading his innocence. In it, he compared himself to Lee Harvey Oswald, the man who is believed to have shot US President John F. Kennedy. Like Oswald, Greg believed he had been framed. "Both guilty until proven innocent," he wrote in the statement.

Greg had even considered changing his middle name to Oswald; presumably he also realised that this would make his initials G.O.D.

The following day, Greg Domaszewicz made his first appearance in the Melbourne Magistrate's Court and was remanded to the Melbourne Assessment Prison in Spencer Street.

Bilynda only found out that Greg had been arrested two days later.

She had been staying in the New South Wales coastal town of Moruya with her friend, Julia Walker, for a week or so. The police, Darren Farr and Katie had convinced Bilynda to get out of Moe for a while. The detectives reckoned that if they could isolate Greg without her support, he would slip up or confess.

It was a difficult time for Bilynda. She was separated from the people in her life – Greg, Breehanna, Brett and Katie – and she had time to think, not about who'd done what but about Jaidyn. Her precious little boy seemed to have been almost

Chapter Sixteen

overlooked for much of the previous weeks, amid the preoccupation with proving the guilt or otherwise of her boyfriend.

She was having nightmares. Several times in the middle of the night she awoke and screamed out Jaidyn's name. Other times she called out for Julia.

She became convinced of Greg's guilt and had refused his plea to come and visit. With time to reflect, Bilynda recalled a few things about Greg's behaviour with Jaidyn. She thought of the haircutting incident the day before his disappearance. She still had Jaidyn's hair wrapped up in tissue paper at home; Greg had given it to her to put in a baby book.

When Bilynda found out on 18 July that Greg had been charged, she was silent for some time, before asking Julia for a pen and paper. Calmly, Bilynda sat down and wrote Greg a stinging, abusive letter. She accused him of killing her child and begged him to tell her where the body was. She told Julia she wanted to visit Greg in jail and put a knife in him.

Brett Leskie picked Bilynda up on Sunday, 27 July and drove her back to Moe. It was the first time the estranged parents, torn apart by the loss of their child, had spent any real time together since Jaidyn disappeared.

When Bilynda arrived back in town, she went straight to Darren and Sheena Farr's house. It was 11.00 p.m. but they were waiting up for her, and they stayed up all night talking about the case and about Jaidyn. She told them about the beating Jaidyn had received from Greg four weeks earlier when Jaidyn had banged his head on the car door. She also told them about the hair clippings.

At 1.20 a.m. Darren drove around to Greg's place to try to find the videos of his interview with the homicide squad – Bilynda said she had stashed them in his front cupboard. On his way over, Darren was pulled up by Moe police for a routine check. Minutes later, the local senior constable was still sitting in his car at the same spot and saw Darren drive past again. He could not find the video tapes.

A couple of hours later, Bilynda realised that she needed more clothes and Darren took her around to her house to get them. She dug out the tissue wrapper of Jaidyn's hair, and found his dummy and a toy phone in the lounge room. She also found photos torn up and left on the kitchen table and in the hallway. Bilynda was mystified as to who had been in her house.

Darren told Bilynda that passing on these stories about Greg to them was pointless; she needed to tell people who could do something about it. The next morning, he and Sheena drove her to the homicide squad office in St Kilda Road.

They were there from 10.00 a.m. to 6.00 p.m. Mick Roberts was rostered off, but came in for the interview. He put a blown-up picture of Jaidyn on the table in front of Bilynda; the toddler's dummy was on the table as well. Bilynda giggled inappropriately at times during the interview.

The trio returned to Moe the next day, and went around to Greg's house. Darren and Sheena checked the messages on the answering machine, while Bilynda walked through to Greg's room. She came out minutes later holding a small, neatly folded jumper that smelt of vomit. She said it was Jaidyn's and that she thought it was the one he was wearing the day he went missing. She said that it had been neatly folded and left on a pillow on Greg's bed. It was different though to the description of clothing she had given police on the first day.

The discovery didn't seem to shake Bilynda's new-found belief in Greg's guilt. She was at Darren's place when he rang from jail once. She didn't want to talk to Greg but she picked up another phone in the house and listened in. She was upset. Greg didn't talk about her during the whole conversation.

Bilynda wrote a couple more abusive letters to Greg while he was in prison and pleaded with him to tell her where Jaidyn was. But her resolve didn't last.

Chapter Sixteen

In early August, she rang Julia Walker in New South Wales and told her she had been to see Greg. She now believed he was innocent.

"The police are all bastards," she said.

On 11 August, Greg applied in the Supreme Court to be released on bail. His lawyers claimed that the case against him was circumstantial and very weak, arguing that Bilynda's discovery of the clothes in Greg's house was evidence that he was not involved. The application was refused.

By 21 October, Bilynda had changed her mind yet again, telling social worker Lucille Atkinson that she was convinced Greg was responsible. She even said that she wanted to coerce him into telling the truth by having his three beloved bull terriers put down.

In one letter Bilynda sent to Greg late in 1997, she poured out her pain and bitterness:

"Grishka, when you go to bed tonight, and every night after that, you close your eyes and remember ... remember my little boy. You look him in the eyes, and you feel his pain, you see him cry. Look right into his eyes Greg and go over and over and over and think what you did that day. Smell him Greg, remember the look on my poor Jaidyn's face and think about what you did to my boy ... and ask yourself Greg, what the hell did that little boy do to deserve to die?

"You have lied to me repeadidly (sic), you let me make a complete fool of myself by telling the world that I believed my baby's killer 100%. I stood by you, I lied for you, you let me sleep with you. I am embarresed (sic) and ashamed.

"I feel sick. I nearly committed suicide you fucking cunt."

In another letter, she begged him to tell her what happened.

"I have to know because although I'm laughing and carrying on with life, and hiding what I feel, I'm dying inside. From now, don't call me, don't write to me, don't lie to me and don't pretend you love me.

"So the only reason you have now to contact me is when you tell me the whereabouts of Jaidyn. I'm sorry it has to be this way, but it's over. All I ever did was love you Grishka. The worst part about it, I still do."

Bilynda's relationship with Greg was impossible to read accurately. At one point, it was reported that the two were engaged, a rumour that Bilynda quickly denied. The story started after a visit she had made to Greg in jail, in which he had given her a ring that his mother had smuggled into the prison. It was reported to be a $3,000 engagement ring; in fact it cost about $1,500 and was later described as a friendship ring.

Legg was no longer surprised by Bilynda's swings in attitude.

"This whole case has been full of that swing in emotions from her. The whole case has been full of it," he said with understandable frustration.

Bilynda had her own troubles with the law. On 5 November, she appeared before the Moe Magistrate's Court for a raft of offences relating to her behaviour since Jaidyn had disappeared.

After Bilynda once again swung back to Greg's "side", Julia Walker accused her of stealing CDs and other small items from her place in Moruya. There were charges over abusive phone calls that Bilynda had made to Sheena Farr. And then there was an ugly incident outside Moe Magistrate's Court on 7 October, when Bilynda had pushed Yvonne Penfold face first into a television camera.

She was released on bail until early in the new year.

CHAPTER SEVENTEEN

It was New Year's Day, 1998, and Sam Payne and his family were starting the year with a family picnic up at Blue Rock Dam.

The 14-year-old was bored and restless; he wanted to go exploring. Lunch was over, so he headed off along the dam wall. He was ambling along, thinking about nothing in particular, when he looked into the water and saw something floating. He couldn't work out what it was, although it looked a bit like a pillow. It was only a metre or so from the dam wall, so Sam moved down to take a closer look.

It looked to Sam like a baby's body, greyish blue and obviously dead. It appeared to have a gash in the side that looked like it had been cut open. The body was listing onto one side and one of its legs was sticking up out of the water. Was it the right one? It was hard to tell.

Sam raced back to get his grandma, who was strolling along the wall as well, and told her what he'd found. Patricia Yocklunn went to see for herself, thinking that her grandson may be joking but noticing that he looked serious. As she got closer, she could definitely see something in the water. It looked like a doll but it was too big to be a doll; maybe Sam was right. The little legs and the socks convinced her.

"Every now and then I could see the little hand," she said of the body rolling gently in the water.

Mrs Yocklunn sent Sam back to his grandfather with a message to call the police, while she stayed with the body.

Rowland Legg was paged by the officer in charge of the homicide squad at the time – Detective Inspector Sergeant Jeff Maher – at 3.45 p.m. on New Year's Day whilst on holidays, to be told that a child's body had been found at Blue Rock Dam. He didn't need to be told where it was; he had been there before. And Legg knew who it was. It had to be.

He immediately arranged for the on-call forensic pathologist, Dr Shelley Robertson, to go to the dam with support services. His directions were simple: the body wasn't to be touched until the water police, or search-and-rescue unit, arrived.

The body was only a short distance from the bank but it was badly decomposed and police didn't want to tug at it, or lift it unnecessarily. The dam wall at that point was steep, and the only practical means of access was from the water.

The water police launched a "rubber ducky" from the boat ramp at the southern end of the dam, motored across to the body and slipped a body bag underneath the toddler. At 6.05 p.m., Gippsland officer, Brian Hall, carefully lifted the body out of the water, placed it in the bright red boat, and took it to shore near the spillway.

Legg had arrived at 7.40 p.m., checked the body ten minutes later and recognised it instantly as that of Jaidyn Leskie. The extreme cold of the water had preserved the body.

Dr Robertson arrived soon after, and made a preliminary visual examination. She asked that the body be packed in dry ice to preserve it, knowing that it would deteriorate rapidly once it reached the relative warmth of air. The police helicopter arrived at 10.40 p.m., and the body was flown to the Alfred Hospital. From there, it was taken by government undertaker to the mortuary at the Victorian Institute of Forensic Medicine for an autopsy the next day.

Chapter Seventeen

Bilynda Murphy had just arrived home from a trip to Lakes Entrance with her friends, Dave and Sue Havis, when the phone rang. Dave took the call in the bedroom. As a joke, Sue and Bilynda pressed a glass up to the door to hear what Dave was saying. They heard him say, "Well, I'll have to tell her".

He emerged looking ashen faced and told them that the call was from friends who had been out at Blue Rock Dam.

"A little boy's been found out at Blue Rock," he said.

Bilynda assumed it was another practical joke; there had been so many, from the chicken carcasses, to the cardboard cut-outs.

"Ring the police," Dave said.

Moe police confirmed that a body had been found at the lake, but stressed that it had not yet been identified.

"Ignore it until you hear from us, if we need to contact you we will," the officer told Bilynda.

She broke down, sobbing and hugging Sue. They ignored the copper's advice and headed out to Blue Rock Dam. Bilynda wanted to be near her little boy, to see him one last time and to say goodbye. Maybe they'd let her hold him.

Bilynda was met at the side of the dam by police, who stopped her from going down to the bank where the body had been found. She wept and shook, as she looked across from the carpark to the point a few hundred metres away where the police were guarding the body.

Steve Fyffe took her aside and sat with her in the back seat of a police car. He told her about the body; Fyffe was satisfied that it was Jaidyn.

"He is in a state that you can identify him," he told Bilynda.

Bilynda never got that final hug; the police would not let her down to the body.

Police divers returned to the dam the next day to search for items that may have been dumped in it.

The cold water was murky and visibility was extremely poor. Two divers entered the water and began searching the sloping dam wall. They were tied to a rope a few metres apart, one searching along a fixed area about twelve metres deep, the other about nine metres underwater. The motion of their swimming stirred up the silt in the water making it even more difficult to see. Progress was slow.

Senior Constable Robert Manks had reached the edge of a steep slope underwater when he noticed a white plastic bag. Remarkably, it wasn't covered in silt. He picked it up and looked inside; there was a baby's bottle in it. He turned to the left to alert his fellow diver to the find and caught sight of something else. It looked like a pink feed bag, some sort of industrial bag perhaps.

Manks handed the white plastic bag to his partner and they agreed, through hand gestures, that Manks would stay underwater while the other diver surfaced with the bag and bottle.

Manks felt around in the mud and silt and came across a length of blue rope. He realised that the industrial bag was weighed down by something, some sort of steel or metal bar. He lifted the bar out of the mud and measured its location in the water. He then swam to the surface, and waited for the homicide squad.

The item turned out to be a small sleeping bag tied to a crowbar. The sleeping bag had burst open, its zip still closed but its stitching torn away. It carried the putrid and distinctive smell of rotting flesh, as did the plastic bag. It was clear that the plastic bag had been stuffed inside the sleeping bag along with the body. The sleeping bag had then been tied to the crowbar and dropped into the dam.

The reservoir keeper estimated that the temperature of Blue Rock Dam at that location was between just nine and ten degrees Celsius during winter. During summer, the water temperature would rise slightly and accelerate the decomposition process. As gases built up in the body, it began pressing hard against the bag,

Chapter Seventeen

trying to rise. Eventually the bag's stitching gave way, and the body was released to the surface.

Dr Robertson concluded that, had Sam Payne not found the body when he did, it would probably never have been found. It would have broken up overnight, or within a short period, and disappeared.

The items taken out of the lake were laid out on a sheet of white canvas on the dam wall. The plastic bag contained various things that Bilynda had packed for Jaidyn on the day he had disappeared.

It included a baby's bottle, an apple, and a bib with pictures of the cartoon characters, Roadrunner and Wyle E. Coyote, and the words "BEEP! BEEP!" on it. There was also a pair of tracksuit pants, emblazoned with "Winner of Baby Games" and stars down the front of the left leg.

The police were anxious to see the effect that the discovery would have on Greg. Legg made enquiries with the prison squad and learnt that at 3.30 p.m. on New Year's Day, Greg had been laughing and joking during a telephone conversation with Bilynda's friend, Sue Havis. Three hours later, after he learnt that Jaidyn's body had been found, Greg collapsed and had to be taken to the prison medical centre. The next morning, he threw a tantrum in his cell and refused to see his barrister John Lee and legal aid solicitor Steve Drazetic.

Paul Lietzau was asleep on 3 January when he was woken by his mother, who came into his room crying. She had a copy of the *Herald Sun* in her hand. On the front page was a picture of a police diver emerging from water with a crowbar under his arm and a bag attached.

"There's your crowbar Paul," she said between tears.

"Lizard" had not been able to find his crowbar or his tree loppers since he'd left them at Greg's while doing some gardening in the week leading up to Jaidyn's disappearance. A week after Jaidyn went missing, he had rung Greg, then called in to see him. He'd asked Greg about getting his tools back, because Greg's brother needed some gardening work done. Greg had told him that the tools were in the back of his car, which the police had in Melbourne for testing.

Later, when Lizard knew Greg had his car back, he asked again. This time Greg told him that the tools were at Darren Farr's, but when Lizard went around to collect them, he could only find the tree loppers. The Farrs were adamant that the crowbar was not with any items dropped at their house.

Lizard wrote off the crowbar as lost, until he saw the newspaper that morning.

On 2 July 1997, a friend of Yvonne Penfold's, Cheryl Stubley, had lodged a complaint that Greg was harassing her. She told the homicide squad that Greg had threatened to kill both her and Yvonne. Greg had told her he was going to tie bricks to their legs and throw them into Blue Rock Dam.

There was little the homicide squad could do with the information and they handed the matter on to the Moe Police. Greg was not charged over the claim. At the time, it hadn't seemed relevant.

CHAPTER EIGHTEEN

The discovery of Jaidyn's body sparked a public brawl between the Leskie and Murphy families. Jaidyn could now be buried, but a peaceful conclusion was as elusive as ever.

The families argued over the type of service, the type of minister, the location of the service, who was to attend, who wasn't, the location of the grave, and whether or not Jaidyn would be cremated.

At one point, negotiations between the families were carried out by ministers while the Murphys and Leskies sat in separate rooms in a church hall. It was even suggested that, as a compromise, Jaidyn should be cremated and half his ashes given to each parent, an idea that was quickly rejected.

Funeral details were released to the media at a press conference held by the two ministers. Jaidyn would be buried at Yallourn North cemetery after a joint Baptist-Anglican service. Helium filled balloons would be released at the grave site.

For a little boy whose disappearance had attracted so much attention, and whose death had touched so many people, not many came to say goodbye. Perhaps 400 people crammed into Moe Baptist Church, but it was hard to tell who were mourners and who were media.

It was also hard to tell how many came but did not want to get too close. There were those who hung around the edges of the carpark, under trees, and on the nature strip, listening to the service relayed through speakers outside. They wanted to be there, but obviously didn't want to be part of it. With so many people jockeying for the limelight, their discretion was noticeable.

For all the bickering and feuding before the funeral, it was a beautiful service. A small white casket with teddy bears on it sat at the head of the altar. Kind words were spoken and prayers offered; there was a cry for justice and truth.

"Jaidyn, who with his big brown eyes and cheeky grin, in his short life touched all who knew him," said Anglican Reverend Bruce Charles.

"As Bilynda said 'to know you is to love you', but Jaidyn's life has so deeply touched not only his family but a community and to some extent a nation.

"People who have never known him have come to know him through the circumstances of his tragic death. Many people in our nation have seen some of those beautiful pictures of Jaidyn in his tuxedo ... those big brown eyes and beautiful smile."

Those few photographs, images of a short life, were all that many knew of Jaidyn. Here at his uncle's wedding, teetering as he held his big sister's hand, his bow tie twisted and off-centre. There, giggling and bright-eyed in his red overalls and playful jumper.

The minister also made a poignant reference to the great sadness of Jaidyn's death.

"The vulnerability of a young child, and Jaidyn's own vulnerability, touched us deeply. It reminds us of the fragility of our own lives. It reminds us of our sacred responsibility to care for all the vulnerable in this life," he said.

It took just four pall bearers to carry Jaidyn's tiny coffin from the church. Jaidyn's uncles, Glenn and Stuart Leskie, Glenn Murphy and a friend, Peter McMaster, crowded close together to get a corner on their shoulders.

Chapter Eighteen

The coffin was carried out to the anguished pleading of Eric Clapton's *Tears in Heaven*, written by a parent who had also lost a child in tragic circumstances.

At the graveside, Brett and Bilynda, who had sat on opposite sides of the church, embraced. As Jaidyn's coffin was lowered into the ground, Bilynda reached across and the pair hugged and cried together.

CHAPTER NINETEEN

Bilynda had been a study in confusion, her emotions swinging wildly since the moment she learnt that Jaidyn was missing. She had fought violently with her sister in the days following his disappearance. And more than once, their fighting had spilled into the street outside Katie's house, where Bilynda was staying. Yet although Katie had stated earlier that she would break up the relationship between Bilynda and her ex-husband, Brett, she had never imagined things would turn out this way, and she couldn't walk away from her sister.

Greg's presence, and Bilynda's confusion in dealing with him, was compounding the tension between the sisters. At first, Greg was instructing Bilynda in what to do.

"Everything was so sneaky … we had to run from the media, when we went to Melbourne it was 'Don't tell anybody we are here, you can't ring your mum, you can't do this'. I felt like 'Why can't I? I haven't done anything wrong'," Bilynda said.

"Why is everyone so sneaky? Everyone is driving around in different cars. Why?

"I nearly stabbed him. He was sitting on the end of the bed. It was the night he got the video tape done, the video interviews, and homicide said to me, 'If you can get hold of the videos and watch them, you will know just from the look on his face that he has done this'.

Chapter Nineteen

"I said to Greg 'I want to have a look at the videos' and he made up every excuse under the sun. You know, 'You can't, you will get fingerprints on them,' and I believed it.

"But he was sitting on the end of the bed and I went to get the videos and they were gone and I said, 'You friggin arsehole'. I was in a state of mind, I went in there and I went to get him with the knife and he turned around and I put it behind my back. I don't think he saw the knife.

"I just didn't know who to believe. The cops were telling me one thing, homicide telling me a different thing and then Greg would just balls the whole thing up. But I had my family saying 'No, Greg wouldn't have done it,' my friends saying, 'No, Greg wouldn't have done it'. Actually, Darren Farr was one of the only ones who said that he did it. That was after a couple of weeks."

Another reason for Bilynda's confusion was that she had become close to Greg's mother, Helen, after Jaidyn disappeared.

"I didn't want to break her heart. But I have always had doubts right from day one [about Greg's innocence]," she said.

Bilynda explained that she was pressured to leave Moe, to place extra stress on Greg while she was away.

"The cops said, 'If you go away for a little while and get out of Moe he might break while you are gone'. I thought, 'Well if he is going to break I don't want to leave Moe while my kid's missing'. I didn't agree to go, I was made to go."

When she returned to Moe following Greg's arrest, she refused to see him, convinced of his guilt. "Then I changed my mind back a bit because we [with mutual friends Sue and Dave Havis] kept sitting around together putting a few scenarios and, no matter what you come up with, Greg is never guilty, it's always the Penfolds. He's got an answer for everything," she said.

This conversation took place in a household that had always been sympathetic to Greg – Dave Havis had grown up with Greg and always supported him, and Bilynda was reluctant to say that she now believed that Greg had murdered her son. When questioned by Sue's mother-in-law, Helen, she offers simply, "I have doubts". This takes Helen somewhat by surprise and the robust woman offers her unsolicited opinion across the table: "No way could he have done it".

Moments earlier, Helen had admitted that she'd only met Greg twice, but he had come across to her as "very caring".

"I have always said that if he has done it, it was an accident, because you just don't do that to a kid. He has just lost it with Jaidyn and the rest has been a cover-up," Bilynda said.

"The question people always ask is, 'Why did he tell me he was burnt?' I think it's because he didn't know what to say at the time about what he was doing with Jaidyn. He said that when I got home and saw Jaidyn on the couch, he wouldn't get in trouble for leaving Jaidyn at home by himself."

"I think two weeks after the day Jaidyn was found, I went down to the jail and the cops thought I was going to bash him. All these screws came out. I felt like it but I didn't [bash Greg]," Bilynda said.

"I said, 'You broke his fuckin' arm,' and he just cried. He couldn't come up with an answer. He just kept saying, 'I didn't do it, I didn't do this'. It doesn't matter what question you ask him, he has got an answer and he doesn't have to think about it, he just answers and when you go and check it out, it's true."

Bilynda went to the jail just two weeks before the committal hearing and made an extraordinary proposition.

"I went down to the jail and I went in by myself. I said, 'The committal is coming up in two weeks, if you want me to lie for you I will'. He turned around and said 'No, lies shouldn't have to come into it,' he said, 'if lies come into it we will never know who's done it.'

"When you spoke to homicide, you were convinced Greg had done it, then when you spoke to Greg's defence, you think homicide are liars. But when homicide asked me, 'Where do

Chapter Nineteen

you think Jaidyn could be if he's around this area?' and I said to them [that] the only place I knew of Greg taking him was Blue Rock.

"I think as soon as he was found at Blue Rock, everyone said Greg had done it because Blue Rock was a place that Greg went with his dogs and fishing. I cut ties with him in June [1998]. I don't believe the shit that comes out of his mouth now."

What changed her mind?

"I read the brief. I just got the feeling that, I mean there's nothing in there to say he is trying to blame me for it but that's the way I read it. That's how I felt reading it and I'm thinking, 'No way'.

"In or out of jail, it doesn't matter, there is no relationship. If he gets off, I want someone else to be put in straight away. Somebody did it. Sometimes I just don't think the whole truth will ever come out, we will never know what happened. I do want someone to hang for it ... unfortunately you can't do that any more."

Sue Havis sat patiently listening to Bilynda's views on the case and held her tongue. Sue believes Greg is innocent and has done all along.

"I have my doubts [about Greg's innocence]. I don't know what to think any more, I'm beginning to think that it was an accident. I still say he has had one of those mental blockages, how you can block things out. He has just blocked it out, doesn't want to remember it. Either that or he knows that he has done it and he is hiding it."

It worried Bilynda that Greg had never actually stated what he believes happened that night, other than vaguely suggesting that Yvonne Penfold was involved.

"Greg has never really pinpointed what he thinks happened. He just says [to] check out this one or check out that one, but he never really says what he thinks happened," Bilynda said.

And Bilynda is adamant there will be no rekindling of her affair with Greg, regardless of the verdict. "I think I owe it to Jaidyn at this stage to just say 'Piss off'. I often think, what would Jaidyn be thinking? You bitch mum. I don't want Breehanna hating me for the rest of her life.

"On Jaidyn's birthday, I came down and went to the cemetery and cried my heart out, I have never cried so much in my life. That's when it really started hitting me that it's real; he is not here on his birthday."

Bilynda admitted that she'd had doubts about Greg's innocence from day one, but the more time she spent with him, the more confused she would become.

"It's like he's got me. I am losing Breehanna because of Greg, and he doesn't seem to care, he is still writing [to Bilynda from prison] saying, 'You've got to talk to me'. You think, 'Well I've already lost one, I'm not going to lose the next one for you'.

"You look at him again and you feel sorry for him, then you come home and you hate his guts, then you look at him again. It's like he's almost able to tell you what to say.

"Jaidyn would always run to Greg, that's why I can't understand when people say he bashed Jaidyn, why would he go to him? You just sit there and think, how could someone do it? You think maybe it happened this way, maybe it happened that way.

"It's just a coward act. If it was a 20-year-old person, that would be a different story but a little baby can't even talk. I just can't believe he has got two neighbours and none of them heard any screaming, because a little kid, and he screamed ... and they say he would have been in horrific pain."

CHAPTER TWENTY

It was October 10 and Colin Lovitt Q.C. had organised to meet with his junior counsel, John Lee, and his instructing solicitors to finalise the defence strategy. The trial was to begin in two days' time.

Greg had pleaded not guilty to the murder and as an accused person he was presumed to be innocent until a jury found him otherwise. The jury had to be sure of his guilt beyond any reasonable doubt, but it was best not to leave anything to chance. The strategy was simple: don't leave it to the jury to find reasonable doubt – show them there could be alternative killers, others with an opportunity to have committed the crime. It is not up to the defence to find the killer, but finding a plausible alternative to the accused could raise doubts in the minds of the jury.

In the notorious case of Eddy Lewis, charged with murdering motoring writer Paul Higgins and his wife Carmel, it took five trials for Lewis to be convicted. Why? Many believe it was because Mr Lovitt presented the many juries with a different scenario, pointing the finger at the Higgins' daughter, Amanda. Two of the trials were aborted midway during proceedings for legal reasons, but juries were deadlocked.

Similarly, when Drouin veterinarian Mark Campbell Neilan locked himself in the boot of his car after murdering his wife, the defence claimed that masked bandits had murdered the woman and locked him in the car.

The alternative killer wasn't on trial, so that evidence couldn't be rigorously examined. It was the possibility of an alternative that was important.

In the Domaszewicz case, finding alternative killers was the easy part; settling on the most likely and the best to build this defence strategy around was more difficult. The fact that a pig's head had been thrown and windows smashed meant that there would already be some doubt in any jury's mind. The defence needed to tease it out a bit further.

The decision to point out that Greg was not the only potential killer in this case was helped by the multiplicity of criminal characters involved. Some were known to be extremely volatile and likely to be menacing in the witness box. Who was the jury to say that one was a more likely killer than the other?

Clearly, the killer must have a connection to the pig's head gang. The defence knew that Yvonne Penfold was friends with men in biker gangs and had done some modelling for biker magazines. They were sure that she was sufficiently close to some bikers who might mete out a bit of revenge for her.

Hence, the plan developed to point the finger at a biker gang for the abduction. The throwing of the pig's head was a ruse to cover for the gang.

That was the plan, right up until the October 10 meeting. Then Tubby Hopkinson entered the picture.

The defence team had done some checking and knew that Tubby's background made him a possibility. As Kenny's housemate, he was well connected to the group. He had a history of violence, compared to Greg's minor criminal record. He was a drug user and possibly a small-time dealer. He had a history of mental illness that, while undiagnosed, was thought to be close to schizophrenia. He looked tough and was feared around town. He was there when the pig was killed and its head

Chapter Twenty

cut off. And, above all, he was at home on the night that Kenny had announced that he was off to throw a pig's head through a window.

The biker gang was out; Tubby was in.

Bill Morgan-Payler Q.C., of the prosecution team, presented a complete contrast in style and manner to his opposing number. Similarly, the prosecution's case contrasted with that of the defence.

While the defence may be helped by complicating the evidence and proffering alternatives, the prosecution needed to keep the facts as clear as possible. Kenny and the pig's head gang were a coincidental distraction, little more. The evidence they felt inexorably pointed to Greg. It was a circumstantial case, yes, but then so are the majority of murder trials.

The strongest weapons that the prosecution had were Greg himself, and the forensic evidence; they mixed fiction and fact. Greg's rambling, illogical and irrelevant answers to direct questions, and his unusual behaviour on the night, were important to the case. His history of maltreatment of Jaidyn further illustrated his poor character and propensity for violence against the toddler.

The defence's strategy regarding the pig's head could be countered with science, which would prove irrefutably that no one could have entered Greg's house without a key.

Bill Morgan-Payler Q.C. is a tall, thin man with a ginger-flecked beard and greying hair. He is polite, with a gentlemanly formality and timbre to his speech.

He was not about to be drawn into discussion of irrelevant scenarios. If the defence wanted to irritate the jury with laborious questioning, throwing in some red herrings, they could do so alone.

The prosecution wanted Greg to take the stand. They knew that they couldn't pin their hopes on this, but it would certainly be a bonus.

It is often a gamble for defence barristers to allow their client to give evidence. A jury is not supposed to read anything into the silence of an accused person in the box. But it is difficult to imagine a jury not thinking that, were a truly innocent person standing in the dock before them, they would be champing at the bit to scream their innocence.

Mr Lovitt knew that his client would struggle under cross-examination, but the very act of Greg's rambling answers may be what the jury should see; there was nothing sinister in his indirect answers, it was simply his manner. The jury would also have seen hours of Greg's interview tapes by then: what would be left for him to answer?

Greg was in jail for fourteen months and twenty-five days – roughly the length of Jaidyn's life – before the trial began.

Supreme Court Judge Justice Frank Vincent had instructed the opposing counsel, prosecutor Bill Morgan-Payler Q.C. and defence counsel Colin Lovitt Q.C., to settle all legal issues before the trial started. He did not want interruptions, and had already brought forward the starting date in an attempt to ensure that the trial was over before Christmas.

On Monday, 12 October 1998, amid intense public interest, the trial of the Crown v Gregory Nicholas Domaszewicz got underway.

Every major media outlet in the state had at least one journalist covering the trial, and cameramen and photographers hovered at every entrance to Melbourne's Supreme Court. Inside, a crush of reporters and court artists queued at the sturdy wooden door to Court Four, before squeezing into the cramped pews in the well of the court or spilling into the public gallery.

The sad tale of Jaidyn's short life may have fascinated the nation, but to most observers it had retained an air of unreality. Now, stories almost too peculiar to be true were being repeated in court.

Chapter Twenty

The accused is no longer brought from the cells beneath the court, up the wrought iron staircase and into the dock. So Greg Domaszewicz appeared from a door next to the judge's chamber.

Dressed smartly in a suit and tie, Greg looked a small and fragile man, too small to be a killer. His brown-blond hair, balding at the front, was swept forward in the fashion of a Roman centurion and worn long so that it fell over his collar at the back.

Greg showed his trademark, impish nervous grin as he walked into court. His wide eyes darted around the public gallery, searching for people he knew. His picked out his mother, Helen Chervev, who would only miss one day in court, and smiled and waved.

But the mood was predictably bleak. During the desperation of the search and the drama that followed, many had all but forgotten the awful tragedy at the centre of this drama: the death of a child.

Bill Morgan-Payler Q.C. rose to outline the case against Greg. It was simple really, he said. On New Year's Day, a body had been found in Blue Rock Dam. It was that of Jaidyn Raymond Leskie, aged thirteen months and two weeks. When the body was found, it answered the only vexing question left about the toddler's murder: where was his body?

The rest was elementary. No one else could have done it. No one else had a motive, and no one else had an opportunity to carry out the horrible crime. No matter which way you looked at it, Greg Domaszewicz was guilty.

Colin Lovitt Q.C. is one of the most experienced and talented criminal lawyers at the bar. He was defending Greg free of charge; problems with Legal Aid funding had threatened to leave his client without a lawyer.

Mr Lovitt's list of former clients reads like a who's who of killers, thieves and muggers over the past thirty years. But naturally, his reputation has been built on his success at getting the right result for his clients.

Mr Lovitt started as he intended to continue, rebutting several prosecution points immediately. And within minutes, he had casually raised a critical point. Why was it that Jaidyn was wearing plastic pants when he was found? Wasn't it true that Jaidyn's mother had sent him to Greg with four nappies? And that Jaidyn didn't wear plastic pilchers? He paused. Surely then, someone else had cared for the child before he died.

It was the defence's smoking gun.

The following day, in drizzle and cold, the jury, lawyers, police and judge drove to Moe to see first-hand the places they would have to consider in detail over the coming weeks.

They visited Bilynda Murphy's former house, looking at Jaidyn's bedroom and at the lounge room where Bilynda had been sprawled on the floor that Sunday morning. They looked at the driveway and across the road to the front window of Kim Wilson's house.

They went on to 150 Narracan Drive, taking the most direct route possible, down the road where Kenny Penfold and Darrin Wilson had run, throwing rocks. They stopped outside Greg's house and filed into the garden. The house had been sold months earlier and police had not been able to contact the new owner to arrange access. But they could see enough.

They could see the front windows that had been smashed, the side gate and the condition of the property. They saw the vacant lot next door, the paddocks out the back and the proximity of Mariann and Michael McKinnon's house across the block. They saw the railway line and scrub opposite the house, and the BP Service Station at Gunn's Gully, just a few hundred metres up the road.

The jury passed briefly by Yvonne Penfold's house in Austin Avenue, before travelling out to Blue Rock Dam and across the dam wall.

The Supreme Court is an intimidating place, by nature and design. Drawn from an era of servitude, pomp and protocol, it is

Chapter Twenty

an archaic reminder of heritage and nobility. The dark wooden panelling and cathedral ceilings, with their ornate trim and grand canopy over the judge, resemble an old theatre more than a modern dispenser of justice. And like the black robes, horsehair wigs and antiquated rituals, the speech of those who perform within it seems distant from the world upon which it passes judgment.

Both in architecture and in ritual, it is designed to create a mystique that suggests the accused is being judged not by people, but by the law itself. You do not attend court and give evidence; you are summoned. Your name is called by several people, whereupon you are quickly ushered through doors, turning around corners before appearing centre-stage. After ferreting through the well of the court, you climb the three steps of the witness box and stand on the pedestal to be scrutinised.

There are those among the police and at the bar who love the Supreme Court for this very reason. It is an overwhelming experience to take centre-stage, to have your evidence scrutinised and your word questioned.

The directions sound simple enough: keep your answers brief and tell the truth. But then comes the cross-examination. The bluff and bluster of barristers can be terrifying to witness and there is no doubt that it works. Those who attempt to wrestle with a smart barrister do so at their peril. Where every word is examined, every contingency considered, attitude is as important as accuracy. Intent is as important as content.

Bilynda Murphy was called as the first witness on day three of the trial. She appeared to have little love for Greg Domaszewicz and left court crying, in a rare public display of her pain. She had spent much of the day fighting back tears.

Bilynda had come to court dressed conservatively in a black pants suit, her long blonde hair pulled tidily back, a small silver brooch on her lapel and her ears bare, except for two silver rings looped through the left one.

She barely whispered as she told the court her story. Feeling embarrassed and guilty for having been out drinking when her son was killed, Bilynda talked gently about her pain. Colin Lovitt was determined to point out that he did not agree with the view that she was somehow implicated, by neglect, in her son's fate.

"There have even been rumours that you have been somehow responsible for Jaidyn's death?" Mr Lovitt asked.

"Yes."

"That has hurt you greatly hasn't it?"

"Yes."

But it was less a time for emotion than for fact. Bilynda was asked to detail her background and her friendship with the man accused of killing her son. It was "a casual sort of relationship" she agreed, one in which she "didn't go out with him in public".

She quietly explained her movements on the day and night in question, how she'd desperately tried to ring Greg, but had given up and got drunk. She was forced to admit how many drinks she'd had, and how she had watched her sister kicking a woman in the head in a wild pub brawl.

Bilynda Murphy made several statements to police about her phone calls from the pub. In the first three statements, she did not mention hearing Jaidyn in the background of the first phone call she had made, some time between 11.00 p.m. and 11.15 p.m.

However in her fourth statement, made in the Melbourne homicide squad offices on 28 July, her memory was different. She said that she recalled hearing Jaidyn in the background during the first phone call.

"Jaidyn was crying, not screaming, but grizzling," she said.

"I went off at Greg and told him to put Jaidyn to bed. I know that I did ring and he, Jaidyn, was crying and I said to him to put him to bed because it was too late for a baby to be awake."

Chapter Twenty

In court, however, she was once again confused. Bilynda admitted that she had made several phone calls that night, one in which she was told that Jaidyn was burnt and at least one other in which she claimed to have heard Jaidyn grizzling in the background. She said that, during the call, Greg had told her about Jaidyn's burns and his being in hospital.

Bilynda could not remember whether the phone call with Jaidyn "grizzling" was before or after the call outlining his burns. Katie and Brett McGrath, who were with Bilynda at the hotel, appeared to agree that it was after the first phone call that Bilynda reappeared in the bar, upset because Jaidyn had been burnt. That had happened just minutes after the group had arrived at the pub.

It appears incongruous for Bilynda to have believed the hospital story until the next morning, if she had heard Jaidyn grizzling in the background of a subsequent telephone conversation.

"I was drunk, I don't remember how many calls I made," she said. For two days Bilynda was on the stand, explaining why she had let Greg Domaszewicz continue to mind Jaidyn, despite his previous admission to her that he had "lost it" with the boy. She explained the injuries Jaidyn had suffered at Greg's hands, even the unusual haircut he had given the toddler.

She chronicled what Jaidyn was wearing on Saturday 14 June, and the things she had packed into a bag for him. And Bilynda was also pressed on her own background, her difficulties in dealing with Jaidyn and how she had taken him to doctors on two occasions because she couldn't cope with his crying. She was also forced to admit to lying to Brett Leskie, about how she was suffering postnatal depression, so that he would leave her.

She tried to explain how, even after Greg told her that Jaidyn was in hospital, she didn't go to see him and, regardless of her condition, wanted to go home to sleep.

For many observers, Bilynda's explanations weren't the only puzzle. Every day saw new revelations, which were often shocking and bizarre, sometimes even amusing.

John Hamilton, associate editor of the *Herald Sun*, comments:

"As witness followed witness, there was the pig's head team and smoking cones ... I mean, cone smoking is well known to a certain section of the community but certainly foreign to most people," Mr Hamilton said. "So a fascinated court heard how cones were smoked."

"The judge said, 'I presume you are not talking about ice cream cones'. One was given evidence in very matter-of-fact terms, as though there is nothing unusual about this ...

"Then, on top of that, I think people felt a bit guilty that that sort of lifestyle exists in our community and somehow we are a bit responsible for it ... this situation where you have endemic unemployment in a community, which has led to all sorts of social problems which this case touched on, and this is now accepted as the norm ... "

People came to see for themselves. And, before long, the line at the door each day would extend up to twenty metres, three and four people wide. Court staff could not recall a case that had drawn such crowds.

The public gallery at the back of the court would fill quickly, followed by the balcony layer. Normally, only a small number of people share the long pews. Some attended every day, others called in once or twice. A young barrister was a regular spectator; she just wanted to be part of this "great case". Another student turned up to see what all the fuss was about.

The court staff who take school groups through the courts normally steer away from violent cases, but even they came in when there was room. There was more than a touch of voyeurism in the public interest, a sense even that the trial was Moe's travelling freak show.

Chapter Twenty

Katie Ellen Leskie made an instant impression when she replaced her sister in the witness box, stomping into court in chunky shoes that filled the small platform.

Jaidyn had been "a mummy's boy" she said matter-of-factly. "If he didn't have food in his mouth he cried." And Greg "spoiled him rotten, but then at other times he could be, you know, grumpy". Like when Jaidyn was crying, Greg was a bit short tempered: "He just used to tell him to shut up."

She told of one occasion at her place when Jaidyn was crying and Greg "put him in the hallway, turned the light out and closed the door". Jaidyn screamed.

Then there was the haircut. "Greg shaved it . . . he had like a patch where he had gone to shave it but it was too short," Katie said.

She explained her movements on the Saturday, and how her drunk sister had wanted to go home when she heard that her boy had been burnt. "She was stressed."

She told of ringing Greg at home. "It was right next to the disco. It was pretty loud. I said to him, 'I can't hear you, you'll have to yell'," she said.

"I said to him what Bilynda said, that 'Jaidyn's been burnt, what's going on?' He said, 'We've been to the hospital, he fell up against the heater and he's burnt his bum,' and I said, 'How bad is it?' and he said, 'They put cream on it, it'll be alright'. I said, 'Is everything alright, do you want us to come home?' He said, 'No, you stay there, there's no need to come home, you stay there'.

"I went back and told Bilynda not to worry about it . . . everything was fine."

This was at odds with Bilynda's recollection, but Katie was sure of what had happened. She wasn't as drunk as Bilynda. Katie said that she didn't believe Greg was joking when he told her about the burns; even by Greg's poor standards of humour, that was beyond the pale.

"We never played sick jokes on him."

Maybe Katie had been stirring Greg when she tried to organise a bed for Bilynda in the back of Brett McGrath's panel van that Saturday night. The court learnt that Katie was fond of stirring people up. Then there was the fight at the pub.

"Anyone that had anything to do with the fight got thrown out," she said. "They stopped Bilynda's drinks, they wouldn't serve her, and then they stopped my drinks because they thought I was buying drinks and giving them to her."

Katie recalled only three phone calls to Greg's from Ryans. One by Bilynda at about 11.00 p.m. telling her that Jaidyn was burnt, one by Katie after that, and then the call she made telling Greg to come and collect Bilynda. Katie had told her boyfriend Neville that they couldn't leave until Greg turned up; the fight was still on and Bilynda was drunk and loud.

Bilynda's neighbour, Kim Wilson, gave her evidence on day four. The committal hearing had been traumatic for her, but she wanted to appear at the trial to make sure everyone understood that it was Greg's car she heard and saw early that Sunday morning.

She was asked where exactly Greg's car was parked: what street number it was parked outside, whether it straddled two houses, whether it was on the street or in the driveway. Under cross-examination, Ms Wilson again became upset and wavered about street numbers.

"All I can say is that I seen the car, that's all I can say," she said.

When Kim Wilson left the court, she started to cry. She knew it was Greg's car, she just knew it. But everyone was twisting what she'd say and confusing her. She felt she'd let the police and the prosecutors down.

The trial moved on to one of the few undisputed facts of the case: the night Greg was pulled over by police. Senior Constable Farnham Molesworth took the stand and explained

Chapter Twenty

that he had stopped Greg at 3.35 a.m., and greeted him again almost two hours later when he had stormed into the Moe police station.

He explained how his mood in the station was markedly different from the sullen way he had dealt with police on the road.

A sense of anticipation surrounded the arrival of the pig's head team, Darrin and Kenny, in the witness box. The San Remo butcher was up first. Darrin tried to explain quietly how he came to be involved in the fiasco.

He was a family-oriented type, going to his cousin's twenty-first birthday with his parents. He drank the half-dozen beers he had taken to the party before his parents had dropped him back at the tennis courts in Haigh Street, where he met up with Kenny. Yvonne's trouble with Greg had triggered Darrin and Kenny's departure from the party with revenge on their minds.

Darrin appeared cautious and his evidence later conflicted with that of both Kenny and Yvonne. Darrin said that he grabbed the axe handle from the boot of his car when Yvonne dropped them off. But he didn't really enter Greg's property, didn't smash any windows, and was scared off by the noise. He turned "around and left", throwing his broken axe handle under bushes across the road as he fled.

It was all Kenny's doing, throwing rocks at the local teenagers walking by, Darrin said. He had no part in that, no way. He remembered dropping Kenny and Deano back at their house in Gladstone Street, before he and Yvonne went back to her place where he stayed. They had sex, and he remembered Yvonne receiving two phone calls, the second at about 4.00 a.m.

Darrin left Moe at about 6 or 7 o'clock that Sunday morning. He didn't know about Jaidyn's disappearance until he saw the news at about 6.00 p.m. that night. The police arrived at his house minutes later and asked him to come to the station to make a statement.

Darrin said he had twelve or thirteen cans of beer on the Saturday night, but no dope. He also said that he and Yvonne had stayed in the car when Kenny went in to get the pig's head, and that the pig's head was only mentioned when they were driving around in the car after leaving Haigh Street.

And Tubby Hopkinson, Colin Lovitt asked. Was he at the house when the pig's head throwing was going on? "I suggest to you that he was there."

"No," Darrin replied, somewhat baffled.

"He came the back way over the fence didn't he?"

"No ... he had nothing to do with it that I know of."

"Tubby Hopkinson wouldn't have wanted to be left out of an incident like this, would he?"

"I don't know."

CHAPTER TWENTY-ONE

Kenneth Stephen Penfold swaggered into the Supreme Court, sniffing. Dressed sharply in a dark suit jacket, white shirt and dark tie, he could have been an office worker dropping in for a look, maybe even a young solicitor.

He was ready for his day in the stand, so ready that he was two days early. Kenny had been told by police that they'd call him when he was needed. But he thought he'd come anyway, just to be sure.

Kenny ducked into a bathroom and quickly changed clothes. Out of the formal wear and into the more familiar worn jeans, flannelette shirt and beanie. Kenny had been advised that the beanie wasn't appropriate court attire. "But look at what them judges wear."

For a year, Kenny Penfold had provided some light relief in a tragic story. For a year, people had heard about the extraordinary coincidence that the night a baby went missing, this peculiar chap admits to having thrown a pig's head at the house. Kenny was here to say it was so in his own words.

Kenny readily admitted his extensive criminal history: burglary, theft, assault, assaulting police, criminal damage, resisting arrest, indecent language, possessing cannabis, possessing and using amphetamines, intentionally and recklessly causing injury, and theft from a motor vehicle.

"You will find lots of things there Mr Lovitt," he told Greg's barrister, "but you won't find murder, especially of a child. I know I have been to jail, I haven't been the best of boys, but I didn't kill no kid, so get off my case."

Among the many charges was one of criminal damage for the attack on Greg's house. The penalty was a six-month community based order and 100 hours of community work. Later, this was varied to a fine of $1,200 for the criminal damage, $500 for driving an unregistered vehicle and $100 for a couple of minor traffic offences.

Kenny had already told one court of his role in throwing a pig's head and smashing a house, but that was in Moe, in a court he knew better than his own home. Now he was in the Supreme Court.

Mr Morgan-Payler questioned Kenny, who was willing to oblige. As he told the story, a cheeky smile spread across his face, exposing the gap in his teeth. There had been enough skirting around the issue of whose idea it was, and who had played what role. Kenny wanted the cards on the table.

"It was my harebrained idea to throw a pig's head through Greg's window and go home," he told the court, nervously drumming his fingers on the rail of the witness box.

"Why?" Mr Morgan-Payler asked.

"Because he was hassling my sister all the time, as simple as that. I left the party, went back home and had a few more beers at home and had a few cones..."

He was interrupted and asked to clarify a few details. What followed was almost an "Abbott and Costello" exchange.

"Who is Deano?" Mr Morgan-Payler asked.

"Deano Dumdum," Kenny replied.

"Deano Dumdum?"

"That's about as much as I can give you on Deano."

"When you left [your house] did you take anything with you?"

Chapter Twenty-One

"Yeah."
"What did you take?"
"Darren. That's Darren Millane."
"There's Darrin Wilson and there's Darren Millane?"
"Yes."
"Who was Darren Millane?"
"That was my pet pig."
"What was left of Darren the pet pig at that stage?"
"I guess not much."
"What did you take?"
"The head."
"Where was the rest of him?"
"In my shower block."
"Let me ask you this – a lot of us are not accustomed to butchering our own meat – if you kill a pig or any other sort of animal to eat, do you eat it straight away?"
"Not unless you are hungry I suppose."
"What did you do with the carcass?"
"I left it hanging in the shower for about three days ... I bleed it for three days, hang it up to bleed it."
"You used your shower at your place for this purpose?"
"Yes, my sister wouldn't let me use hers."
"The carcass was in your shower?"
"Yes."
"Where was the head?"
"I think the head was sitting on my front door."

The packed public gallery tittered and shook their heads in disbelief. Kenny looked around the gallery. He knew it sounded odd, but to him it was just one of those things that you do.

Kenny explained how the group left his house and drove to the BP service station where he bought two hot dogs. They sat in the car outside the 24-hour garage while he ate, then did "a quick U-bolt" and went up toward Morwell, to the driveway that runs beside the railway tracks. Darrin and Kenny got out a short distance along and organised for Yvonne and Deano to collect them up at Narracan Bridge in five or ten minutes.

He told of crossing the road to the fence in the vacant lot, of Greg coming out of the house after his dogs started wildly barking. He "hit the deck" he said.

Greg's car had been reversed into his driveway. "Never seen him back his car in his drive before," he said. Kenny saw Greg come out of the house a second time and go to the bin to put a white bag in it.

"Where were you when you saw him [Greg] come outside and put something in the garbage?" Mr Lovitt asked in cross-examination.

"Like I said, kneeling down backing one out – having a crap. I saw him go to the bin a couple of times, but didn't put nothing in."

Mr Lovitt marvelled at the coincidence that Kenny and Darrin appeared to know Greg was leaving his house in the early hours of Sunday morning. He queried whether they had been tipped off on Yvonne Penfold's phone by someone in Traralgon.

"Had anybody contacted Yvonne on her mobile phone and told her that Greg Domaszewicz was going to leave and drive to Traralgon to pick Bilynda up?"

"I don't know, I don't carry Yvonne's mobile phone. That's why it was Yvonne's. If it was mine it would be Kenny's phone," Kenny replied.

Kenny explained how he and Darrin had run over to attack the house once Greg had left, lobbing the pig's head twice at the window before it smashed. "As far as I knew I thought it went inside the house, but obviously it didn't," he said.

The dogs "went troppo" but had he heard any other noises coming from the house? "No. No baby noises."

"You've been asked that before haven't you," Mr Lovitt said.

"Sure have."

Chapter Twenty-One

Inevitably, questions turned to Kenny's liking for beer and drugs.

"You haven't had anything to drink today have you?" Mr Lovitt asked Kenny.

"No," Kenny replied.

"You haven't had any cones or any drugs?"

"Yes, I had a couple this morning, but I have a couple every day."

"What time was that?"

"Probably six o'clock this morning."

Kenny went on to explain how Tubby Hopkinson had been with him during the slaughtering of the pig.

Mr Lovitt began to scratch at the idea of a police conspiracy case, which he would later build on, by asking Kenny about his sister's relationship with Sergeant Russell Fraser of Moe police. Kenny denied any knowledge of an affair.

He explained that, although Yvonne suffered years of abuse at Greg's hands, the final straw had been Greg ramming her car in the driveway. Kenny rang Greg and warned him to leave his sister alone or he would belt him.

"I thought we were mates," Greg replied.

"We're not mates after what I saw you do [to my sister's car]," Kenny replied and hung up. He said he had "seen enough" of the trouble Greg caused Yvonne. On other occasions of violence between the couple, Kenny had been indisposed, generally in jail, and only learnt of the trouble after the event.

"I have been in and out of jail all my life. I can't get to see all those things, I can only get to see them when I get out," he told the court. He wanted to strike while the iron was hot.

The longer Kenny faced the questions, the more agitated he became. He wanted to go home, back to Moe. When he was nearing breaking point, he pleaded with Justice Vincent, "Can I go home? I've really had enough."

"Mr Penfold, this is..." Justice Vincent began, but Kenny cut him off.

"I have come here to try and bust my gut for you and for all I have done is get it thrown in my face. I would have done a lot of things to Greg. I would have belted him, but I didn't belt him for the simple reason that he would have given me up to the coppers. That's why the pig's head went through the window."

Kenny told the court that, at about six or seven in the morning – only hours after he had attacked Greg's house – he rode down to inspect his handiwork on Tubby Hopkinson's motorbike. He was stunned to discover the area crawling with police.

He approached a police officer in an unmarked police car.

"What's going on boss?" he asked the officer.

He was told it was a crime scene and he couldn't go up there.

"The first thing I thought was, 'Shit, all this over a pig's head?'"

Kenny was only too willing to tell police of his role in damaging the house. He didn't want to be associated with this talk about child abduction. Besides, he had expected to be charged with criminal damage. What he hadn't expected was the national media coverage that the case would attract.

When a Queensland policeman saw Kenny's face on the news in Brisbane, he twigged that it was the same man he wanted over an assault.

"I was shanghaied [extradited] to Queensland. Yes, first plane I've ever been on. Gee it was good," Kenny said enthusiastically of the ordeal that had landed him more prison time. However, Mr Lovitt was more interested in Kenny's mates.

He asked why Kenny had said that Deano sat on the floor of the car when he drove up to Greg's house that night.

"I don't know, ask Deano ... he's a weirdo person," Kenny said.

Chapter Twenty-One

"Had Deano been given a hiding by Tubby?" Mr Lovitt asked.

"I don't think so. There's always stuffing around in my house – boys will be boys, so what? There might be a little blood here, somebody might get a blood nose, boys will be boys. I do whatever I like in my house. If we want to fight, we'll fight; if we don't, we won't fight."

Colin Lovitt again asked Kenny about arriving home to collect the pig's head. "When you went in, everyone smoked marijuana?"

"No."

"You didn't?"

"No ... I can't mention nothing about marijuana because every time I do it gets mentioned in the paper. It's just a deadset mess, your honour. That's all. I'm caught up in the middle of it and I'm sick of it."

Tub Hopkinson had been brought into the scenario by Mr Lovitt and Kenny couldn't work out why. His face was all over the papers and TV and he felt ridiculed. He'd been extradited and jailed in Queensland on charges he'd have otherwise escaped and now his housemate, Tubby, had been brought into it. When would it stop?

He had to explain to Tubby that night how Greg's defence was pointing the finger squarely at Tubby as a possible murder suspect.

"He ain't a happy man, or should I say he ain't a happy boy. I wouldn't be either if stuff like that was printed about me," Kenny said.

"I didn't take any child from no house. I think it would be a pretty sick joke for someone to take any child. I have kids of my own, four of them ... I threw a damn rotten pig's head through the window. If I could bring little Jaidyn back I would. I'm deadset spewing because it has devastated my life when this happened."

Colin Lovitt then took Kenny by surprise with a startling claim.

He put it to Kenny Penfold that, days after Jaidyn went missing, he was seen with another man and a small child in the area near his father and step-mother's property in Mountain Creek Road, Holbrook, New South Wales.

He suggested to Kenny that the child he had been seen with was about Jaidyn's age. They had apparently run out of petrol and had borrowed a petrol can from a local farmer. It sounded plausible.

Kenny doubted it was true, but couldn't recall his precise movements and whether he had visited his dad at that time.

"If I was there it was probably only my little sister anyway," he reasoned.

Kenny has a two-year-old sister who would have resembled Jaidyn in size.

"If I suggested to you that you were seen with a child who looked to be about fifteen months old, what would you say to that?" Mr Lovitt asked.

"I would say that you are tripping."

Colin Lovitt pursued Kenny and his mate Tubby about their drug taking habits.

Asked if Tubby dealt in amphetamines, Kenny replied: "Definitely not, might have a cone every now and then, that's about it."

"Were you involved in any drug dealing while you lived with Mr Hopkinson?" Mr Lovitt asked.

"No, definitely not. If I was involved in any drug dealings it was with him over there [Greg], or hasn't he told you?"

"Did Darrin talk to you about going into the house to do a proper job?"

"He did, yeah."

"But you wouldn't be in that?"

"No way."

Chapter Twenty-One

Mr Lovitt was adding some doubt to the mix of claim and counterclaim. He clearly understood the dynamics of the case: nothing should be taken at face value.

Fortunately for Kenny, others could recall his movements better than he could. Myself included. When Mr Lovitt said Kenny was supposedly seen in New South Wales, I had interviewed him on both days for the *Herald Sun*. Consequently, two days later I was subpoenaed and gave evidence to that effect.

To Colin Lovitt, I was a distraction and an annoyance. He could not dispute the accuracy of the evidence, however journalists were fair game.

"Mr Gleeson, I take it you are not an old family friend of the Penfolds?" he asked.

"It's pretty safe to say that, yes," I replied.

But the friend Mr Lovitt was interested in was Tubby.

CHAPTER TWENTY-TWO

Despite his prominence in one of the most conservative of Melbourne institutions, Colin Lovitt, Queen's Counsel, has the common man's touch. His career in criminal law has meant dealing with meat-and-potato characters, who do not respond to the superior demeanour typical of the law. Mr Lovitt swaggers in court, physically and verbally, blustering and groaning, yelling and intimidating in the knockabout style of a bloke from the pub up the road. Juries are supposed to relate better to someone who speaks to them on their own terms.

It was stated early on that there would barely be a person from Moe to Melbourne that Colin Lovitt wouldn't suggest could have killed Jaidyn by the end of the trial. To achieve reasonable doubt, toss up an unreasonable number of possibilities and demand that the jury throw their hands in the air and say, "Well how do we know?" It is a successful approach for, while duty to the court demands the pursuit of justice be paramount, a barrister's role is also to defend his client.

The adversarial system of justice in Australia is not a search for the truth, however, it is an assessment of someone's involvement in a crime. If you can mount enough evidence against someone, they will be proved guilty; if the defence can establish a reasonable doubt, they will be acquitted.

Chapter Twenty-Two

In Tubby Hopkinson, Colin Lovitt believed he'd found his reasonable doubt. Mr Lovitt had not represented Domaszewicz at the committal hearing, but even if he had, it's unlikely he would have raised the possibility of Tubby Hopkinson's involvement then.

Tubby was not listed as a witness. He hadn't even made a statement that was worthy of inclusion. He was a bit player in the police view, a bit player, in fact, to everyone but Colin Lovitt.

Tubby Hopkinson is a violent man. The court heard that he was mentally unstable, took "speed", dealt drugs, had a string of criminal convictions and admitted once using a baseball bat to attack someone, though police were his normal targets. He's a burly menacing character, not gifted with great intelligence and with a reputation as a standover man.

Tubby was at home in the house he shared with Kenny Penfold the night Kenny and his mates called in to collect the pig's head. He'd been in bed when Kenny came in to see what he and Dumb Dumb Deano Ross were doing. As is normal for Tubby, he had been smoking marijuana and drinking beer. When Kenny woke him to ask whether he could take his pig's head, Tubby agreed but that was the end of his involvement. He rolled over "wasted" and went back to sleep.

When Kenny Penfold told this to the packed Supreme Court, he was visibly moved when Colin Lovitt began to suggest that Tubby had played a more sinister role.

No one had suggested this before. And even Colin Lovitt admitted there was absolutely no evidence to suggest Tubby ever went to Greg's house that night, or even left his own house.

Colin Lovitt put it to Kenny that Tubby had joined the plan to steal and murder Jaidyn. While Kenny and Darrin created a distraction at the front of the house by smashing windows, Tubby was coming in through the back door, he suggested.

The theory was that Tubby had arrived separately, approaching the house by motorbike from the rear. He allegedly carried an axe handle. After the attack, Kenny and Darrin would flee in one direction while Tubby fled in the other with the baby.

Mr Lovitt's rationale was simple. Tubby's background would suggest that it was inconceivable for him to deliberately miss out on a bit of hell raising. If there was trouble, Tubby would be in it – the last thing he would have done is go to bed.

Tubby was present for the slaughtering of the pig. However, to Kenny's knowledge, that's where his role ended, save riding back out to the scene to collect the head.

"You were asked about Hopkinson [in relation to killing the pig]," Mr Lovitt said to Kenny.

"What do you mean asked about Hopkinson? Where is his name even coming from?" Kenny had asked, perplexed.

"It's coming from me," Mr Lovitt replied.

The judge, Justice Frank Vincent, intervened to calm Kenny down: "Mr Penfold, just be cool and answer the questions please."

"After you sat around smoking dope with Yvonne and Deano and Darrin and you and Tubby, all of you left, leaving Tubby on his own?" Mr Lovitt again picked away.

"Yes, pretty much like that, yeah," Kenny agreed.

"And Tubby was the bloke who had gone back to pick up the head because you left the head behind when you slaughtered this pig?"

"Yes."

"How on earth did that happen?"

"Because it wasn't thought about then, when we killed it."

"That's not what you told the police."

"It wasn't thought about until that night at the party."

Kenny is then forced to concede he had earlier made a statement admitting that he had already thought of throwing the pig's head through the window when they killed the pig.

Chapter Twenty-Two

"Tubby was looking forward to this wasn't he?" Mr Lovitt asked.

"I couldn't say he was looking forward to it. If he was looking forward to it, he would have been right beside me too."

"Wasn't there an arrangement that you were going to go, you in the car were going to go one way and he was going to go the other way?"

"No."

"He was going to come via the back of Domaszewicz's house?"

"He wasn't even there … he didn't have a baseball bat. I don't know why you keep saying he went there, because it didn't happen."

"The last thing you want to involve yourself in is the murder of a helpless child?"

"Of course because I didn't do it, it's as simple as that," Kenny said.

When Mr Lovitt claimed Tubby wouldn't miss "a bit of sport", Kenny replied that, if that was the case, Tubby would have been hurling stones and smashing windows with Kenny, not sneaking in back doors.

For the defence it was a strong line of questioning; it fuelled the conspiracy theories and was plausible, if not verifiable.

Colin Lovitt had been able to introduce the theory through another witness. Now he needed Tubby. As Kenny Penfold was finishing his testimony the next morning, he gave the court an indication of Tubby's mood in a typically understated way.

"Tubby ain't a happy man, he ain't a happy boy. I wouldn't be either if these things were said about me," Kenny said.

For Colin Lovitt, it was perfect. When Raymond Tub Hopkinson finally stomped into court, he was bristling mad. It was exactly the mood the defence had been hoping for. The court was silent as Tub began giving evidence, his anger palpable.

"Kenny was always complaining about being hungry so I said, 'Let's get rid of Darren' and then we were getting complaints by the neighbours, the council and he was getting a bit too big to be keeping as a pet any longer," Tub said.

"I went back out there to get it, because I was going to get it 'taxidermied'."

When Tubby arrived home he had "put it in a bucket of water to preserve it" from the ants and left it on the doorstep.

"[Kenny] come back, woke me up and asked me if he could take Darren Millane's head," Tub said.

"Did he say why?"

"He wanted to pay Greg back. He said he was going to throw it through the windows. I said 'you can only take it if you are going to throw it through the windows'."

He claims he didn't get out of bed.

Tubby was asked about Dean's role.

"Deano's not even around when he's around ... like I said, he's a shadow, he's nothing. Stupid."

Kenny came home later, Tub said, "very happy" he had finally got Greg back. He woke Tub up and had a few cones with him before they went to bed.

The questioning became more personal: "Do you have any mental illness?"

"Yes I do."

"Schizophrenia?"

"I don't know, I'm getting tested for it ... I've been tested, they can't find nothing, that's why I've been referred to a higher doctor from Moe courts."

Tub admitted he had once overdosed on drugs prescribed by a doctor and that led to "schizophrenic spasms". When pressed on this, Mr Lovitt appeared to be risking Tubby having one in the witness box.

"You're fucking pissing me off," he yelled. "What happened to me, what I done to myself is nothing to fucking do with you,

Chapter Twenty-Two

you know? Now you're trying to tell me I'm schizophrenic mate. What are you on? I don't know. I read the papers ... I get told I'm a fucking amphetamines abuser, drug user, dealer, standover merchant ... lucky I even turned up here today, mate, you know?"

Tubby has a history of convictions for assaulting police, cultivating cannabis, unlawful assault, threats to kill, firearms offences. However, he denied to the court ever hitting someone in the head with a baseball bat. He had hit them in the arm, he explained.

"He was standing over me. It was either belt him with the baseball bat or get the shit kicked out of myself you know. I'm only five-foot ten, he's like six-one. A bigger person gets me a little bit scared."

"Did you tell someone you had been inside Greg Domaszewicz's house that night?" Mr Lovitt asked.

"No. I've never been there at all, never even spoke to the fucking dog maggot cunt because he's a kid-killer. As far as I'm concerned he's a fucking dog."

The outbursts didn't stop there. He knew he was losing his temper, and struggled to control it. "You're making me angry and I'm getting frustrated with you – I'm starting to call you a dickhead again."

While Tubby was protesting to the court, Greg sat in the dock, a striking contrast. He was a pathetic and diminutive character compared to Tubby's barely contained rage in the witness box.

Greg sat nervously leaning forward in his seat, looking to the ground during much of Tubby's evidence. He would nod a lot throughout the trial, and talk to himself or mutter, repeating what was said as he followed the evidence. It was like a child who mouths the words as they read to themselves.

Greg has a range of facial movements, like ticks, but was quite composed in the dock. Sometimes he would catch the eye of a reporter or lawyer, his mum or the jury and he would smile and nod. Several times he asked for water and once he was given permission to take medication for asthma, which he said had been denied him by prison authorities.

On the witness stand, the case again touched on the bizarre as Mr Lovitt asked Tubby about a period he lived in Moorabbin, in Melbourne's south-eastern suburbs.

As if from nowhere, Mr Lovitt brought up the murder of two police officers in Moorabbin and asked Tubby about his connection to that.

"You are aware that the police became interested, after two policemen were killed in Moorabbin, in mobile phone calls that they could trace to people connected to you, aren't you?" he asked.

"No I haven't. I have got a mobile phone. I just received it as of lately."

It was a stunning question that was not followed up but it had the desired effect.

Mr Lovitt persisted with his line of questioning on Tubby's decision to stay in bed that night while his mates went out to play.

"If I did, I would have breached my ICO [intensive corrections order] and I would have been back in jail and I didn't want no part of that episode whatsoever. I was asked if my pig's head could be taken and I said yes.

"I smoke cannabis so I don't go out to do those sorts of things. That's why I don't drink alcohol," Tub reasoned.

He was then forced to deny ever having held his family hostage, or having cut off the head of a former housemate's dog. Tubby again worked to control his temper, telling the seasoned barrister to "cut out the shit". But the shit was exactly what Mr Lovitt needed. Tub Hopkinson appeared for all the world, and particularly to the stunned jury, like a man perfectly capable of extreme violence.

Chapter Twenty-Two

According to veteran *Herald Sun* journalist, and associate editor of the newspaper, John Hamilton, who was covering the case, everyone was scared of Tubby that day.

"Tubby in the whole case was the most riveting character and the most frightening character," John said.

"The contrast between Greg sitting in the dock mouthing to himself and Tubby in the witness box shrieking at the counsel and banging the witness box with his fist, just on the verge of losing control . . . very real fear was that Tubby was about to let fly. And that's a pretty big factor in the mind of the jury."

Tubby gave evidence over two consecutive days. Leaving court on the night of the first, he was mad, seething mad, and felt trapped. The media were waiting outside to photograph him and even though the questioning had stopped, he felt pursued.

Court security officers tried to usher him out but he ran off screaming through the corridors of the courts. Eventually, after climbing a side wall, he was corralled in a courtyard by security staff, screaming obscenities at the top of his lungs and carrying a large rock. Detective Senior Sergeant Legg arrived with another member of the homicide squad as things turned nasty. The court staff had drawn their batons and were preparing to advance on the equally terrified Tubby. The detectives approached and were able to calm him down.

The detectives sat Tubby down that night and the next morning and reasoned with him that he was overreacting. They steadied him sufficiently that the next day in the box, he was decidedly more placid. However, they weren't taking any chances; the next morning a large policeman was positioned behind him in case he lost his temper again. But the damage, as far as Colin Lovitt was concerned, had been done.

One problem with the conspiracy theory was that it required one to accept that there had been a high degree of planning by Kenny and his mates. More importantly, it required one to accept that the goal of the night wasn't to scare Greg Domaszewicz, or to damage his house, but to kill Jaidyn. If the plan had been to bash Greg Domaszewicz, they wouldn't have been likely to go to such elaborate lengths to enter the house from two angles. And they would surely have seized their opportunity before Greg left. This theory would also render the pig's head redundant, as this was meant to be a warning to Greg.

Another problem with the theory is that few people knew that Jaidyn was with Greg that night. Even if they did, Tub Hopkinson would have had to ride a loud motorbike behind Greg Domaszewicz's house in the early hours of the morning. Neighbours who reported cars coming and going would have heard a motorbike behind the house. Tubby would have had to jump over the fence into the backyard, where Greg's three bull terrier dogs were loose.

He would then have entered the house through the back door, although Greg Domaszewicz admitted that he had bolted the door from inside before he left, and that was how the police found it the following day. Then Tubby would have had to smash a window to get in. But the only windows smashed were at the front of the house.

The theory arrives at the same problem faced by Kenny and Darrin entering the house; forensic experts claim there was no way anyone entered the property through the windows.

Even if all of the above were possible and Tubby was able to get Jaidyn with his nappy bag and clothes, he would have had to flee with him over the back fence to the motorbike. He would then have had to carry him, probably already wrapped in a sleeping bag and tied to a crowbar, while riding the motorbike.

Finally, a key tenet of the defence case was that a forensic photograph taken days after Jaidyn disappeared showed what

Top: Bilynda Murphy, mother of toddler Jaidyn Leskie, who was snatched from his home at Newborough, near Moe.

Left: Bilynda Murphy leaves the Moe police station after questioning by police.

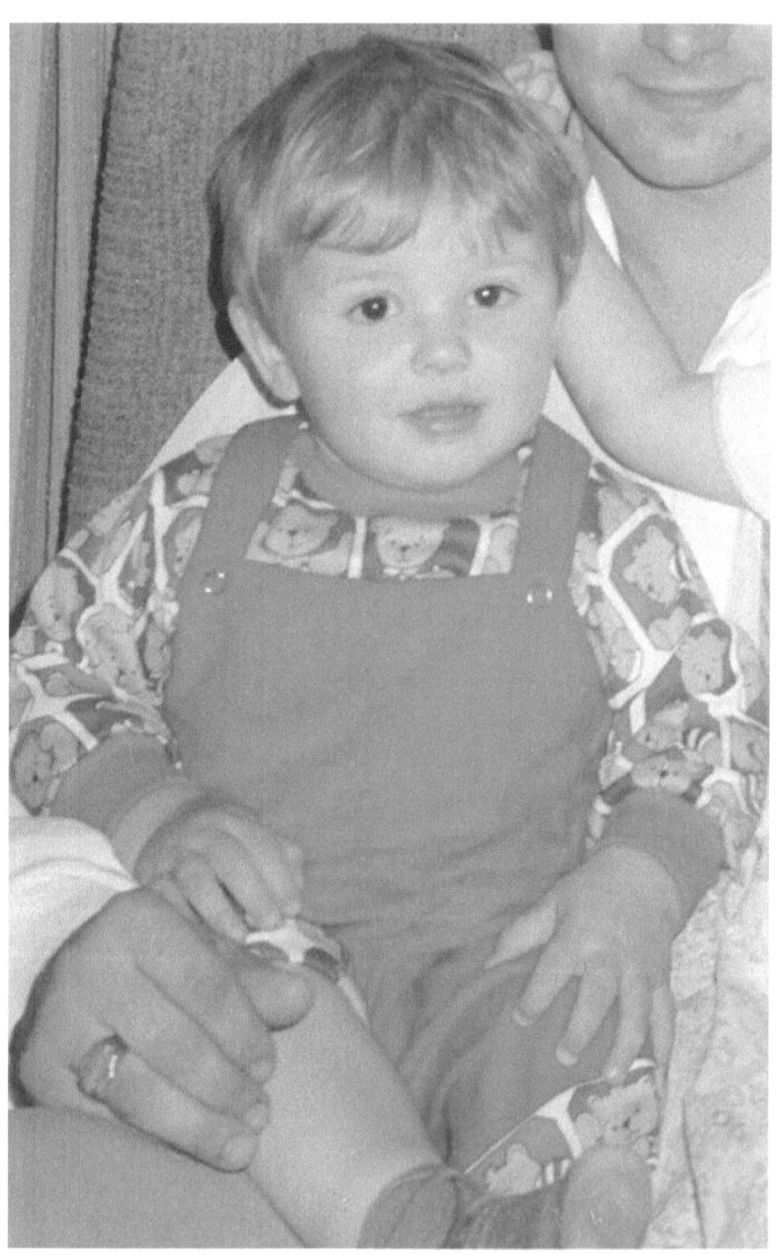

Jaidyn Leskie with dad, Brett Leskie.

The family: Breehanna, Bilynda, Brett and Jaidyn.

Jaidyn Leskie's dad Brett.

Top: Greg Domaszewicz's vandalised car.

Left: Police remove a hangman's noose, found on the veranda of Greg Domaszewicz's house.

Opposite Page: Greg Domaszewicz with his vandalised car. He was Jaidyn's babysitter and the main suspect in the murder case.

Left: Police searching for the body of Jaidyn Leskie at Yallourn Tip near Moe.

Search-and-rescue squad divers retrieve a plastic bag containing clothing out of Blue Rock Dam at Moe.

Senior Sergeant Rowland Legg, leading officer in the Jaidyn Leskie investigation.

Bilynda and her husband, Jeremy, attend the Coroner's inquest at the Melbourne Magistrates Court complex in 2003. Both were wearing T-shirts campaigning for Jaidyn.

Bilynda at Jaidyn's grave in Yallourn cemetery with her sons Caleb and Corran in January 2003.

Chapter Twenty-Two

they claimed was the crowbar that was used to dispose of his body. If this was true, then Tubby – or one of his mates – had to go back to the house a second time, while police had the place under virtual twenty-four hour surveillance, and get the crowbar before disposing of the body.

The most important thing about the theory, however, was that it fed doubt. Tubby Hopkinson looked a lot more capable of murdering a child than Greg Domaszewicz.

CHAPTER TWENTY-THREE

Yvonne Penfold looked a picture of sweetness and innocence as she tip-toed to the witness box. Yet this image dissipated as she started to tell of her miserable life with Greg. No one could doubt she had had an awful time, although culpability seemed evenly apportioned as details emerged.

"Very recently before Jaidyn disappeared, someone spray painted on my [car] bonnet," she told the court. "I went to the police station and demanded they make some sort of a ... a write-up because, I don't know, there was things happening all the time. There wasn't a day of the week that went by that I wasn't getting some sort of harassment. I was constantly getting phone calls at work – I had two lines at work that Greg Domaszewicz and Bilynda Murphy were both having their fun and games playing [with].

"Burnouts on your nature strip and your petrol tank full of dirt that's been, I don't know, off a tree that's been ripped out of your garden and sprinkled into your petrol tank – there wasn't a day went by when something didn't happen."

They were the pranks, but things became violent when Yvonne had smashed the glass shower screen in Greg's bathroom, after he had locked her in.

"[He] locked me in till I went mentally insane because he

Chapter Twenty-Three

wouldn't let me go ... at this time Mr Domaszewicz would not let me out of his home because we were fighting."

On another occasion she had been forced to spray Greg with a capsicum-type spray. She denied it was capsicum spray, saying that it was a self-defence spray she had bought at Ryans Hotel to protect herself against Greg. She vehemently denied that Sergeant Russ Fraser, of Moe police, with whom the defence claimed she was having a sexual relationship, had given it to her.

"I'm saying that I squirted him with something. What it was I don't know, because he was strangling me in my kitchen sink," Yvonne said.

"He was holding me around the throat, my head was in the kitchen sink." She claims she managed to break free, grab the spray and use it.

She admitted that Greg had always hated Sergeant Fraser because "he thought I was, I suppose, screwing around with him". Which she hastened to add, she wasn't.

It had been in this environment that the pig's head plan was hatched.

"We were having a little bit of a joke and a bit of a conversation about the pig's head but there were no plans or anything that I recall being made," Yvonne said.

They had gone to Kenny's after the party, Yvonne said. She disagreed with Darrin Wilson that they had stayed in the car, saying that they went inside and had a few drinks. Yvonne also claimed that it was Darrin, not her, who drove to Greg's house that night. She had climbed behind the wheel, when Kenny and Darrin jumped out, and driven off with Deano while they had attacked Greg's house. They were small points of divergence, but discrepancies nonetheless.

Both agreed that Darrin had stayed with her on the night of the attack. At one stage, Darrin had gone outside after hearing a noise. "He had gone outside to see if anybody was out there ...

and there was another time where Mr Domaszewicz's vehicle had also drove past and tooted his horn," she said.

Yvonne's first statement said that she had offered Darrin Wilson $20 to put the pig's head in Greg's letter box. This was untrue, and she admitted as much, but she had wanted to take responsibility for the attack herself.

"Kenny, like he did something and he doesn't need to cop all this shit for something he has done to me. It's taken – it was like a-year-and-a-half, two years of harassment and no one had the balls to do anything, not even me, except Kenny. Kenny was the only one willing to do something and that's what he did," she said.

Yvonne and Greg didn't look at each other much as she gave her evidence. Bilynda and Greg were also at pains to avoid eye contact, with Greg preferring to stare at the floor as he followed their evidence.

Yvonne's behaviour since the incident has not always been consistent or easy to follow. On 26 August, she was at the house of Greg's cousins, Michael and Jacinta Korbut, with a man known as AJ – Arthur Oliver. Yvonne admitted she had said something along the lines of "if I help him, I will finish up where he is".

"Why did you say that?"

"Because he is guilty as far as I am concerned. I am not going to help someone who is guilty."

For all the venom Yvonne directed at Greg, however, she exposed a more tender side when she wrote to him in jail.

"Babe what can I say, everything is to (sic) much, I'm blown away. Are you guilty or not, which is probably exactly what you are thinking of me.

"I don't now (sic) if I'm doing the wrong thing by writing this note or not, so many things are being (sic) said and all I know is I didn't take, see or hear nothing about little Jaidan (sic).

"I need some communication or answers from you to solve the problems in my head, or to see your (sic) or prove you're

Chapter Twenty-Three

inocent (sic) to me, as I'm not sure to trust what you say as I don't now (sic) what is going on with you and fuckin Boo.

"As you have said so many lies to me, prior to this whole disasterous (sic) situation. If you didn't do it babe the truth will be found out, and then whatever happens you deserve to be happy.

"Thinking of you and only you, (DIDO xx)

"I'm so tired,

"I can't sleep

"I love you

PLATE FACE."

The letters DIDO are understood to represent the phrase: Dick In, Dick Out. PLATE FACE is said to refer to her flat face.

Yvonne was offended by the suggestion that she had been behind the prank in which Bilynda's children were swapped over in their beds.

"It's stupid for anyone to even think of that. I wouldn't even know where she was living ... it is a very bizarre [allegation]."

Mr Lovitt was affronted by this response. "You are going to shake your head and say 'I am a little girl and I didn't do that?'" he snarled at her.

"Yeah."

"That's the way you try to portray yourself isn't it?"

"This is me. What you are looking at is what you get."

"There is more than one you isn't there?"

"So Greg used to say, yeah."

So much had already been said of Dumb Dumb during the trial, not much of it flattering, that there was an expectant silence when he took the stand.

It gradually became apparent, however, that in a relative sense, Dean Ross was far from the dumb one. Deano was the classic placid soul from whom heavy marijuana smoking had taken its toll. He had passed his VCE and gone to university to study teaching, but then dropped out of his studies, and pretty much out of life. He had worked at the Ranger Uranium Mine at Jabiru for short periods but was back on the dole.

"Too much choof, Mr Legg, too much choof," was how Kenny described Deano's state to the policeman.

It came as no surprise to learn that Deano – like most in the case – suffered from a mental disorder; in his case, it was mild schizophrenia. Deano was nonetheless articulate and composed, appearing comfortable in the formal court in tracksuit pants and flannelette shirt. He was unfazed by the cross-examination, telling the story of how he came to be in the car, but had played no part other than that, plainly and directly.

He was hungry at the time. That was all. He had wanted something to eat and, as they were going down to the service station, he'd gone with them to get a pie.

"Kenny came in and I was sitting in the lounge room and he came in from the car and asked me if I wanted to come for a drive to throw a pig's head through – I can't remember the exact word – this prick's window or something, referring to Greg I suppose, because Greg was hassling Yvonne.

"I just wanted to go for a drive because I wasn't doing nothing. I didn't want to get involved."

Deano was also among those who believed that they had gone to the service station before the attack. However, he agreed with Darrin that it was only Kenny who had come into the house to pick up the pig's head.

Mr Lovitt's questions then took a strange turn, asking Deano if he knew Greg's mother, Helen Chervev.

"No, the only time I've been acquainted with her is one day she gave my mother's house a call and we had quite a long conversation," he explained.

"She had a conversation with my mum and then I got on the phone and, you know, she sounded upset. I didn't know who it was, you know, and we had a conversation. She was obviously upset. She was asking me, you know, putting across

Chapter Twenty-Three

like how upset she was and she eventually got on to ask me whether I could help her with anything else and I just said no, because I've already told the police, you know, everything I know and she was quite upset.

"She seems like a nice lady. She offered me, indirectly like, she said to me something about she could give me money if I could help her out with anything to clear her son's name or something."

Colin Lovitt knew it didn't sound good and suggested, without stating it outright, that it wasn't a bribe she was offering. More of a reward.

"In other words she was offering you a reward if you would provide more information, wasn't she?"

"She didn't say it in those exact words," Deano replied.

"But a reward?"

"But she didn't say reward, she just, you know, she was in tears yeah."

CHAPTER TWENTY-FOUR

A procession of witnesses gave evidence that placed Kenny and Darrin outside Greg's house that Saturday night.

A fitter and turner, Chris Allford was driving home with his wife after a cards night, when two men ran across Narracan Drive in front of him. He remembered, because he had to slow down to avoid hitting the second as he followed his mate south toward the train tracks. He thought the behaviour suspicious, so he checked the clock in his car. It was 2.14 a.m. Both men were wearing dark clothes and beanies; neither was carrying anything.

Butcher Paul Reid explained how he was walking home from the party in Haigh Street with his mate, John Sellens, when they were pelted with rocks.

"We couldn't see where the rocks came from; they just came at us from towards the railway line." They walked on to the BP to buy a Coke and some food.

Teenager Ben Stubbs was also walking home along Narracan Drive with his mate, Daniel Halstead, when they noticed two men walking towards them.

"As we passed, the taller guy came up and said 'boo'. He jumped in front of us and we ignored him and just kept going. Then rocks started being thrown at us," he said.

Ben's mum knew Greg Domaszewicz, and Ben had played cricket with Greg and even bought one of his dogs from him. So

Chapter Twenty-Four

he knew Greg's house when he walked past it. He saw that the front porch light was on and could tell that the lounge room light was on. The dogs were barking and he could hear music, but couldn't be certain where it was coming from. Ben had originally made a statement that he thought music was coming from inside Greg's house, but later changed it to say that he couldn't be certain.

He mentioned the house to his mate, Daniel, because of the dogs and the fact that Greg used to have a pet pig called Stimpy. When they got to the BP service station, Ben recognised Kenny Penfold as the bloke who'd said "boo" to him. Ben said "boo" back as they stood near the hotdog stand.

The shop assistant at the BP service station that night, Wayne Koning, had gone to school with Kenny Penfold, so he knew who he was and could verify the time.

Mariann McKinnon is a short round woman with a rough edge to her personality. Her ex-husband was, at the time of the trial, serving time in jail for the axe-murder of a local drug dealer eight years earlier, so Mariann was familiar with the court system. Mariann and Greg had been close and spoke regularly. She recalled that she had rung Greg at 8.00 p.m. on the Saturday and he had called back at about 10 o'clock. She knew the time because the clock was near the phone. She also confirmed that Greg had asked her for nappies, but that she didn't have any. Her husband had suggested using a towel, or picking some up at the BP service station.

Mariann told the court that, during their half-hour conversation, she heard a baby and a dog in the background. Greg explained that he hadn't answered the phone at 8 o'clock because he only answers calls if he knows who's calling. He also said that he had called Mariann's place earlier and got the answering machine, which cut him off. Mariann admitted she had cut the machine off.

Greg ended the conversation, Mariann said, because Jaidyn "had spilt something or he had done something and he had to clean up whatever Jaidyn had done. I don't know if he spilt a drink or something. He said he was going to leave him with no nappy on, just put a pair of tracksuit pants on him."

Mariann recognised the bark of the dog in the background as that of Greg's bitch, Sammy. She had also heard Jaidyn in the background and said, "Are you looking after your son again?"

At about 1.00 a.m., as she was playing computer games, she heard Greg's car start up. She knew it was his car, as it was coming from his house.

"The sound went away from my house from where I was at the time when I heard it start up," she said.

She had also heard loud music coming from Greg's house or that general direction between about 2.00 a.m. and 2.30 a.m. It had been the song Slice of Heaven, from the Footrot Flats movie. Greg vows that he never played his stereo and was probably on his way to Traralgon at the time.

Darren Farr was also familiar with the courts from his own brushes with the law, but had never done anything serious enough to land in the Supreme Court.

From being one of Greg's closest allies, Darren had turned on him. He believed that Greg was guilty and that put him in the other camp, the coppers' camp. But it was the period between Darren deciding on Greg's guilt and Greg learning of Darren's opinion that troubled the defence. They believed Darren had been acting as a police informant.

"You effectively were deputised by the police on or about 15 June, if not the 15th the 16th, but probably the 15th, to keep an eye on the accused man and keep them informed, weren't you?" Mr Lovitt asked.

"No I wasn't."

Darren later admitted that he had given evidence at a committal hearing for a man charged with murder years earlier who had confessed the killing to him.

Chapter Twenty-Four

Darren explained his phone conversation with Greg on the Saturday afternoon, following the death threat rumours. They had resolved the matter and arranged to have a few beers the next day, he said.

After a heavy night drinking, he was woken at 8.00 a.m. by his wife, Sheena, who'd heard some trouble on the scanner. Darren explained that, despite falling out with Greg a couple of months earlier, he had become his closest confidante in the weeks after Jaidyn's disappearance. He had asked Greg if there was anything to worry about at the house, and Greg had mentioned that there was a pair of jeans with blood on them. This had resulted from a cold sore he'd had, or a cut to Jaidyn.

This new closeness with Greg surprised Darren. But it was the comment Greg had made during the search of the rubbish tip that most alarmed him. "They won't find anything there," he'd said.

Darren explained how he and his wife Sheena were with Bilynda when she returned from New South Wales. She had wanted to go to Greg's, to find the video of his interview with police. It was then that Bilynda had found Jaidyn's windcheater, folded on the pillow of Greg's bed. Darren hadn't seen her make the discovery.

"It was ripped and it sort of ponged a bit," Darren recalled. "She said it was a jumper Jaidyn was wearing and I said, 'You had better get it down to the police'." It was given to the police and analysed; it was Jaidyn's vomit.

The police believed that someone who was sympathetic to Greg had planted it.

Darren was no official informer, but he thought that Greg was guilty of killing a small child. So when the police asked him questions, he volunteered any information that came his way, and encouraged anyone else who knew something to call the police.

Darren recounted how Greg one day had dropped around a pair of tree loppers to be collected later by Paul "Lizard"

Lietzau. Tree loppers, not a crow bar. It had seemed odd to drop the tree loppers at Darren's house when Lizard lived only five doors away.

Mr Lovitt also put several unusual propositions to Darren Farr. One was that he had allegedly said to a girl, Vicki Philp, in July or August of 1997, that Jaidyn was dead and that Yvonne had told him she watched two men kill Jaidyn. Darren denied making the comment, or knowing where it came from.

After Darren had finished giving evidence, Greg's mate, Glenn Walker, was called to explain Greg's previous babysitting mishaps with Jaidyn. He told of Greg's troubles in dealing with Jaidyn's grizzling, of the fishing incident at Blue Rock Dam when Jaidyn ended up scratched and bruised.

Glenn, like Matthew "Spider" Walsh, who was next on the stand, was clearly uncomfortable giving evidence against his friend. Spider told how Greg had turned up the stereo loudly to drown out Jaidyn's crying and how he had put the boy out with the dogs.

"I went out the back and brought him inside."

Spider also gave an explanation for the money that was found under Greg's bed. Two days before Jaidyn went missing, Spider had sold a boat that he and Greg owned. Spider had given Greg his share of the money, about $500. Greg, however, could never satisfactorily explain why the money was wet.

Paul Lietzau had been asleep on 3 January, when his mother came into his room crying.

"My mother woke me up with the newspaper with the crowbar on the front," "Lizard" told the Supreme Court.

"She was crying ... and she said, 'There's your crowbar Paul'."

Lizard had just told the court how he'd been doing some gardening at Greg's in the week leading up to Jaidyn's disappearance, and how his tools had gone missing afterwards.

He recalled talking with Greg about the police search and, in particular, the search of the tip.

Chapter Twenty-Four

"Did he say anything about the police search of the tip?" Morgan-Payler asked.

"Yes, he said they wouldn't find anything there."

Lizard recounted how he'd asked Greg for his tools, only to be told they were in his impounded car in Melbourne. He'd asked again when Greg had his car back, and was told this time that they were at Darren Farr's place. However, when he'd gone to get them, Sheena Farr gave him his loppers back, but there was no crowbar. They looked everywhere but couldn't find it.

He was sure it was his crowbar when he saw the photo on the front page of the *Herald Sun*. The coincidence was too great.

"My reaction was more or less definitely [that the crowbar in the picture was my crowbar]," he said.

He called the police and identified the crowbar as his.

CHAPTER

TWENTY-FIVE

In the absence of a murder weapon, an eyewitness or a confession, police, prosecutors and the jury would have to rely on forensic science to fill in the blanks.

Trevor Evans believed he had a lot of those blanks filled in when he gave evidence to the court. The senior constable was a crime scene examiner, an expert at reading the signs and deciding what had or had not happened. He'd done all the tests, examined all the evidence and had come to one vital conclusion: no one went into Greg Domaszewicz's house that night without a key.

Evans had arrived at Bilynda's house on the afternoon of Sunday, 15 June and, after a ten-minute preliminary assessment, had noticed a green wheelie bin knocked onto its side on the nature strip. He had also noted tyre impressions on the nature strip and the front lawn. (The judge later ruled that the results of the tyre marks were too inconclusive to indicate with any certainty that Greg's car had made them.)

Detective Senior Sergeant Legg had organised for the scene to be video-taped and photographed before they had gone to Greg's house.

All of the front windows had been smashed, and there were two small bloodstains on the eave of the house along with some fine hairs that looked like pig hairs. Evans concluded, after testing, that when Kenny had first thrown the pig's head, it had

Chapter Twenty-Five

not bounced off the window as Kenny suspected. Instead, it had smacked into the eave and dropped. This had probably happened twice, before it smashed the window on the third attempt.

The two left-hand window panes had external fly-wire screens attached. Both were damaged, but still intact, and the windows behind them were smashed. Evans examined the large broken window for any possible trace evidence – fibres, material or hair – that might indicate someone had gone in.

"Being the type of edge that the glass had, I examined that for any such evidence, such items, and nothing was there. I also examined the glass both inside and outside which had fallen on the ground for any trace evidence such as dirt, vegetation or indeed shoe impressions and I found none," he said.

"Were you looking for anything that might have been left, for example, by a foot that subsequently stood on it?" Bill Morgan-Payler asked.

"Yes."

"Were there any scuff marks or anything of that nature on the walls, either interior or exterior?"

"None that seemed obvious to indicate someone had certainly gone in."

"What about inside on the carpet; again was there any indication of any dirty feet or anything?"

"No there wasn't."

"The actual aperture of that window, are you able to give us a comparison in size between that and an ordinary adult?"

"I would suggest it would be very unlikely that an ordinary adult would have got through that window at all. It's too small."

Justice Vincent asked: "The one thing you didn't seem to do was to actually measure the width of that aperture?"

"No I didn't." Senior Constable Evans hadn't thought it was necessary. He had already concluded that no one could have climbed through the window because of its size, its height from the ground and finally, because there was no trace evidence.

Inside, Senior Constable Evans had found the house to be unkempt. There were two rocks on the lounge room carpet, the curtains had been pulled aside and the venetian blinds raised. The television was on with a Nintendo game plugged in, asking on-screen if the player wanted to continue. He examined a gas space heater in the room, and found a small amount of skin tissue and hair fibre on it; tests indicated that it was Jaidyn's.

A footstool stood in the lounge room with a telephone directory and dictaphone on it, just in front of a join in the heavy drapes. Senior Constable Evans examined its upper surface and found "nothing to indicate any movement or that anyone had stood on that area".

Further, there was a pot plant on top of a speaker and "no evidence that it had been disturbed – should it have fallen over, there was no evidence of dirt or clean-up on the floor". In front of the pot plant on top of the speaker were small toy figurines of Simpsons characters "which had just been set up neatly in a row".

"Were they knocked over or apparently disturbed in any way?"

"No, they appeared to be as you would expect to find if they had been lined up in a row."

"Was there any mark in dust or anything like that in the vicinity of that broken window to indicate that somebody may have entered or not?"

"No, there is nothing there."

A brickies' hammer was found beneath the lounge room window but, after examination, Senior Constable Evans believed it was irrelevant to the smashed windows. He didn't know if it had been fingerprinted, but no fingerprinting had been done inside the house.

Mr Lovitt would later launch into trenchant criticism about this oversight, but Evans maintained that, once he had concluded that no-one had broken into the house through the

Chapter Twenty-Five

windows, what was the point of fingerprinting the inside of the house? If no one got in, how would relevant fingerprints be found inside? Well, only if they got in through the front door with a key perhaps.

There was also a cigarette butt in an ashtray in the lounge room. Senior Constable Evans didn't take note of its brand, nor take it away to be analysed. He had noted from smoking gear he had found in the kitchen – marijuana and a "bong" – that Greg was a smoker, so he thought nothing unusual of the find and didn't believe it relevant at the time.

Mr Lovitt countered. Greg wasn't a smoker. People who smoke marijuana are not necessarily cigarette smokers, he said. The cigarette in the ashtray was most likely smoked by the person who had abducted Jaidyn, Mr Lovitt said.

"Taking items from the house because they could be relevant, we would have had to have packed up the whole house," Senior Constable Evans replied.

Along with the cannabis, "bong", pipe and mixing bowl in the kitchen, he had found a pair of latex surgical gloves with a white powder inside. A similar white powder was found on the steering wheel of Greg's car, and on the peak of his cap.

The problem with this evidence, however, was that Greg's car had been driven by a Moe police officer an hour or so after he had arrived to report Jaidyn missing. The car was, in forensic terms, partially contaminated. There could be no reliable test of the steering wheel and the suspicious white powder.

The Crown wanted to suggest that Greg had worn the gloves when disposing of the body, and that, because of this, little forensic or DNA evidence was found. Justice Vincent ruled this out, saying it was too speculative.

Senior Constable Evans found blood splatters on the bathroom wall which turned out to be Yvonne Penfold's.

There was no sign of forced entry to the house through either the front or back doors. At the front, there was a steel security door with a deadlock and a solid timber door with a cylindrical lock. The back door was timber and the lock didn't meet, so it couldn't be shut properly.

"It has a padlock type bolt on the base of the door and inside, the bolt slides into the floor," Senior Constable Evans said. "I was satisfied at the time no entry had been gained into that house," he said.

When he had been at Bilynda's house, Evans had been surprised to find a baby's wet disposable nappy in the bathroom. "[It] had been placed behind a number of clean towels underneath the vanity unit or inside the vanity unit at the rear."

He noted that bedclothes in Jaidyn's cot were disturbed and that the wet nappy had been found behind the towel, but said "there was no indication of like a break-in or anything like that".

He explained to the court how he returned to Moe police station that Sunday and examined Greg's green XC Falcon, IRS 680. It had a baby's car seat in the back with a toy block on it. On the floor in the back, he found a baby's plastic jacket that was as wet "as if someone had been caught in a shower of rain with it". There was also a wet wallet in the front driver's side footwell, underneath the accelerator pedal.

"It had been soaked through," he said. An appointment card inside the wallet was so wet that the ink had smudged. The floor of the car and the carpets were also damp, but the wallet seemed wetter than both.

Splashes or sprays of mud were found on the underside and mudguards of the car but he had been unable to deduce anything from this.

The forensic specialist was also present at Jaidyn's autopsy. He noted the clothes Jaidyn was wearing and examined the tape, wrapped around gauze, that had been used to bandage the boy's broken arm. "The tape was a fibrous-type tape. It looked like the sort you buy at chemist shops. It certainly wasn't your

Chapter Twenty-Five

normal sticky-type tape that you have at home for wrapping papers or parcels or whatever," Senior Constable Evans said.

But he was unable to connect the tape with Greg's house in any way.

He also examined the sleeping bag that was found tied to the crowbar. "It was in an advanced state of deterioration. The zipper was closed but where it was actually stitched on to the bag itself, that had come away from it and it was only attached to one part of the bag itself," Evans said.

The sleeping bag was tied to the crowbar using two pieces of rope and a series of elaborate knots: reef knots, single loops, a clove hitch, a series of loops, a picket line hitch and a single half hitch were all used.

Senior Constable Evans told the court that he went to Yvonne Penfold's house but didn't examine or search the inside; he didn't go to Kenny Penfold's house.

On 29 April 1998, Detective Sergeant Steve Fyffe had rung the forensic specialist and asked if anyone had used any shovels in Greg's backyard during the searching of his house. Yes, Evans said, he had used a shovel in the trench of freshly turned soil where Lizard had been working the previous week. He had wanted to satisfy himself that the fresh soil was not part of a shallow grave.

Mr Lovitt presented Senior Constable Evans with a photograph of the back of Greg's house taken by the forensic team. During the committal hearing, the defence had claimed that the photograph featured a crowbar. If so, this would be irrefutable proof that the crowbar found with Jaidyn's body was still in Greg's backyard when police were searching his house and Greg was at the police station.

Senior Constable Evans had not been asked about the photograph at the committal hearing, but he remembered now that the forensic team had used two shovels in the backyard search. He believed that the photo showed one of the shovels.

The photograph had been blown up and enhanced, and a white line drawn down the length of the shaft showed "a distinct deviation at the base. If that was a crowbar ... [it] would continue in a straight line..." Senior Constable Evans said.

"I say it is a shovel."

His view was supported by Dr Edgar Smith, professor of mathematics and dean of the faculty of science, technology and engineering at Latrobe University. He was called in to examine the photograph, to try to gauge if the height of the tool could be estimated.

Dr Smith concluded: "The maximum that I think it [the tool] could be, I would say, is 1.58 metres."

"Is there any way we can make it 1.8?" Mr Lovitt asked.

"Certainly not," Dr Smith said.

Asked if part of the crowbar could be imbedded in the ground, disguising its true height, Dr Smith replied: "It should be difficult to drive a crowbar one foot into the ground".

"Why do you say a foot, Professor?" Mr Lovitt asked.

"...because the object that I see there, however I interpret it, keeps coming out at 1.6 metres when I do conservative estimates of positions."

It was the most unusual piece of evidence in the trial to date. If Dr Smith had concluded that it could have been a crowbar, it would also have been one of the most important.

CHAPTER

TWENTY-SIX

Senior forensic pathologist Dr Shelley Robertson has a reputation among police for taking some time to come to an autopsy conclusion. Meticulous and precise, Dr Robinson is also known for her unshakeable resolve once she has reached her conclusion.

However, the Jaidyn Leskie autopsy was an exception, one of the rare occasions where Dr Robinson would have to accept an oversight. It was an oversight that could have truly damaged the prosecution case.

Detailed examination of clothing is conducted by specialist forensic scientists, not by Dr Robertson. However, as she undressed Jaidyn, she noted some decomposing plastic matter and concluded that the boy was wearing plastic pants, known as pilchers. She was on her own in this observation. Of all the police and forensic scientists and assistants present, including a forensic pathologist for the defence, no one else detected the pilchers.

This may not have been particularly important, except that Bilynda never dressed Jaidyn in pilchers. His chubby legs would chaff badly if he did, giving him red marks. Thus, the defence contended, Jaidyn must have been in the care of someone else who had dressed him in pilchers after taking him from Greg's house.

Mr Lovitt dwelt on this point during his lengthy opening to the trial. Indeed an impartial observer could think a large part of the defence relied on the presence of the pants. So when Dr Robertson took to the stand, the defence was ready to present what it believed to be some of its strongest evidence.

"There is no record of the plastic pilcher in existence," Dr Robertson told the court somewhat sheepishly.

"Therefore, I think I may have been mistaken regarding that ... one of the photographs shows the disposable nappy to have had what looks like an outer plastic layer and I think that is what I may have been referring to."

Mr Lovitt was seething and asked Dr Robertson in cross-examination whether she had been contacted by anyone with regard to the pilchers. He obviously feared collusion.

Dr Robertson admitted that Detective Senior Sergeant Legg had contacted her and told her that there was no record of a pilcher. He had asked her to have another look, which she had done, and it was then that she realised her deductive error.

It would be the only point on which she was swayed.

When Jaidyn was discovered in Blue Rock Dam on New Year's Day, Dr Robertson was taken directly to the scene at about 7.45 p.m. to oversee the removal of the body from the water. She would also inspect the body. She had stressed at the time the need to use ice to slow the onset of decomposition.

The following day, she carried out an autopsy in the presence of another pathologist, Dr Collins, who was there on behalf of Greg Domaszewicz.

The autopsy report is shocking because of the banality of the language used to describe Jaidyn's broken body. It points to the terrible suffering he went through before he died. In a monotone, Dr Robinson listed what she had found.

The body was 84 centimetres long and weighed 18 kilograms. He had fair hair and, according to the report, his eye

Chapter Twenty-Six

colour was indeterminate. He was dressed in dark green tracksuit pants; dark green tracksuit top with checked cotton-type trim largely intact; a long-sleeved top, possibly blue but badly damaged, with the words "Mish Mash" on it; and white socks with a blue motif.

"I have noted scant fair hair with some bare areas covering the scalp," she explained to the court in clinical detail.

"There was loss of skin over the left frontal and parietal skull, that's the left front and side region of the skull exposing underlying bone. Loss of skin from the right cheek, around the right eye and the right temporal region. Remaining skin edges were ragged and irregular, but there was no obvious bruising. The nose and mouth were distorted. There was superficial skin loss across the anterior [the front] and there was dark discolouration behind the right ear.

"There was blotchy blue discolouration of the trunk and superficial skin loss over the anterior aspect of the right shoulder, the front of the right shoulder, the right lateral chest wall, and an approximately fifteen centimetre split in the skin over the left lower abdominal quadrant, through which protruded loops of bowel."

As the court became more ill at ease, Bill Morgan-Payler interjected.

"Just so that nobody gets the wrong idea here, that is due to decomposition?" he asked.

"Yes. Patchy bluish discolouration resembling bruises were present over the buttocks. The right hand was intact, there were some changes which were consistent with decomposition. The left arm was bandaged from the region of the elbow to the wrist with an elastic type bandage covered by tape."

Had she noted anything significant about the skull?

"There was a Y-shaped linear fracture of the right occipital bone (that's the bone at the base of the skull where the head joins onto the neck) with fracture lines extending superiorly and to the left across the midline to the right into the right occipital bone and medially into the foramen magnum (that's the large hole in the skull where the spinal cord passes)," she explained.

Jaidyn had a fractured skull. After examining the muscle and tissue in the area of the fracture she noted "there was some dark discolouration which I was unable to determine whether it was bruising or due to decompositional changes".

"...the brain was extensively softened and decomposed, so no assessment as to brain injury could be made on this material. There was, however, a two centimetre diameter area of haemorrhage on the inner surface of the dura (the membrane covering the brain) in the region of the right occipital lobe."

After this clinical description, Dr Robertson described the injuries in terms the court could truly relate to.

"I have said the nature and site of the skull fracture is such that it would normally almost have been associated with significant underlying brain injury of a similar severity to that seen in motor vehicle fatality," she said.

"The nature and site of this particular injury is such that the only way I can conceive it would be caused is by a direct blow to that area."

She explained that the arm had been fractured in two places: "This fracture is of both the bones of the forearm in this region which is approximately the mid forearm level. There is some displacement of one of the bones and there appears to be a loose fragment of the other bone."

However as there had been no "callus formation", the process by which bones heal, Dr Robertson deduced that the injury was suffered soon before death.

"...probably within twenty-four hours but perhaps a little longer," Dr Robertson explained.

She believed that a direct blow to the region with a blunt instrument would also normally cause this type of injury. If

Chapter Twenty-Six

anyone was in any doubt, she assured them "it would be extremely painful".

"The splint or the bandage that was applied around the forearm in this particular case would have produced no significant splinting of the injury at all, of the bones. They would have been free to move against each other and would cause considerable pain."

The most puzzling aspect of the autopsy, however, was the discovery of the drug, benzexhol, in Jaidyn's liver.

"Benzexhol is ... a therapeutic drug used predominantly in the treatment of Parkinson's disease, a neurological disorder, and also to counteract the side effects of major tranquillisers such as the phenothiazine group of drugs which are used in the treatment of psychotic disorders, in particular schizophrenia," Dr Robertson explained.

Commonly known by the brand name, Artane, the drug is also used recreationally for its euphoric effects.

"It is what is called a parasympathetic inhibitor. It inhibits parts of the nervous system, which enables some features of muscle activities to be relaxed. It has no analgesics, that is, pain-killing properties, at all that I am aware of."

Toxicologist Ian McIntyre also gave evidence about the drug, but was unable to tell what quantity the boy had ingested.

Dr Robertson concluded that the most likely cause of Jaidyn Leskie's death was head injury. Death would have come within "a relatively short period" after the blow to the skull, she said. But Dr Robertson's analysis did not seem to give any clear pointer as to who had killed Jaidyn.

The immersion of Jaidyn's body in the dam was a vital factor in the forensic case against Greg Domaszewicz. It had slowed the decomposition, but no one knew to what extent. If it could be scientifically proven that the body had only been in the water for a month or so when it was found, then clearly

Greg could not have been the killer. Precision in these estimates was almost impossible.

"It is more likely given the temperature of the water, which was quite cold, and the nature of the water, which was fresh and not near a sewage outlet for example, it is more likely to have aided the preservation of the remains rather than hastened the decomposition," Dr Robertson told the court. She was informed that water officials measured the lake's temperature regularly and that it varied between nine and fifteen degrees Celsius, depending on the time of year.

"Nine degrees, the lesser of the two in the range, is not known or recognised as a preserving temperature. In other words it is not low enough to be a temp. whereby a body would be preserved, is that right?" Mr Lovitt asked.

"That's correct."

"Could it have been in the water six months?"

"Yes."

"Could it have been in the water two months?"

"It's possible."

Dr Andrew McLoughlin, the specialist radiologist consultant to the Institute of Forensic Medicine, felt after his examination of x-rays that there was some suggestion that Jaidyn had a healing rib. Dr Robertson, however, was unable to confirm this in the autopsy. She was not surprised at the notion, because decomposition had made that sort of visible observation difficult.

There was one further matter. Under Mr Lovitt's questioning, Dr Robertson acknowledged that she could not rule out that some sort of epileptic seizure or asthma attack might have caused Jaidyn's death. Despite all the other injuries, she could not say that this was impossible because it could not be categorically assessed whether the skull fracture took place before or after death.

Jaidyn's hair was not closely shaven. It was "...at least a couple of centimetres long".

Chapter Twenty-Six

"Hair doesn't grow after we die does it?" Colin Lovitt asked.

"Not to a significant extent," Dr Robertson said.

It had been the task of forensic scientist Dr Maxwell Jones to examine Greg's house and Jaidyn's body for traces of DNA.

He had examined the five bloodied tissues, finding human blood on each.

"One of the pieces had been twisted at two points in a manner of which I believed was to aid the insertion into some orifice: nasal cavity or perhaps the ear. That's what it appeared to me," he said.

Dr Jones tested the blood against Jaidyn's Guthrie card – the hospital record that keeps a blood sample from every newborn baby – and found that the blood on all the tissues was Jaidyn's. He further tested five hairs taken from Greg's heater and found three of them to be Jaidyn's. No human blood was found in Greg's car.

Dr Jones had also carried out a "luminol" test in Greg's garage and backyard. Luminol is a chemical fluid that can be sprayed over a wide area to detect the presence of blood not visible to the naked eye. Dr Jones found only dog's blood.

Kenny Penfold's clothing was tested; there were no cuts to it other than general wear and tear, and no glass fragments. Blood was found on the top of his shoe, but it was pig's blood.

Deano Ross's jumper had blood on it, but it was Deano's own.

Dr Jones examined the sleeping bag that contained Jaidyn's body, but found nothing of any biological significance.

Jaidyn's bib, which was found with the body, was found to have traces of female DNA that didn't match any samples Dr Jones had. It definitely was not Bilynda's. A small sample of DNA taken from the child's pants was also female and did not match Bilynda's profile, or any other given to Dr Jones.

Contaminants in the water and the length of time the body had been there affected how much DNA could be drawn from the items.

Only two items in the shopping bag found with the body suggested proof of DNA. Presumptive testing indicated that a darker stain may be blood, but this was inconclusive.

"Given my understanding that the exhibits may have been in water for a very long time, I was very sceptical as to whether or not I would get a result [from DNA tests]," Dr Jones said.

CHAPTER TWENTY-SEVEN

Sergeant Max Hill was in the witness box for two gruelling days. Unlike the homicide detectives or senior officers, the country copper was not used to being questioned by a Queens Counsel in a big trial. And Colin Lovitt was giving his behaviour on the morning of 15 June – the morning Greg and Bilynda reported Jaidyn's disappearance to the Moe police – a good going over.

Mr Lovitt contended that the entire investigation that morning had been "a ham", claiming that the whole station knew that Sergeant Russell Fraser was having an affair with Yvonne Penfold. They also knew that if Sergeant Fraser was implicated in the case, the entire force, not just the Moe police, would be brought into disrepute. This meant that police were out to protect their own that morning, rather than conduct a proper investigation, he claimed.

It was a wild shot.

Max Hill had immediately sensed something awry in Greg's description of events when he entered the police station that Sunday morning. In Hill's mind, Greg shifted from victim to possible offender in an instant.

"I drew conclusions from that [the two different stories] that there was something very suspicious going on," Sergeant Hill told the court.

"The 'something very suspicious' was linked to Greg Domaszewicz right?" Mr Lovitt asked.

"He was the one with the conflicting story and the last person to see the child alive," Hill explained simply.

"Why did you accept Bilynda Murphy – she was drunk and he wasn't? It's because he was who he was?"

"No. His whole demeanour, the way he presented himself to the watch house counter . . . the conflict, the story about the pig's head, the initial conversation where he speaks over Bilynda Murphy when she tries to say the bit about the child being in hospital, raised to me serious suspicions about his involvement.

"He did appear to have something to hide."

Justice Vincent then asked: "Why, if you thought a baby was missing, didn't you ask Mr Domaszewicz where he thought the baby might possibly be?"

"I guess I didn't take the credibility of Mr Domaszewicz seriously at that initial time because of conflicting stories," Hill said.

"He didn't seem to be full and frank with me. He was beating around the bush. He did not appear to be honest and I guess with hindsight I should have, but it wasn't something that came to me at the time."

Colin Lovitt asked why no effort was made to have anyone go around to Yvonne Penfold's place, to investigate Greg's claim that she was behind the abduction and attack.

"Well my understanding at that time would have been that if Yvonne Penfold had have, or anyone, had have taken a baby, they wouldn't have it at their address. If they had just stolen it from a house, if that was a legitimate explanation as to what had happened, then it would be at some other location. I didn't have any resources to deploy in that area. I could only do what I could with the limited resources I had, and that was to inspect the crime scene."

Chapter Twenty-Seven

To suggest that he wouldn't send police around to a suspect's house because they would be unlikely to have the baby there seems farcical. If the police were suspicious of Greg Domaszewicz, they would almost certainly have gone to Yvonne's house. However, it does seem reasonable to suggest that there was serious concern about Greg.

Max Hill denied any knowledge of his colleague Russ Fraser having an affair with Yvonne Penfold.

The prosecution also seized on a suggestion by Bilynda that she and Greg were left waiting in the police station for "some time" between their interviews with Farnham Molesworth and Sergeant Hill.

Senior Constable Molesworth had not noted the time that the pair entered the station but believed it was about 5.15 a.m. He spoke to them long enough to get the basic details, before going out to tell Sergeant Hill. Hill did, however, note the time he spoke to Greg and Bilynda. It was 5.18 a.m. Mr Lovitt contended that the pair had entered the station closer to 4.45 a.m.; they'd then been left alone for about half an hour.

Sergeant Hill was obviously unable to comment on when his deputy had first spoken with the couple.

Mr Lovitt's line of questioning concentrated on the timing of Greg's movements. Greg claimed he went to Bilynda Murphy's at 4.05 a.m. It would have taken at least fifteen minutes to get her up and to the police station. Mr Lovitt claimed this was proof that the couple were at the police station at 4.45 a.m.

The only irrefutable timing on the night was that Greg had been pulled over by police at 3.35 a.m. Mr Lovitt provided his own version of events from that time on.

"... Greg goes home, he searches the home. He is probably, if one assumes he is telling the truth, probably in a somewhat frantic state at that stage. He searches the house for whatever ... and I wasn't making an estimate of time, I wasn't there.

Ultimately, he then goes to Yvonne's, parks the car wherever he parked it, wanders around there and, according to what we have heard, hangs around for a period of time.

"Then, he ultimately leaves and goes to Bilynda, has to wake her up, has to tell her that a child is missing, has to get her to come to realise the gravity of everything and then tells her 'we've got to go to the police' or words to that effect. Then she does whatever she needed to do in order to get ready to go to the police station and then we have got a question unresolved from your evidence of how long was he there before he sees you. There is really not much time missing at all is there," Mr Lovitt said.

On Sergeant Hill's calculations, just half an hour was missing, Mr Lovitt said. These timings, however, were based on Greg's estimates, which appear exaggerated.

The prosecution case is that there is a lengthy period of time Greg cannot account for, be it an hour-and-a-half or forty-five minutes. Police believe that Greg used this time to drive out to Blue Rock Dam – a trip of about eighteen minutes each way at the speed limit – and dump the body.

The argument over times, however, ignores the fundamental question of why Greg failed to tell police when he was pulled over that Jaidyn was missing.

The prosecution had no intention of calling Sergeant Russell Fraser to give evidence in the trial, believing he played no real part in events.

Mr Lovitt thought otherwise. And in any case, once Mr Lovitt had suggested in court that Sergeant Fraser and Yvonne Penfold had been having an affair, prosecutors had to call Russell Fraser. If nothing else, it would give him the opportunity to clear his name.

It was with no small measure of disgust that Russell Fraser attended court. He was defending himself against the serious implication that, because of an alleged affair, he had covered up

Chapter Twenty-Seven

Yvonne's involvement in an abduction. Not only that, the alleged relationship had led Fraser to influence other police to aid his so-called cover-up.

While Russell Fraser admitted that he had known Yvonne's parents, Ellen and Hugh, for ten years, he was adamant that there was no sexual relationship between the young woman and himself.

On Sunday, 15 June, after being told the basic details of the case, he had recalled a conversation he'd had with Yvonne Penfold weeks earlier.

"I can't recall the specifics of that conversation, other than during the conversation a pig or pig's head was mentioned," he told the court.

"I went and approached Detective Sergeant Ian Riccardo who, at that time, was in charge of the investigation pending the arrival of the homicide squad and I spoke to him about my beliefs that she may have had some involvement and that I believe it needed looking at. I'm sorry ... I spoke to Paul Cripps [of homicide]," he corrected himself.

Paul Cripps discussed the matter with Ian Riccardo and it was decided that Fraser should bring Yvonne in for questioning. When he did so, he told her something had happened at 150 Narracan Drive involving a pig's head "and that I vaguely recalled something in a previous conversation"; she had to come to the police station to clear things up.

Why did he have no further involvement in the investigation?

"It was a deliberate action because of my association with the family. I felt it improper for me to be in any way associated," Fraser said.

Mr Lovitt claimed that Sergeant Fraser had conspired with other police to invent his statement.

Fraser said he had been separated from his wife for six years, although they were technically still married. He had approached

Detective Senior Sergeant Legg during the trial and asked to give evidence "because I was deeply upset about remarks that had been published".

Russell Fraser's appearance in court was widely covered by the media. The following Monday, he was recalled to the witness box. Mr Lovitt claimed that, during the weekend, a woman had contacted the defence team and told them that she had seen Russ Fraser in uniform, leaving Greg's house with two other suited men. They were carrying a crowbar.

"Were you ever approached by any member of the Penfold family to assist in the disposal of the body of Jaidyn Leskie?" he was asked.

"No, absolutely not sir. That's ridiculous. Good Heavens!" Fraser said.

Then he was asked about the date in question, the last Sunday in September. Did he go to 150 Narracan Drive that day? "Not that I can recall sir. I would have no reason to." He also denied being at the house with two other men, or carrying a crowbar.

"Were you ever told by Yvonne Penfold or any other member of the Penfold family, or indeed, any associate of the Penfold family, that they had taken Jaidyn away from 150 Narracan Drive back on the morning of June 15 last year?

"No sir."

"Were you ever told that the child was being kept somewhere?"

"No sir."

"Were you ever told the child was dead?"

"No sir."

"Did you either offer or were you prevailed upon to provide some assistance?"

"In relation to what?"

"Covering up?"

"Absolutely ludicrous."

Chapter Twenty-Seven

"I am suggesting to you that the crowbar was taken from the home in order to effectively provide a link or thought to provide a link with Domaszewicz."

"That's a ridiculous suggestion, sir."

After lunch, Fraser was recalled. After doing some checking of work records, he had been able to verify that, on that particular Sunday, he started his five weeks annual leave. He had collected his two kids from his wife, and had not been in uniform at all that day.

Mr Lovitt then accused Sergeant Fraser of having argued with Detective Senior Sergeant Legg outside court after the morning's evidence.

"I have spoken with Mr Legg, expressing my disgust at my involvement in these proceedings," Fraser replied.

Mr Lovitt quizzed him about driving to Melbourne to collect his kids from his wife, and Fraser said that they met at an agreed point. The Q.C. suggested that there was "some difficulty with your ex-wife in going to the home".

At this point, Justice Vincent intervened.

"I can answer that if you wish," Fraser said.

"You don't have to," Justice Vincent said.

"It is a convenience matter [that he drives halfway to Melbourne]."

The following morning, before the jury arrived, Justice Vincent gave his own view of the wild claims that Colin Lovitt was making.

"I must say Mr Lovitt, in view of the large number of allegations that you have thrown around in this trial, sometimes like confetti at a wedding..." Justice Vincent said.

After some discussion with the Judge, Mr Lovitt said: "Your Honour says allegations floating like confetti. I have got certain instructions..."

"I understand and they range far and wide. I have said nothing about these matters. It is not my task to intrude in front of a jury, but at one stage I thought the only thing that Sergeant Fraser wasn't guilty of was being on the grassy knoll," Justice Vincent said with a patronising smile.

"Very funny your honour."

"I don't want to pursue it, Mr Lovitt. That's my impression; it is not an impression that I indicated to this jury and it is not one that I ever would."

By the time Mick Roberts took the stand, the trial was getting to the business end. For the prosecution, the unpredictable personalities had departed and the more manageable facts were now being adduced. The video-taped interview Greg had done with detectives on Thursday, 19 June was considered the most damning evidence.

The court was told that the interview began at 3.38 p.m. and continued until 10.37 p.m., when Greg left with his lawyer, Paul Vale. He went to Narracan Drive, where he was met by Mick Roberts, to collect a box of tissues and some clothing.

"What clothing was it you were anxious to collect?" Mr Morgan-Payler asked the detective.

"The clothing that the accused was wearing on the night in question," Roberts told the court. "He took us into the laundry area of his house to try and locate the clothing he was wearing and he would pick up an item of clothing and sniff it and then shake his head and say, 'No, that's not it'. And I think he was unable to locate the actual items at that time."

The prosecution and defence had agreed previously that, because there was so much duplication during the interview, they would use an edited version of the video. They worked out which parts could be cut, and the jury watched the video, following dialogue from written transcripts.

Greg sat in the dock, his heavy brow creased, as he stared at the large screen. He nodded at times, occasionally mouthing the words to the tape, apparently still agreeing with what he'd said at

Chapter Twenty-Seven

the time. Sometimes he rubbed his eyes, through either weariness or emotion. His face would twitch at times and his head would droop.

After the video, Mr Lovitt resumed cross-examining Detective Roberts.

"Why didn't you instruct [forensic fingerprinter] Letson to take fingerprints from areas inside that lounge room, for example?" Mr Lovitt asked.

"I could see no reason to. There was nothing disturbed and there was no indication that anybody had been in there other than the accused," Roberts said.

Mr Lovitt then returned to his assertion that the police had persecuted Greg because he had a relationship with the same woman (Yvonne) as a police officer. Roberts confirmed that Greg had received one unroadworthy "yellow canary" sticker by Moe police for his car, before June 1997. Other infringement notices had been issued by police outside Moe, two were from outside the valley and five were from within the valley, between April 1992 and June 1997.

Roberts said that police had explored the idea that Greg may be covering up for Bilynda or Yvonne, and conceded that "information was given" by Darren Farr to the police. Was he a go-between then?

"He provided us with some information, yes," was as far as Roberts would go.

"In addition to the accused being followed, to your knowledge were a number of listening devices placed ... is that right?" Mr Lovitt asked.

"Yes."

"Was a listening device placed in the accused man's car?"

"Yes it was ... I am not sure what date it went in, I think it was the twenty-seventh of June".

"Was a listening device placed in 150 Narracan Drive?"

"Yes."

Roberts said that other listening devices had been placed, including one in Greg's psychiatrist's consulting rooms. Two other devices were installed, but police were reluctant to reveal their locations. Police conceded that bugs had been used in the prison where Greg was being held – not in his cell but in a visiting area – and in a general area "where prisoners congregate". The one in the visiting area was a personal-type listening device worn by certain visitors.

The defence was already convinced that police had been bugging their conversations with Greg in jail. What made them suspicious was that detectives had learnt in advance of the defence's intention to use the forensic photo, showing the crowbar or shovel, at a bail application. Homicide was found to be asking questions of the forensic scientists and photographic department before the defence had formally indicated this line of attack.

Detectives could only know this information if they had been listening to Greg's conversations with lawyers, they reasoned. But there was one other way: Greg had been telling other prisoners what was proposed in his defence.

Police decided to put an end to the claims that they had been bugging Greg's conversations with his lawyers. Two officers were dispatched to speak to a prisoner we can refer to only as F. He was the man who had been telling police about the strategies and plans of Greg's defence.

Police had known F for some time. He had given them information about Greg and his case, albeit anonymously. In fact the information he had given them already was far greater than anything about shovels or photographs.

It was years earlier, on Tuesday, 10 February 1998, to be precise, Detective Inspector Chris Enright had gone to the Melbourne Assessment Prison to see a prisoner. The Ethical Standards Department Inspector met with a convicted armed robber who for legal reasons we can refer to only as F. It was just

Chapter Twenty-Seven

another visit to the prison for Inspector Enright when he sat down with the prisoner and an ESD colleague, acting Chief Inspector Mark Stubberfield. As they were talking F mentioned Greg Domaszewicz was in his area of the jail. Nothing surprising in that, but police were extremely surprised when F said that the day before he had been sitting at lunch when he overheard Domaszewicz, only a metre away, confess to another prisoner that he had killed Jaidyn.

F told Enright he heard Greg telling the other prisoner – whom we can only refer to as M – how he had been in the driveway working on a car with the boy. Then F heard something about a jack and a lot of blood.

Chris Enright made a few notes and moved on to other matters for it was not his case, nor his immediate concern. After leaving the prison Enright called Rowland Legg and two days later Mick Roberts was dispatched to join Enright back at the jail to talk to F. Was F prepared to repeat to homicide what he had told Enright about Domaszewicz?

"Yes," F said. He would tell them for their benefit, but he would not make a statement. He went on to relay the detail of the lunchtime conversation. When he heard Domaszewicz say how he'd killed Jaidyn his ears had pricked up. "I heard him say 'I should never have tied the kid to the crowbar,'" F said.

He told them how Greg had been working on the car when it rolled forward or fell off the jack onto Jaidyn's arm. Panicked, Greg had taken Jaidyn inside the house, bandaged the arm and given him drugs for the pain. The toddler was knocked out from the drugs and slept briefly on the couch before waking up screaming.

"Greg was playing the Nintendo game when Jaidyn woke up screaming. Greg picked him up and was shaking him. I don't know if it was while he was shaking him or he threw him but Jaidyn's head hit the fireplace," F said.

A week later Roberts was back at the prison, this time with Detective Sergeant Steve Fyffe. They spoke again with F. Domaszewicz was still talking, though so far only to M, F said.

Greg had allegedly told M he had accidentally killed Jaidyn, and said something vague about the involvement of a female but said no more. Greg had said that after the initial accident everything he had done was to fix it up, or cover it up, but things had snowballed fast. Now it seemed to be getting out of hand and he was trapped and didn't know how to get out.

F told Roberts and Fyffe that if he had a fortnight he could try to get to know Greg and talk him around, perhaps drawing a full confession. Maybe even on tape? Police were keen for him to do so, but not wear a tape recorder. It was too risky.

A couple of weeks passed and Roberts returned to the jail, this time with Senior Detective Russell Sheather. The pair saw F but he admitted having made no ground on Greg. Apparently Greg was wary of F and had so far only confided in M.

F, however, had had discussions with M, and M was prepared to talk with the police and tell them what he knew. At 3.50pm the next day Roberts and Sheather were back at the jail to meet M. He knew what they wanted and launched into explaining Greg's behaviour. He told of the moment Greg returned from the prison hospital after collapsing upon hearing that Jaidyn's body had been found in Blue Rock Dam. Greg had sobbed into M's arms, "What have I done?" M presumed he meant he'd killed a young boy.

M was prepared to talk to the police and tell them what he knew for their information, but he also would not go on record. He would not make a statement. He agreed to try to coax a further confession out of Greg.

Despite what seemed to be explosive allegations, with the committal having already started, they meant little to the police without formal statements. As a result the prosecutors did not attempt to introduce evidence of the alleged confessions at the committal.

Chapter Twenty-Seven

At the trial it was a slightly different matter. Police had given up hope of convincing the prisoners to make statements, but then the territory shifted. When the allegations surfaced that police had been bugging conversations between Greg and his lawyers the police were required to refute the claim. As a result one of the investigators, Senior Detective Paul Cripps, was sent to talk with F again to see if he would be prepared to confirm for the police that he had agreed to the placement of the bugging device in his cell. F was out of jail by now and a free man. The pair met at Melton police station and F agreed to talk, and this time to make a statement. Being out of jail, it seems, might have emboldened him that it would be safe to turn "informer". He made a signed written statement with Cripps telling about Greg's confession.

On 13 November Cripps went to see M. The pair chatted and M said Greg had told him how he and Jaidyn were playing Nintendo when Jaidyn interrupted and he "lost it". When a prison guard entered the room occupied by M and Cripps, M said he didn't want to talk any more and would not make a statement. Cripps left, but three days later he was called by the prison and told M was ready to speak with him. He went back to the jail with homicide detective Mick Daly. This time M was prepared to make a statement. He told them again about the Nintendo and how the car had fallen off the blocks while he was working on it and Jaidyn's arm had been crushed underneath.

As Cripps and Daly sat there taking the statement a prison officer walked in.

"Are you blokes from homicide?" one of them asked Daly.

"Yep."

"There's a bloke here who wants to talk to homicide."

Daly left and a prisoner, known only as R for legal reasons, was brought in to see him. Daly asked him what he wanted and R said Domaszewicz had talked to him about the case.

As Daly began to question him R butted in, saying: "Look, I'm only going to tell you this once. I'm doing time for murder. I'm due for release in a couple of years. You can't offer me anything, I don't want anything, I'm only going to tell you this once so start writing."

So Daly did. He wrote up the statement then read it back to R. The prisoner couldn't read or write so the detective had to read it back to him before he signed it.

The detectives left the prison that day, with three prisoners all telling how Greg had either confided directly in them or they had heard him do so with others. There were inconsistencies, but substantively they told a similar tale.

Police had reservations about R's statement, but set store by F's and even M's statements. They were particularly persuaded by the fact F was now out of prison, had nothing to gain from talking, but was prepared to sign a statement and give evidence anyway.

On Monday 16 November, day 24 of the trial, copies of the prisoners' statements were given to Justice Vincent in the absence of the jury. The statements, however, were not tendered in evidence nor presented to the jury, the prosecutors deeming it to be too late in the proceedings to attempt such a move. Further, the inconsistencies in the stories could reduce their value, to say nothing of the scepticism with which prisoners' statements are always held by courts. To introduce these so late in the trial might have appeared to be a desperate act.

Colin Lovitt said the confessions amounted to little as there was evidence both incriminating and contradictory in the statements and he set little store by them. The jury never heard from the prisoners.

CHAPTER TWENTY-EIGHT

When the jury returned, Mr Lovitt wasted little time in attacking Mick Roberts and Steve Fyffe's interview with Greg. His main concern was why they had waited so long to ask about the bloody tissues.

"We wanted to establish what had happened during the night, during the evening and during the day. We wanted the accused to give us his version of events before we started putting things to him," Roberts said. "We wanted to give him the opportunity to raise it himself, which he didn't do."

"Would you say when he was talking about the tissues and what injuries Jaidyn had that he was effectively 'bulldusting' you, to use a well-known expression, right?" Mr Lovitt asked.

"That's what you are saying."

"What do you say?"

"I am saying he was evasive in his answer."

Mr Lovitt then made another extraordinary statement. He claimed that he hadn't wanted the video to be edited but had been forced to agree.

"I mean the Crown didn't want..." he began.

Bill Morgan-Payler leapt to his feet in indignation. "Could we have that question again please your honour?"

"The Crown didn't seek to have any questions from 870 through to 1872 where it ends, apart from three topics..."

"Really your Honour this is ... I am happy to play the whole darn lot and my learned friend knows well that we discussed this matter together in an endeavour to shorten it. To criticise the Crown now for presenting a shortened version to this jury is inappropriate in my submission."

Mr Lovitt countered in part that it "wasn't my idea" to edit the tape and he had been brow beaten into agreeing. Justice Vincent sent the jury out and the judge and lawyers angrily discussed the edited tape.

Mr Lovitt complained that he wanted the whole tape played so that the jury could see his client, warts and all. "But I complied because it seemed to me there was an atmosphere by last Friday afternoon where the defence would come under some criticism, implied or actual, if we didn't." He further suggested that Justice Vincent had given him the impression he would not be popular if he made the jury sit through another full interview, following the Hill interview.

"But I told you Mr Lovitt, if you wanted it played in its entirety it would be ..." Justice Vincent said.

Eventually, the court agreed that the tape should be listened to again, this time in its entirety. This did not appear to greatly impress anyone present, particularly the jury.

The last prosecution witness was Rowland Legg.

He was soon asked about the windcheater – which tests had shown had Jaidyn's vomit on it – that Bilynda had found in Greg's house on 28 July.

"It is an item that Miss Murphy has indicated the child was wearing on the day that she last saw it on 14 June last year," Colin Lovitt asked.

"I understand that is not what she told us originally. It doesn't fit with the description of any item that was left with the child on that day," Legg explained.

Chapter Twenty-Eight

"So what?"

"So she told us at the time he was wearing a different piece of clothing. She assured us it had no hood."

"Really?"

"That's correct."

"And therefore, what, the item wasn't significant as far as you were concerned?"

He admitted that the item was of interest to police, particularly given it had Jaidyn's DNA on it. But Legg was suspicious of how it came to be in Greg's house.

"Mr Legg, let us not beat about the bush. Are you suggesting that somebody put it there?" Mr Lovitt asked.

"I am suggesting that is quite likely."

"Who? The accused, or somebody else, or don't you know?"

"I have no idea."

Legg was asked why he left Greg at the police station until about 2.00 a.m., ten hours after the end of his interview with Sergeant Hill.

"I wanted other inquiries to be conducted at the houses. I wanted to totally familiarise myself with what both of them [Greg and Bilynda] were saying and I didn't want him to leave the police station until I knew where he was going."

It was put to Legg that this was taking a particularly high-handed approach to the investigation.

"At that stage they were both strong suspects in the disappearance of a young child, in connection with a child's death, and as far as I was concerned I had a lot more to do before they were going to leave the police station," he said.

"On what legal basis were you going to retain them there?" Mr Lovitt asked.

"The fact they were suspects and the fact that there were great contradictions in their stories, massive gaps in the accused's, and I wanted to absolutely assure myself that we were getting to the bottom of the story."

Unlike some previous police witnesses, Legg was forthright in stating that he considered Greg a suspect virtually immediately.

"You were looking at the accused as a suspect before the ball had been bowled in this test match, weren't you?"

"Certainly," Legg said, with no hint of doubt.

Mr Lovitt kept after the police. He claimed that the police media releases on 16 June, which asserted that the group who had thrown the pig's head were not suspects, indicated their impatience.

Legg disputed this statement, claiming that it simply meant the investigation's focus was moving away from those people.

After Jaidyn's body had been found, Legg wanted to note the impact that the news would have on Greg, so he asked the police prison squad to monitor his behaviour.

Greg heard the news on TV. Leigh Ashworth, a crime analyst from the prison squad, told homicide detectives that, at 6.30 that night, Greg was taken to the prison medical centre. He had "thrown a wobbly" after hearing the news.

"Did you think there was any significance in that? If he is innocent he would be pretty upset?" Mr Lovitt asked.

"Yes, I have merely noted what I was told. I am sure different people would put different connotations on it," Legg said.

Mr Lovitt continued to probe Legg's investigation. He even asked Legg about what he referred to as a ridiculous and unsubstantiated police theory. Mr Lovitt was taken aback when Legg wholeheartedly agreed with the theory.

"Did you ever subscribe, in the history of this case, to a hypothesis that the accused man went around to the deceased child's mother's home some time after midnight on the morning of 15 June, in order to place the body of the deceased child in the cot, in the hope or expectation that Bilynda Murphy, suitably drunk, would then think that somehow she had killed the child?" Mr Lovitt asked.

Chapter Twenty-Eight

"I am a strong proponent of that theory actually," Legg said.

"I beg your pardon?"

"I believe that is what happened."

Prosecutor Bill Morgan-Payler was permitted, after legal argument, to ask on what basis he held that view so strongly. It was agreed that he would not comment on the tyre marks found outside Bilynda's house, as they had already been ruled inadmissible.

"There were a number of elements involved in forming that view," Legg said. "I have always been concerned about the fact that the people who broke the windows would not have had the capability of entering the house, that they would not have known in the first instance the baby was there, that they would not have been in a position to identify items that were left with the child on that day, and the bag, and to remove them from the house and all trace of the child; the fact that we had an hour-and-a-half gap during which time there was no effort made to report the matter, and when the accused was pulled over by the police he didn't report the matter, and that led me to strongly believe that at that stage the body hadn't been disposed of."

"The fact that the greatest credibility that I placed on Bilynda Murphy was, on that first day, her description of items and her movements. The fact that . . . she assured us that the cot was made up on the Saturday afternoon. The fact that we found it strewn. There was another point but they are the main points," he continued.

"You are aware that some evidence has been excluded from this matter; did that operate or not operate on your mind, that material?" Mr Morgan-Payler asked, referring loosely to the tyre marks.

"I have difficulty with – it is not so much what was excluded – but I have difficulty with discussions with Kim Wilson outside both courts," Legg replied.

"I'm sorry, I don't follow you," Justice Vincent said.

"If I can be fully frank your honour, what happened outside the committal after she had given her evidence was [that] she was in tears and said that she became confused under cross-examination [and that] it definitely was the accused's car. At the conclusion of her evidence here, she again left the court in tears and said it was definitely the accused's car and [that] she was confused under cross-examination."

Legg also placed great importance on one item found near Jaidyn's body.

"You are talking about the tape around the bandage, are you?" Mr Lovitt asked.

"No."

"What are you talking about?"

"I am talking about the bag of clothing."

"You mean the plastic bag?"

"The plastic bag."

"Why was that significant?"

"That always had enormous significance to me, from the beginning of the inquiry."

"Why? Because it was white? Because it was plastic?"

"Because it was white and plastic, because he [Greg] described a white plastic bag."

"What sinister significance did you place on that Mr Legg?"

"I was always interested in the fact that no one else would have known to remove all trace of the child from the house ... that you would remove those items that no one else would know about."

"What significance did you place on the fact that he said a white plastic bag?"

"Because of what we found, and it contained clothes that were described to us by Bilynda Murphy on that day, and a bottle that was described, and some shoes that had been described, and the fact that every item that was removed from the house ended up with the body."

Chapter Twenty-Eight

The Crown closed its case against Greg Domaszewicz. Mr Lovitt, predictably, was not finished. In the absence of the jury, he moved to dismiss the charges on the grounds that there was no evidence for a jury to be satisfied of his guilt beyond reasonable doubt.

Justice Vincent dismissed the motion.

Mr Lovitt then told the court that Greg would not give evidence. Under Victorian law "no inference of any kind can be drawn against him" from this decision. However, the media was forbidden from reporting this fact – which had been stated in open court before a jury – by Justice Vincent, who placed a suppression order on it.

The prosecution had called forty-seven witnesses in all. Over the next two days, the defence called just eleven. Much of its case had already been conducted in challenging prosecution witnesses and rebutting evidence in cross-examination. Witnesses would be called to substantiate claims made by the defence during the Crown case.

The defence called Professor Gale Spring, a photographics lecturer from Royal Melbourne Institute of Technology, to interpret the forensic photograph that contained the "crowbar". A lecturer from the same institution, Christopher Bellman, made some further calculations, the results of which suggested that the tool in the photo could quite feasibly be a crowbar.

A knot expert, Colin Dowd, an instructor with HMAS Cerberus, was called to explain that the knots used to tie the sleeping bag and the crowbar were extremely elaborate, and not of the type used by novices. Greg, the court heard from a fishing mate, David Mallia, was not well versed in knot tying.

A private investigator, Michael Dunn, who had been hired by Helen Chervev to find the real killer, was called. However, he could not offer the child killer. He had conducted some tests using a crowbar against the fence, and proffered to the court that the tool in the photo could be a crowbar.

Greg's friend, Sue Havis, was called to explain how she had hunted through his garage and found three shovels. She was also forced to deny that, during the trial, she had been with Bilynda and that she had made an anonymous call to police, claiming Tubby Hopkinson had been involved in the shooting of two police officers. The call had been traced to a Moe phone box. When police had arrived at the box minutes later, Bilynda Murphy and Sue Havis were walking away from the phone. She denied making the call.

Perhaps the most extraordinary evidence, though, was that of Moe woman, Sue Haslam. The office administrator had been watching television the week before testifying, when she had seen Sergeant Russell Fraser on a news report, walking from court after giving evidence. She believed that she had seen the same man walking from Greg's house a year earlier, with two other men.

Mrs Haslam said that on that day – she couldn't be certain of the date – she had slowed down in front of Greg's house to prepare for the intersection some 300 metres ahead; she was doing about 10 kilometres per hour when she passed the house. She saw a man in police uniform, along with two other men in suits whom she believed were detectives. They were walking out of the house carrying an item she thought at the time was a golf club; she later realised it must have been a crowbar.

In that fleeting moment she was able to see that the car was a large six cylinder type, Holden or Ford, the distance the men were from one another, even the police officer's haircut.

When this claim had been put to Sergeant Fraser, he was able to refute it. He had been on leave on the supposed date, the last Sunday in September. However, Mrs Haslam was sure it was any date but that Sunday – that was the day after the 1997 Grand Final and, as a St Kilda supporter, she would have remembered.

A week of closing submissions followed. The prosecution opted to take just half a day to recap, while the defence took

Chapter Twenty-Eight

three days. Colin Lovitt fastidiously addressed every aspect of evidence and argument.

The prosecution's problem was that there was no overwhelming direct evidence to connect Greg with the murder. There was supposition, and reasonable conclusions could be drawn, but there was no eyewitness and no murder weapon. There was Greg's previous behaviour in handling Jaidyn, which suggested violence and maltreatment. There was the crowbar and the bag of clothes from his house, which perhaps only Greg had known about. There was even Greg's intellectual limitations and communication problems. But, as Mr Lovitt contended at the opening of the trial, his client was not on trial for being an idiot.

The judge had disallowed the admission as evidence of the surgical gloves found in Greg's house. The gloves had talcum powder inside them, powder that was later found on both the steering wheel of Greg's car and his baseball cap. The Crown claimed that Greg had worn these gloves, reducing any forensic evidence that would have been left.

There was precious little forensic evidence in the car, especially in the boot where it was claimed Jaidyn had been transported – admittedly wrapped in a sleeping bag.

Against this weight of evidence was stacked the episode with the pig's head. It seemed too much of a coincidence that, on the very night Greg was accused of killing a child, a gang of thugs went to his house, and threw a severed pig's head through his window. Yet the events were supposedly unrelated.

Colin Lovitt had raised so many possible alternatives to the Crown version that he felt sure there must be reasonable doubt. He argued that it would be "too convenient" to ignore all of these alternatives and say it must have been Greg. He even used the name Azaria in his closing address. The name of Australia's most notorious child death was intended as a reminder of the perils of jumping to conclusions.

The Jaidyn Leskie Murder

Finally, Justice Vincent was left to sum up the eight weeks of evidence. He explained the process of the law, and by which rules the jury must be governed in coming to their decision. He talked about a vague and difficult concept called "beyond reasonable doubt". What was reasonable? That was for the jury to decide.

Justice Vincent spent three days explaining this responsibility to the jury, and canvassing the evidence.

At 3.12 p.m. on Tuesday, 1 December, the jury retired to consider its verdict.

CHAPTER TWENTY-NINE

The jury had been a curiosity to everyone involved in the trial. As in any trial, both defence and prosecution camps analyse every movement, gesture and expression made by jurists to get a feel for how they are responding.

The jury appeared to be divided on Greg's guilt.

Some jurors took copious notes, covering every utterance noted. Others giggled with each self-deprecating wisecrack Colin Lovitt made. Then there were those who rolled their eyes in annoyance when the defence counsel asked for Greg's six-hour interview tape to be replayed in full. Was that derision? Was Mr Lovitt losing them? How did they take it when the tape was being played? Were they reading the transcript, or looking at the screen to watch Greg's manner and demeanour? Did they look at Greg when they came into the court, or did they avert their eyes? If they looked at him, did they smile or scowl?

For weeks, lawyers, journalists, Greg, his family and the public, had been searching for a sign. Other, less serious, questions had been asked about the jury too. Such as how long would it take each day for one particular juror to fall asleep? One morning he lasted just seventeen minutes. Why did two of them come in eating Chuppa Chup lollipops one day? What about those other two: was there a flicker of romance between them? And the juror who withdrew toward the end of the trial after the sudden death of her own son? Which way would she have gone? Most considered she was in the Mr Lovitt camp.

But now there was only one question left to answer.

Quick to acquit, slow to convict, that's how it's said to go. But as the days passed, this was of no comfort to either side. The police began to feel sure it was a hung jury. There was little chance a jury could stay out for three nights and come back with an acquittal; for it to take so long must mean division in the ranks. But the jury had eight weeks of evidence to trawl through and, as shown by the note taking, they were certainly thorough.

When the jury finally returned to the court, they had two questions. First, they wanted to re-hear details of evidence that neither the defence nor the Crown had given much weight to. They asked for an interpretation of a conversation that may have suggested Darren Farr was with the pig's head gang at the time the head was thrown. This surprised most in the court as no-one had considered the evidence particularly crucial. Both sides agreed he was not with the raiders.

The second question, asking for a finer definition of "reasonable doubt", suggested more yet revealed little. Many felt the jury was looking to acquit. They had doubt, but was it reasonable? Who knows? They didn't. Which way was their doubt falling? Did it suggest they were permitting themselves a modicum of doubt and would convict? Or were they looking the opposite way?

Maybe they were not thinking about a murder charge at all, but looking at manslaughter. Justice Vincent had offered the jury the option of a manslaughter verdict, suggesting that there was evidence enough to support a claim that, if Greg Domaszewicz was involved in Jaidyn's death, he may not have intended to kill the boy. Was the jury looking to compromise?

When jurists were heard to be laughing loudly in the anteroom in which they were deliberating, the mood swung

Chapter Twenty-Nine

further to the defence. Would a jury be so amused if they were about to convict a man of murder?

At 5.06 p.m. on Friday, 4 December, word filtered through that the jury was returning with a verdict.

For four days, scores of journalists, lawyers and the public had hovered around the door to the court, waiting. They sat on the benches patiently, reading and talking. They sat on the stone floor, in the passageways, or stood in groups. Rowland Legg smoked endless cigars in the courtyard, chatting with reporters and lawyers. By late Friday afternoon, most were resigned to sacrificing a Saturday sitting outside a court room. An announcement of the jury's return was expected; it was also expected that they would be sent out again for the night.

Colin Lovitt had spent that lunchtime and part of the early afternoon in the Essoign Club, a barristers-only retreat. He was at ease and content he had done enough to get his client off. Bill Morgan-Payler had been less relaxed.

The prosecution team gathered nervously at the bar table. Rowland Legg, Mick Roberts and a couple of detectives new to the crew squeezed onto the benches behind. Colin Lovitt took his orange cloth armchair. His junior counsel, John Lee – his wig, never once sitting cleanly on his florid pate through the trial, and not making any exceptions now – sat alongside him.

There was a scrum outside court as journalists jockeyed with the public gallery queue to get inside. Police dispensed with the laborious metal detection process; names would suffice for the press, as most were well known from eight weeks of daily attendance. The press benches filled quickly. Spare chairs were taken. The tipstaff almost lost his spot.

Greg walked shakily in to court. He wore beige trousers and a pale blue shirt. He smiled his nervous, inappropriate smile, looking bewildered and scared.

His mum sat behind him with a young law student.

Justice Vincent arrived a minute later in his scarlet and grey robes, his white wig planted firmly on his head.

"I understand we have a verdict, bring in the jury please," the judge said.

Eight men and three women filed into court and stood in a row in front of the jury box. Not one of them looked up at Greg to meet his eye. A sure sign. He was guilty. They never look when they convict.

"He's going down," a member of the wider defence team muttered.

The judge's young female associate asked the jury foreman if they had reached a verdict. They had.

"Do you find the accused guilty or not guilty of murder?" she asked.

With barely a pause, the foreman replied in a strong and clear voice: "Not guilty".

A few people gasp. Some shake their heads. Someone claps. But it's not a time for clapping.

The compromise verdict. Would he be guilty of manslaughter or would he walk?

"Do you find the accused guilty or not guilty of manslaughter?"

"Not guilty."

Justice Vincent discharges the jury, but no one really hears. The jury shuffle about as stunned as anyone, absorbing the scene in court.

The judge looks up over his half glasses and leans forward on his bench beneath the wooden canopy. "Mr Domaszewicz," he says in a half-whisper so many don't hear, "You may leave the dock."

Greg walks quickly in a stiff-legged jittery sort of stumble to embrace his lawyer. Colin Lovitt is still sitting at the bench, leaning forward on his elbows. Greg kisses him on the left cheek, his arm fumbled over the lawyer's shoulder in a clumsy half hug. "I love you," he says. And at that moment, he ought to.

Chapter Twenty-Nine

Greg turns, his right hand on his heart, and looks back at the court. His eyes blink fast. Journalists rush to make phone calls and deadlines. Greg looks up to the public gallery. He is shaking. His mum is crying. She tries to reach him but she isn't quick enough. She'll have to wait. Lawyers take Greg to the back of the court. There is more business to attend to.

Helen Chervev hovered outside the court in the corridors of the Supreme Court, barely able to contain her glee. Her little boy was coming home. She paced around outside waiting, more waiting. She was wringing her hands with excitement now, not trepidation. Friends hugged her. Backs were slapped, hands shaken. "I knew he would get off," they said.

"Justice has been done," Helen said.

"I knew it. I knew it. I told you all, I told you he was not guilty," she told the reporters gathering around her.

Bill Morgan-Payler, his junior counsel Tony Trood and instructing solicitor walked through the crowd. There was no comment. What comment could there be.

In the small police anteroom outside Court Four, Rowland Legg and Mick Roberts were fuming. Legg called his superiors to give them the news. The defence team had attacked the investigation throughout and now, in their moment of triumph, they were unlikely to let another opportunity slip. They needed to formulate a response, and the detectives were not the ones who ought to provide it. Sitting through the verdict was humble pie enough.

Superintendent Noel Ashby, the head of the serious crime squads, put out a statement. There was no further evidence to take the case on. There would be no further investigation. The case was closed.

The detectives walked from the room, through Greg's exultant family and friends. Nothing was said.

Other large, suited men gathered around. Greg's triumphant walk from court was starting to take on the form of a choreographed stunt. Many in the media recalled the scenes of pandemonium and farce that occurred when those accused of the Walsh Street killings were released. They had walked from the court straight into a waiting limousine with a TV crew on board.

Greg suddenly appeared from the stairs to the cells and was standing in the passage of the court. A free man, but still trapped.

The crowd pressed in. It was agreed that he would make a short statement to the wider media before fleeing to negotiate lucrative deals with those who would pay for his story. He was warned not to let too much slip; his earning potential would drop with every non-exclusive utterance.

There were rumours during the trial that the defence team's pro bono agreement provided for a cut of any money earned by Greg or his family from magazine, TV, book and movie deals, should they arise upon acquittal. The rumours were never substantiated and were fiercely denied.

Greg was overwhelmed. He was familiar with the media scrum by now. But this was something new. Colin Lovitt decided that the media conference should be conducted on the steps outside the court in William Street.

Greg thanked his legal team for their work and their determination.

Asked how he felt, Greg said: "Fine, it's over isn't it?"

"I can't express how happy I am, that's about it. I just hope they go and look into it, I guess."

Then all turned to farce. Greg tried to walk to a car to escape the questions and cameras but the car was nowhere to be found. Nothing could be seen beyond the wall of people, microphones and cameras. The questions came as sharply as the camera flashes, and they became more difficult, more pointed.

"So who did murder Jaidyn, Greg?"

"Who do you think did it?"

Chapter Twenty-Nine

"Do you feel partly to blame for what happened Greg?"

"You left a child alone in the house Greg, what do you have to say to that?"

"What do you have to say to Bilynda, Greg?"

"Will you go back to Moe?"

"What does this mean for Jaidyn, Greg?"

He deflected the questions along with the elbows and shoves. Mr Lovitt tried to shepherd his client along with a deliberate stride but it was a charade. He had no more idea of how to end the rumble than Greg. Eventually, a car was found in Little Bourke Street. Greg slipped into the passenger seat and covered his face with his hands.

The mob moved to a nearby pub in Fitzroy, the Marquis of Lorne. The venue was no coincidence; it was where Greg's defence strategy had been drafted and settled on. There was a beer waiting for Greg. "It tastes good," he said as he drank.

"I still can't believe I am here to enjoy this," he told the *Herald Sun*.

Neither could others. Not far away at a city pub called The Owl and The Pussycat, the annual police media Christmas dinner was on. Rowland Legg was booked in as M.C. along with John Silvester of the *Sunday Age* for the presentation of some tongue-in-cheek awards. He kept the appointment.

Bilynda Murphy required the opinion of eleven jurors to make up her mind about Greg's guilt. She had read the prosecution brief, spoken to police, spoken to Greg. And still she couldn't decide. After reading the brief, she had been certain of Greg's guilt. During the trial she had wanted nothing to do with him; she still felt he was guilty, although she was wavering. Now she accepted that he mustn't have done it.

So who killed my little boy?

That night Bilynda felt she owed it both to Jaidyn and to Greg to visit him for herself. Bilynda said she would keep fighting to find her son's killer. But the fight seemed to have been knocked out of her. She spoke mournfully of her vow to Jaidyn, and her pleading with him to forgive her for getting involved with Greg in the first place. It was her greatest regret.

"I am a victim of my own mistakes and will continue to live with them for the rest of my life," she said in a written statement. "But I realise I cannot change them. I believe I will go through my life never knowing the truth but will continue to be strong for my children."

Despite her anger with herself, Bilynda was anxious to point out that she and Greg were just good friends again; they were not lovers. Bilynda drove down to Melbourne from Moe. No one knew how Greg would receive her, or how she would respond.

It was Helen she saw first. They hugged. Bilynda had wanted to see her as much as Greg that night. The two had grown close in the months after Jaidyn disappeared. And it was Helen, Bilynda had said earlier, who had been central in fostering her doubts about Greg's guilt.

Bilynda later told a women's magazine that she went to the pub after the trial to see if Greg would apologise to her. She was amazed to see people celebrating there. Her child was dead, she said. She didn't think it was something to celebrate.

Greg went into hiding. He had an agent and he wanted money; he wasn't talking for nothing. Leo Karis, who was also test cricketer Mark Waugh's agent, tried to broker a deal. Reports said that Greg wanted $200,000 for his story.

Greg's mum reasoned that he should earn a considerable sum, after all he had been through; it was his reward, she said. Channel Nine's *60 Minutes* was said to be offering the largest sums, along with that station's *A Current Affair* and Channel Seven's *Today Tonight*.

Bilynda also sought cash for her story. *New Idea* paid, but the money went into a trust fund for Breehanna, not into Bilynda's pocket.

Chapter Twenty-Nine

Brett Leskie, who had an agent, Margaret Fletcher, negotiating on his behalf from early on, wanted a similar deal. It was for Breehanna, not him, he said. It would be a legacy to his sister from Jaidyn. There were few offers. Brett spoke briefly to say that he felt numb, and that he didn't believe justice had been served by the result.

When, however, he found out about Greg's negotiations with television stations, he was furious. He spoke out angrily against anyone paying blood money to the man accused of killing his son. The networks trod more carefully; the exclusive story could backfire on them. If there was a perception that Greg Domaszewicz was a lucky man to escape the court system, the deal could do more harm than good.

Brett threatened litigation against Greg for any money earned from media appearances. He felt that Greg would lose a civil suit, where his guilt would be assessed on a lesser standard of proof – the balance of probabilities.

The networks were losing interest. Several figured there was more to gain from taking a higher moral stand and vowed not to pay Bilynda for her story. They were less adamant about Greg.

Leo Karis then decreed that Greg's story was not for sale. Money was not the issue here, he said. Greg just wanted to get on with his life after seventeen months in jail.

Greg had lost his real name in jail; everyone knew him only as 'Moe'. One wonders if Moe will ever get its name back; it will always now be linked with Greg, and with Jaidyn.

Before the trial, when she had sat around Sue Havis's kitchen table musing over Greg's guilt and her son's death, Bilynda had felt used. Used by the police, used by the media, but most of all used by Greg.

She had turned away, with a fading smile of regret and muttered "just a dumb blonde". She had pondered for a while, flicking a cigarette box.

"If Greg has done this he has fucked my life. I have had to go through so much shit because of him. The reason Brett and I split up is because Katie was getting into my head saying 'he doesn't love you' and all this sort of stuff, and I believed it," she said.

"Now you regret it but this, this is just playing games with my whole life. I could have lost my daughter, my family, everything."

"If he has done it he has fucked everything."

Has he done it?

"I dunno."

CHAPTER THIRTY

The trial was over but the story did not die. How could it? So much had been left unresolved by the Supreme Court verdict, so much was still left unsaid and unknown for it to be allowed to stop there, to be laid to rest in the dusty corners we place the difficult and the uncomfortable.

Although the trial was over, the case was not. The acquittal of Greg Domaszewicz did not signal an end; on the contrary, it only added to the intrigue. The verdict begged the question, if Greg didn't do it, who did? In essence the Supreme Court trial established one thing: a group of 11 people could not be convinced beyond a reasonable doubt, based on the evidence before them in court, that Greg Domaszewicz had killed Jaidyn Leskie. It did not establish who did kill him and nor should it, for that was not their job. In the criminal justice system in Victoria the next stage in the process of a sudden or suspicious death after a trial is for the case to be returned to the Coroner. If someone has been found guilty at trial it becomes an academic process for the Coroner to accept the jury's verdict for how a person died and who killed them.

However, in cases where a not guilty verdict has been returned the situation is less clear. The Coroner will read the transcript of the criminal trial, accept the evidence presented and make his own judgment whether further investigation is required or a public hearing held. Normally, the Coroner reviews the evidence and trial transcript and returns an open finding, or a finding that the deceased had been killed by a person or persons unknown.

In Jaidyn's case the Coroner followed this procedure and accepted the advice of the homicide squad that there was no evidence to justify further investigation and that there were no other viable suspects for Jaidyn's murder. Nothing in the trial had changed their opinion that Domaszewicz had killed Jaidyn. So the police investigation was closed. Or rather left open, such is the terminology in these things, that without a conviction the case is left "unsolved" but dormant with no officer pursuing it. This is the way of the system saying: "We know who did it, we just didn't have enough evidence to prove it. Case closed. Next."

In this regard the Coroner seemed to agree with the police. After initial comments following the trial that there would be an inquest into Jaidyn's death, no date was set. The Coroner's Office took time to review the case and decide upon a course of action. Weeks spilt into months, months into years.

Deputy State Coroner Iain West eventually followed the regular procedure and conducted a "record of investigation". He held a private two-day hearing which re-examined the trial transcripts, before producing a two-page report, known as an in-chambers finding. This outlined the facts already known about the case and that Jaidyn had died of head injuries. It apportioned no blame and identified no culprit.

A chorus of protest followed. In June 2002 Bilynda wrote to Victorian Attorney General Rob Hulls requesting a full, open inquest. So too did Brett Leskie and his family. In her letter to Mr Hulls Bilynda identified five possible killers. She was angry and wanted answers and years of legal procrastination would not alter that.

"I didn't need a piece of paper to tell me my son's cause of death was head injuries. I was well aware of that but Jaidyn

Chapter Thirty

didn't break then bandage his own arm. Jaidyn didn't bang his head and take his own life. Nor did he fill his body with the drug benzhexol, tie himself to a crowbar and throw himself into Blue Rock Dam," she said.

Similarly, the Leskie family – Brett, his parents and brothers – wrote an open letter to the Coroner asking him to review the decision. They seemed perplexed that the last known person to see Jaidyn alive the night he disappeared had never been called before a court to account for what had happened. Besides, given Domaszewicz could never be retried for the murder of Jaidyn, nor any other charge extending from that incident, he could not incriminate himself in his evidence. Unlike the Supreme Court trial where Greg could choose not to testify in case he said something incriminating, that was theoretically not the case now. It appeared more than reasonable to wonder why the justice system would not demand at some stage in the process that the last known person to see a child alive be asked to recount the actions of that day. In short, that Greg be asked to tell a court what happened and submit to questioning.

Mr Hulls consulted State Coroner Graeme Johnstone who consented to an "investigation review" before deciding if the case warranted being canvassed in an open hearing. The investigation was carried out by the Coroner's Office and police attached to work with the Coroner, rather than by the homicide squad members who investigated the case in the first place. This was so that fresh eyes and ears could review all material and make up their own minds without prejudice. There was little point asking the same people to go over what they already knew and second-guess themselves.

All players involved were reinterviewed, unidentified female DNA found on the bib Jaidyn had with him when he was fished from Blue Rock Dam was re-examined. The possibility of Jaidyn being alive after the day he disappeared was explored. The police reviewed all forensic evidence and took statements from the prisoners who claimed Greg had confessed to them when on remand.

Greg Domaszewicz publicly welcomed the investigation and the push for a full hearing. "I don't care if I have to give evidence at the inquest, I've wanted that all along," Greg robustly declared.

As word of the "new" investigation filtered through, Bilynda's mum Pam Blackwood spoke for many when she said it would be pleasing if there was a chance for Greg to be made to account for his own movements and Jaidyn's on the toddler's last known day alive. "Why shouldn't he be questioned? Everybody else at the trial was, except him," she observed.

In the meantime the Leskie and Murphy families tried as best they could to reconnect the shattered pieces of their lives and start over.

In 2000 Bilynda learnt she was pregnant again. After all her grief and torment over the death of one son and the loss of custody – albeit temporarily – of her daughter she found joy in the news she was to be a mother once more. She had found love again and with a new baby dared dream of a new, happy and normal life. Nothing could ever hope to truly be the same once you had endured what Bilynda had but this was a step in the right direction. Then 25, she began a new life with sheet metal worker Jeremy Williams, whom she married in late 2001. Bilynda's new baby boy, Caleb Aidyn Williams, was born on 16 July 2000, at Sale's Gippsland Base Hospital. The couple had always planned to incorporate Jaidyn's name in the middle name but, mindful of the burden they could place upon the newborn, they opted against the full Jaidyn name and took the abbreviated Aidyn as their sign of respect.

A young mother's stroll with her new child around her town's streets is normally a moment of pride when fussing neighbours nose in the pram and speculate about who the child most looks like and query how everyone is sleeping, but Bilynda

CHAPTER THIRTY

was denied even this simple pleasure. Callous hearts among some in Moe called across busy streets, asking if Bilynda was "going to kill this one too". It was cruel and cut deeply. The suspicion of her possible involvement, no matter how ill-founded, would not go away. Regardless of her immaturity and the fact she made a raft of poor choices, there had never been any serious suggestion Bilynda was involved in Jaidyn's death. That she left Jaidyn with her drug-taking, socially-limited misfit of a boyfriend in the first place that night betrayed an appalling lack of judgment. That she went out to get drunk and was never entirely certain what was happening with her child throughout stories of burns and hospitals and did little to establish his safety is at best regrettably reckless and at worst culpably negligent. But it does not equate to killing your child. For some in Moe, however, it was tantamount to the same thing.

Perhaps her crime was to have allowed, via Jaidyn's death, the national spotlight to be turned on her own dubious social circumstances and to unfairly establish Moe as a by-word for what in America would be called trailer trash. Consequently life in Moe, more than anywhere else, was going to be an ongoing trial. It was unsurprising she decided to take her new husband's surname after marriage. While it remains a convention to do so, it also afforded Bilynda some degree of distance, anonymity and shelter. The couple soon after had a second baby boy, Corran.

The turmoil that seems to constantly engulf Bilynda's life once more emerged in August 2002 after Jeremy was nearly killed when his car was hit by a train. He was flown to Melbourne in a critical condition but for one of the first times in her life Bilynda caught a break. Jeremy survived and managed to make a full recovery.

Coincidentally in late May 2000 Brett Leskie similarly had a near fatal car accident. Life and death for those in this Moe tale are never far apart.

Greg Domaszewicz meanwhile was out of remand and attempting to establish a new life working as a plasterer in

Melbourne's outer eastern suburbs. He was dogged by the incessant media coverage and the infamy of his name made it hard to lose himself in the community. He was recognised wherever he went in Victoria so he considered moving interstate to Newcastle outside Sydney. At one point he was reported to be considering changing his name. This he later denied, but with Greg you can never be too sure of the line between fact and fantasy.

Greg re-emerged in the oddest places. Members of the Victoria Police's Purana Task Force investigating underworld murders recorded telephone conversations between Greg and suspects they had under observation. It was an oddity to the police that this pathetic, unemployed drug-user from Moe who had achieved notoriety for being accused of killing a baby, then covering it up, should find himself conversing freely with the heaviest members of the Melbourne underworld.

Greg's high public profile ensured he had forever lost his anonymity, and while he would nervously avoid instances where he'd be recognised and potentially ridiculed in public, in prison it had quite the opposite effect. His profile made him someone to know inside and even the most serious of organised crime figures were amused by him. When Greg left remand after the trial he maintained contact with some of these characters. While the underworld figures he rang were largely dismissive of him and treated him as something of an amusement, it made for yet another weird tangent in this tangled tale.

The lives of those involved were changed forever by the events surrounding Jaidyn's death and disappearance yet so much would never change. The subculture of drugs and crime did not magically disappear and neither did the petty feuding and soap-operatic internecine relationships, nor the unemployment, the desolation and regular brushes with the law. It was sadly unsurprising that before long many would reappear before the courts. From Greg to Brett to the pig's head gang, they all

Chapter Thirty

returned to court at various stages on misdemeanour charges. Whatever their movements, the minor celebrity the case provided them ensured they no longer appeared anonymously in court as defendants known only by their lengthy rap sheets. They had public currency so their indiscretions were now also dutifully reported. The pig's head gang appeared on a collection of drugs, theft and possession of stolen property charges.

In early January 2003 Bilynda and Jeremy arrived home after a Christmas holiday in Lakes Entrance to discover the house had been visited while they were away. But it was not quite the small note shoved under the fly wire door that friends leave. This was a little more crass, and disturbing. Indeed, Jeremy didn't notice anything unusual about the house until he walked into the bathroom and there, stuck to the shower wall, was the couple's engagement notice. Next to it scrawled in lipstick was a simple message, "you're fucked". Bilynda didn't need to be told who had broken into her house to have her suspicions. After years of relative quiet it was an unwanted return to the sorts of silly pranks that marked life with Greg Domaszewicz. It was a reprise of the bad old days. Greg started to send Bilynda text messages as the Coroner's reinvestigation drew to a close: on one occasion he sent a text message wishing her a happy Mother's Day.

On 21 July 2003, the principal registrar of the Coroner's Office advised Bilynda and other family members that an inquest would indeed be held.

"I have wanted one from day one," Greg said when it appeared a date would be set for the inquest to begin. "A little kid is dead and they are not looking into it. That is the whole issue. Someone has to be fucking accountable for this, there's so much evidence." Indeed, however most of it appeared to point to him.

The man people had been looking to for answers on Jaidyn said he had them. In a bold move, Greg spoke out about the new inquest to the *Herald Sun*'s dogged Keith Moor, declaring that he not only knew who the real killer was but that there was more than one.

"There were three involved," he said. "I have got three that were involved that I know pretty much 100 per cent. It can't be 100 per cent without DNA, but 100 per cent otherwise."

When told that the prisoners he shared cells with would be called to give evidence Greg erupted, daring them to testify. "I am willing to put a bullet in their heads is what I am willing to do," he said. Which is an interesting response from an innocent man, and one that attracted the attention of the police.

On 26 September 2003, Coroner Graeme Johnstone announced that his office's inquiries into Jaidyn's death had uncovered new evidence which had prompted him to seek orders under section 59A of the Coroners Act to void the Deputy Coroner's findings and to clear the way for a new public inquest to commence in November.

CHAPTER THIRTY-ONE

Jaidyn disappeared again. For a third time the toddler had vanished – not from a couch in a lounge room, but, as at the trial, lost in a fog of deceit, self-interest and self-importance. Nothing else should have mattered more during the inquest than the toddler himself. For once in his miserable life and awful painful death it should have only been about him, but Jaidyn had rarely been the central concern. His mother chose partying over child-care, Greg – at best – chose convenience over common sense. The public and media opted for the soap opera over crushing tragedy. But now those misplaced priorities should have been swept aside as the State took charge to insist the investigation strike to the heart of his death. It was not to be.

While ostensibly the inquest was about Jaidyn, he would become the excuse for the occasion not the occasion itself. The conga line of misfits and miscreants who peopled Jaidyn's parents' lives returned to explain the sorry life the toddler led before he died. Still others, as if drawn to the music, came forth to provide their own versions of events. The circus had returned to town.

On Monday, 17 November 2003, Coroner Graeme Johnstone finally opened the inquest into the death of Jaidyn. It was to become known as "the first inquest". For security reasons the hearing was moved from the Coroner's Court building in

South Melbourne to the busy beige brick Melbourne Magistrates Court complex in the city's legal precinct.

Bilynda and Jeremy, wearing T-shirts emblazoned with *Justice for Jaidyn* above a picture of the toddler, sat front and centre in court near the Leskie family. Finally their day had arrived. The inquest almost stumbled before it began when it emerged that Legal Aid Victoria had refused to fund Greg Domaszewicz's legal representative. The inquest was allowed to venture forward slowly while these matters were dealt with. In the second week Colin Lovitt QC once more emerged, consenting to handle the case pro-bono for Domaszewicz who was by now living on a disability pension. Mr Lovitt made his views on the inquest clear from the outset: it was a pointless sham, a witch-hunt by police, prosecutors and a rabid media all angry at failing to obtain a criminal conviction at trial. It was a modern lynch mob.

Jim Kennan QC, a former state attorney general in the Labor governments of John Cain and Joan Kirner, was enlisted as counsel assisting the Coroner. He opened the inquest with a lengthy summary of facts well known to most after the trial and spelt out the role of the Coroner's Court and the standard of proof that applied there, which differed from the criminal courts.

The Coroner's Court, like the civil courts, must be satisfied not beyond reasonable doubt in a case, but on the balance of probabilities. However this is not so simple as placing competing evidence on a mental scale of justice and coming down on the side that carries 51 per cent of the argument. The Coroner's Court additionally demands "reasonable satisfaction", with consideration given to the weight of the offence in question. Something known as the Briginshaw Test is applied which would demand in this case the Coroner accept that if he was going to say someone killed Jaidyn, he needed to weigh up the gravity of the accusation of murder before simply saying someone probably did it. He would need to be quite sure. It

Chapter Thirty-one

makes the standard of proof here somewhat less than beyond reasonable doubt but more than just a gut feel, or simply reckoning something probably happened.

Mr Kennan promised that he intended for the inquest not to restate the trial but to explore new evidence. Primarily, this evidence was: the source and relevance of the anonymous female DNA on the bib and track pants; Jaidyn's age at the time of death and whether he had likely lived on after disappearing; exploration of the source and reason for the drug benzhexol in Jaidyn's body; examining the statements by prisoners that Greg had confessed to them while on remand; and evidence by two new witnesses, one claiming to have seen Greg's car near Blue Rock Dam on the night Jaidyn disappeared, the other a child protection worker who had been Breehanna's case officer and who had kept quiet about three incidents of abuse of Jaidyn.

The Coroner's worthy determination for completeness and transparency insisted that those who should have been summarily dismissed were examined in ghastly, cringing detail. The inquest peeled back the layers of invention and self-deception to reveal fools and frauds, probing in excruciating detail the barely relevant and eliciting little in the way of new, illuminating detail as to how and when Jaidyn died. And who killed him.

To begin with, the court once more heard of the occasion at the dam when Jaidyn went fishing with Greg and was dropped and left with scratches and bruising to his face. There was a retelling of the times Greg put him outside with the three vicious dogs and when he turned the stereo system up loud to drown out his crying. Then there was the time Jaidyn was left with a bruise on his face in the shape of an adult hand after being left at Greg's house for the night. The court again heard of Jaidyn being kicked by his mum and how he was found after death to have had a healing broken rib. The court heard how in light of this string of troubling incidents no-one took charge of Jaidyn. No-one did anything.

The Jaidyn Leskie Murder

Courts are typically utilitarian places, austere in architecture and purpose. Here sentiment might not be the bedfellow of logic and fact but that does not mean it is not open to entertaining the bizarre and ridiculous. The desire to countenance all possibilities in order to rule them out means ventilation can be given to the absurd and consideration to the preposterous.

The mystery of Jaidyn's disappearance had generated its own industry in urban myth and conspiracy theory. The court and the inquest provided the forum to speculate. Sightings of Jaidyn, like Elvis, had been seemingly more common after his death than before. People who for years thought they knew nothing of the case suddenly concluded they could be the key witness. People like Seamus Hasson.

A hunter, Hasson had been away shooting deer for four or five days – he could not be certain how long – when he drove down from the hills the night Jaidyn disappeared. He was careening along the Thompson Valley and Walhalla dirt roads when he saw headlights on nearby Willow Grove Road. He was so surprised to see another car on the lonely roads at that time of night it spooked him. Maybe after days alone in the hills with a campfire, a gun and his thoughts, he was easily spooked. The roads run vaguely parallel for some distance before meeting so Seamus sped up to fall in behind the other vehicle when the roads joined. The car in front sped up and slowed down. He thought the driver waited for him at an intersection to catch up, as though toying with him. Seamus memorised the car's registration and when he arrived home just after 1 a.m. he sat down for a cup of coffee and contemplated this unusual moment with another car. It all struck him as odd.

Not nearly as odd, you might think, as a hunter coming home late at night, uncertain if it was a Friday or Saturday evening, seeing headlights, believing them to be so unusual as to warrant giving chase, following the car and memorising its

Chapter Thirty-one

number plate, hearing the next day a child was missing – but after all of that deciding not to say anything to the police while they searched waterways, parks and tips. To then see a green Ford Falcon on the television news being examined by police and still not think, "Gee maybe I should tell them I saw that car acting suspiciously out on remote dirt roads in the middle of the night the baby went missing". It is perhaps odder still that you have your moment of blinding clarity seven years later in the lead-up to an inquest and decide to make a statement to police. But it is nowhere near as odd as the fact that when police re-enact the journey there was no way they could see the headlights of another vehicle travelling on Willow Grove Road.

"I can say that I was unable to achieve the results that Mr Hasson did when he drove the same route," Senior Constable John Gibson told the Coroner of his re-enactment of the drive.

For some people the desire to help, or the necessity to be necessary, clouds their judgment. When he gave evidence at Greg Domaszewicz's committal hearing Kenny Penfold told how he had witnessed Greg's comings and goings from his house before he left to collect Bilynda on the night of 14 July. He remembered in acute detail running to the block beside Greg's house and being startled when he looked over the fence to see Greg walk to his car. He recalled vividly Greg's trips out to the car and the fact the vehicle was reversed up the driveway with the boot open.

His memory was clear, his story verifiable – he was able to take police to the pile of his faeces on the railway tracks that proved he had a bowel movement on the train line opposite Greg's house while waiting to launch the pig's head at his house. At once liberating his bowel and his pent-up anxiety. He could show police the tear in his shirt where he ripped his pocket off to use as toilet paper. He told the same story at the trial. Darrin Wilson told a similar tale. As did Yvonne Penfold and Raymond

"Tubby" Hopkinson (unfortunately by the time of the Coroner's inquest Tubby Hopkinson had died of an illness). At no point in any of that testimony did Kenny, or anyone else, make reference to Greg coming out of the house carrying a sleeping bag and putting it in the boot of his car. But he did now.

"I think I said he was carrying something out, but not as a bag," Kenny said. "I've been whingeing and complaining to that many people over the years, and the police just turned up and asked me if I'd like to make another statement and I said 'Yes, I'd like to add a couple of things'.

"I can't say what sort of bag it is, but it's obvious to me it was a sleeping bag ... 'cause that's what the boy was found wrapped up in ... Now it's obvious, Mr Lovitt, it was a sleeping bag. It doesn't take Einstein to work that out now, does it?" Kenny said.

Indeed, it was not hard to work out. It was not hard at all to guess it might have been many things, but Kenny was not being asked to work it out or to guess – he was simply asked what he remembered, not what he thought might have been going on. What might have been was convenient. The term gilding the lily was invented for Kenny Penfold.

Certainly this surprising additional detail added little to the picture of what happened to Jaidyn for it was seemingly fabricated and only served to colour Kenny's earlier evidence. The Coroner made no comment of his own on this astonishing departure from prior evidence, relying on Colin Lovitt's summation of Kenny's new clearer memory.

"This was a startling change from his testimony at the trial, and was, quite clearly, an invention," Mr Lovitt said.

Julie Clarke similarly carried a secret. A big secret. The sort of secret that rattled and scratched around in her head trying to get out until eventually she gave in. Julie had felt she couldn't tell. She had waited so long she had backed herself into a

Chapter Thirty-one

corner – damned if she told, damned in her mind if she didn't. In the end she told. And was damned. Not just for the timing of her statement, but for what she said.

Coming forward doubtless took great courage, even if it paradoxically betrayed her cowardice for being silent so long. Julie Clarke finally spoke out in Jaidyn's defence years after it counted for anything. In that time Julie's recollections percolated with all she had read, heard and learnt of the case to form the one tangled memory. Julie was a child protection worker in Moe and in the winter of 1997 had occasion to see Bilynda Williams (Murphy at the time) over a period of several months as Breehanna's case worker. For reasons known only to Julie she never told the homicide squad how a desperate and emotional Bilynda had come to her and told her that her boyfriend had beaten her little boy.

"When the case was publicised again recently I was plagued by guilt for having this knowledge but not being able to tell anybody. It is for this reason that I have come forward now," she told the Coroner.

Julie Clarke became Breehanna's case worker on about 21 August 1997. It was soon after Jaidyn had disappeared when there was a protection application made for the young girl on the basis that she, too, could be at risk. Soon after this Brett Leskie came to see Julie at her office and confessed he had broken into Bilynda's house in Lincoln Street looking for his clothes and tools. It was then that he found the most awful note next to a drawing of a boy, with the words "mongoloid, poofter, faggot, cunt" written on it. Brett even reckoned if you held the note up to the light you could see Jaidyn's name written there. He grabbed the pad and picture and took them with him along with his other personal belongings. The following day he gave the items to Julie – not the homicide squad as you might expect. Despite his son being missing and this seemingly being a clue, Brett Leskie didn't go to the police, presumably because he was worried he might be done for burgling Bilynda's house. Julie took the things and later gave them back to Brett, telling him to take them to the police, which he did.

The note pad, which contained the beginnings of a range of letters from Bilynda to Greg, included one with the message: "Tell your mates to shut their mouths, because they're telling their mates what you have done." Julie said there was also a crude drawing of a fish with a human leg and foot sticking out of its mouth, but this drawing as she described it was never found.

A photo of Jaidyn with sunken features and a bruise on his cheek troubled Julie so much she confronted Bilynda about it. She was told the bruise occurred during the fishing trip to the dam when Jaidyn had been crying and Greg struck him. For much of Julie's evidence of meetings with Brett and Bilynda the case notes she said she made could not be found. Vital notes of meetings detailing allegations of abuse of Jaidyn by Greg were lost along with the photocopies she took of documents. She could also not produce the freaky fish picture she claimed to have been given. The only thing resembling anything like this was a child's drawing of a shark chasing a smaller fish. Julie Clarke insisted this was something different.

After an exhaustive search none of Ms Clarke's nine superiors or colleagues could locate the documents either. Their recollections of her involvement in the case were somewhat vague. Her claims were starting to unwind. The message on the pad about warning friends to "shut their mouths" could equally have been the lyrics from an Alanis Morissette song, but Julie insisted this was a different page to the one she had referred to.

The Coroner again made no direct finding but relied upon this comment from Colin Lovitt:

Chapter Thirty-one

Put simply, Ms Clarke's imagination seems to have run rampant in the six years between her seeing the note pad, and contacting the police. She claimed to have raised the issues with various superiors and colleagues, but they have all denied any knowledge whatsoever. She claimed to have photocopied the notes – and lost the copies. Counsel acting for Human Services, who had sat patiently through day after day of evidence unconnected with her claims, proceeded to strongly criticise her reliability in his cross-examination of her. In the end, realistically, her reliable evidence amounted to nothing, and I note that Mr Kennan does not seem to have placed any weight on it in his submissions. But she, like Hasson, was opened as a "you-beaut" important piece of new material when counsel-assisting opened the issues at the commencement of the first inquest.

For all her loud outspoken demands for justice for her son in the lead-up to the inquest, Bilynda was almost inaudible once she entered court to give evidence. Having demanded the inquest it was only right that she be called to give evidence.

Of course she was also central to the events of the day and the months leading up to the death. Indeed, after Greg there was no more important witness in this case. It was Bilynda who could best attest to the treatment Jaidyn endured in the last weeks and months of his life, and best describe the bruises and injuries Jaidyn returned to her house with after being babysat by Greg. Bilynda could best explain why she kicked Jaidyn in the chest a month before he died, and should best know how long her son's hair was when he went missing. She alone could explain why it was she agreed to let Greg look after Jaidyn that last day.

It was also Bilynda who rang several times during the fateful night to be told Jaidyn had been burnt, and who went back to drinking at the bar. It was Bilynda who could tell whether she saw a pig's head when she arrived back at Greg's house and explain what happened in the hours that followed. It was Bilynda who could reveal why she chopped and changed her mind about her suspicions of Greg's involvement in the months and years that followed.

As aggressively as she had campaigned for questions to be put to Greg Domaszewicz about that dreadful night, she also had to accept the fact the same uncomfortable questions would be asked of herself. Having endured them at trial she might have presumed they had been asked and answered. She was wrong.

It did not take Bilynda long to become frustrated that the process she had helped instigate should be going so awry. Colin Lovitt quizzed her about answers she had given at trial, about comments made in a range of statements she had given and about her changes of heart. He pointed to the inconsistencies of her behaviour and claimed that each change was designed to present her in a better light, irrespective of the truth.

"I didn't ask for the inquest so that you could sit here and say that I'm a bad mum, all right?" Bilynda snapped.

"I'm not saying you're a bad mum," Mr Lovitt replied.

"Bullshit, you're sitting there and saying it and I don't want nothing more to do with it because it's a crock of shit, and like you said it's a fucking sham." She rushed from the court in tears, declaring she wanted nothing more to do with the inquest. Bilynda, having championed the inquest, wanted an end to it. And once more the drama was about her. Jaidyn, as ever, was lost.

Bilynda was talked around and consented to return to the court. She was quizzed further about the relevant days. Like Bilynda, her sister Katie's allegiances had shifted since the trial. Katie's lot was her own now, she was not throwing it in with anyone, neither Greg nor Bilynda. She had also, since the trial, altered her story. Now she contended that on the Saturday

Chapter Thirty-one

afternoon before going to the party, she and Bilynda had driven past Greg's house several times "hanging laps". Bilynda disputed the claim.

"She can say what she likes. I was driving and I know," Katie said.

Bilynda reckoned the change in the story might be connected to the change in their relationship.

"I don't like the way she brings up her kids," Bilynda said. "I don't want her back in my house ... if I could disown her I would."

Colin Lovitt picked at the scab of Bilynda's unease at the proceedings.

"You sought an inquest in this case, didn't you?" he asked.

"Yes," she replied.

"You wrote to various people, including the attorney general?"

"Yes."

"You asked, effectively, for justice for Jaidyn; is that right?"

"Yes, I did."

"You were hoping for, were you not, a full reinvestigation into the circumstances surrounding Jaidyn's disappearance and death, weren't you?"

"Yep."

"That's not what in your opinion you've seen happen here, is it?"

"No."

"Are you disappointed with the process that's happened here?"

"Well, I just don't see that anyone's been here. There's been prisoners and a DHS worker; there's no Penfolds, there's no-one that's involved in it."

"Did you think if this was going to be a fair dinkum attempt to find out who was possibly responsible that people like Kenny and Yvonne Penfold, and others — let's not call the roll — should have been brought to court to be questioned further?"

"I would have liked to question them, yes. I believe he's [Greg's] told a lot of lies but that is why I asked for the inquest, so I can find out."

"You believe he has told a lot of lies?"

"Yes."

"Of course, the police told you right from the outset that he was lying about all sorts of things?"

"Yes, they did, but I got hold of his video tapes."

"You what?"

"I got hold of his video tapes, his police tapes and he has lied."

"The video tapes of the interview?"

"Yes."

"Your counsel has asked you questions, you have announced to the media plenty of times that there were things you wanted to ask Greg – what do you say he said that was untrue? There is a nice open-ended unleading question."

"Well, for a start ..."

"You tell us what he said that was untrue. Did he ever hurt Jaidyn?"

"Yes, he did."

"M'mm?" Mr Lovitt asked.

"Did he ever hurt Jaidyn?" said Bilynda. "Yes, he did, and he says no, he didn't."

"That's one. Next?"

"I don't know, I would have to watch the video, but there are a few things."

"Can you think of any others?"

"Not off the top of my head, no."

Bilynda had wanted the hearing for the opportunity to publicly condemn Greg Domaszewicz as her son's killer. Yet the Coroner was almost as critical of Bilynda Williams' inaction as he was of Greg Domaszewicz's action. Jaidyn had not been well treated when he was in Greg's care, and Bilynda knew it. But a

Chapter Thirty-one

mother's concern did not overwhelm a young woman's desire for independence. The hardest battle for any new parent is adapting to a changed life circumstance and learning to sublimate their own desires for the needs of their child. For Bilynda, as a young mother these desires were in constant conflict, and too regularly her own needs won out.

The Coroner found: "Ms Williams may have been wary after the incident that apparently occurred in May 1997 [in which Jaidyn was left with the hand mark bruise on his face], in that she was nervous about leaving her son with Mr Domaszewicz. But this nervousness did not translate to preventing her leaving Jaidyn in his care. It did not trigger any real action by way of protective behaviour towards her son. It should have.

"The most she did was try to look for her son in the evening of 14th June whilst he was in the care of Mr Domaszewicz. Apart from a number of attempted telephone calls she appears to have put little by way of effort into this action. On receiving no answer to the telephone calls, she went to a party and then proceeded to the local hotel where she drank alcohol into the early hours of the next morning."

CHAPTER THIRTY-TWO

He had changed his name since leaving jail but in court he was still simply known as Prisoner R. He was the first of the former remand prisoners to give evidence at the inquest. A convicted killer, he was familiar with the court system, but it made his experience no less uncomfortable. He wished he was almost anywhere else. He heard his statement read back to him, telling how he met Domaszewicz when on remand at the Melbourne Assessment Prison. Greg had been transferred to the same unit R was in during his stay and their paths crossed for several days.

"I walked into Greg's cell to ask him for a cigarette," said R in the statement. "He told me to have a seat and have a yarn. We talked about my case and I said I hated Crown witnesses. We eventually got onto the subject of his case, I said not to lie to me and to tell me the truth about his case. He said that he would tell me the truth about how the child died. I asked why would he tell me and he said because I hated Crown witnesses. I think he trusted me.

"I asked how it all eventuated. He said he was working on the car. Greg said the car fell down and the kid's arm got broken. I asked him what he did then and Greg said he panicked. Greg stopped talking about this part of the incident at this stage. We continued talking and he eventually started to tell

Chapter Thirty-two

me how the kid was screaming and he slipped the kid something to keep him quiet. When I say 'slipped the kid something', I mean he drugged the kid. Greg never told me what drug he gave the kid. Greg started sweating while I was talking to him and went real strange. I asked if he was happy to keep talking. He said he was happy to keep talking.

"Greg then told me that he put a pillow over the kid's head and hit him a couple of times with a crowbar. He said he felt the kid's pulse and neck and the kid was dead.

"Greg then said that he didn't want to talk any more about it. I asked why and he said he was paranoid. He said he had told me more than he had told anybody about the case. I walked out of the cell. Over the next couple of days before he left the unit we never discussed his case again. We would only say 'G'day' to each other. I have not spoken to him since he left the unit."

The day R made this statement, another prisoner, M – a close friend of R's in the jail – was simultaneously making a statement of his own to homicide squad detectives. Yet, apparently, neither was aware that the other was talking to police. Suffice to say Colin Lovitt was scathing of this apparently innocent coincidence. He suggested R was making up the statement simply to "back up" M to make that confession appear more plausible.

With what would seem to be significant justification, Mr Lovitt was amazed at the coincidence that although Greg had spoken to R some time earlier, R should choose the very same moment as M to independently go to the governor of the prison and say he needed to speak to homicide detectives about the Leskie case. R admitted M was his mate in jail, but insisted he was completely unaware M was also making a statement to the same effect to police at the very same time. It beggared belief, Mr Lovitt said. These were, after all, prisoners, and their relationship with the truth should be considered a fractious one at the best of times. And the timing of these statements should only further colour an already jaded view of their likely authenticity.

In fact, Mr Lovitt was stunned that three prisoners — R, M and F — all made statements to police about the same matter within four days of one another, yet each of them protested to be blissfully unaware the others were doing so. While R admitted being a friend of M's, he said he was far from friendly with F. He would not have known what F was doing because the pair didn't get along.

"We didn't cross paths much and when we did cross paths we didn't talk," R said.

Mr Lovitt spent a long time cross-examining R about his past and what brought him to being in jail, the details of which still cannot be repeated for legal reasons. He also raised how absurd it seemed that R professed to hate Crown witnesses from the experience of his own trial, yet suddenly had agreed to become one in the Leskie case.

R was a sad man in many ways; pitiful, in so far as a murderer is deserving of pity. He admitted that far from trying to get an early release by making a statement to police about Domaszewicz, he had wanted to stay in jail. There was something of the *Shawshank Redemption* in his argument that institutionalisation was less suffocating for him and preferable to the terror presented by the freedoms of the outside world. "I didn't know if I could cope with the outside," he said. "I didn't want to get out because I was scared of the outside world."

Quizzed over the detail of the statement, R stood by his word. "All I know is the car was on the jack and the baby somehow got its arms caught under the car. That is all he said. He didn't know what to do, so he told me he slipped it something to make it calmer.

"He got hot and sweaty and a bit nervous, a bit paranoid. He started like he was getting flashbacks ... he come across that he

Chapter Thirty-two

was thinking of what he had done very seriously, and as he was talking it made him get hot and sweaty and upset.

"After he told me about the car and the drugs he said that he couldn't shut the baby up so he put a pillow over its head and hit it with a crowbar."

F's evidence was, to be precise, brief. Indeed, it was as brief as his written police statement was long. He was clearly uncomfortable now at being brought to court and even less comfortable with the notion of speaking. Asked to take the oath or give an affirmation he refused. There was no point taking an oath, he protested, because he was not going to say anything else. Not only was he not talking about what Greg had allegedly told him in the past, he wasn't saying anything at all. No statement, no oath, no affirmation. Just get me out of here.

"You've indicated something to me in your witness statement and that indication was that – the general indication was that yourself and your family were in fear?" the Coroner said.

"Yes."

"That's yourself and your family?"

"That's it, yes, in the interests of their safety, yes."

"Of their safety, is that what you're saying?"

"That's correct."

"Has anyone threatened you?"

"I'm not prepared to elaborate any further."

After brief discussion, that was it for F in court. He left leaving as many questions unanswered. For whatever reason – be it safety, or the fact, as Mr Lovitt would contend, that he no longer stood to gain anything – one thing was clear and it was that F would make no comment.

Earlier, at the time he made his statement, he had been most forthcoming:

The Jaidyn Leskie Murder

My full name is F. I am xx years old. In xxx I appeared at the Melbourne County Court on one charge of xxx and one charge of xxx. I was sentenced to two years two months with a nine month minimum. I went straight to the M.A.P. [Melbourne Assessment Prison]. I went to unit xx. I was there for four or five days and then went to unit xx. Both units xx and xx are protection units. I was in protection because I was going to give evidence against xxxx xxxx who had been recorded confessing to a murder to me.

There are about 25 prisoners in each protection unit and you only mix with other prisoners who are in protection. One of the prisoners in unit xx was Greg Domaszewicz. I had never met him before and most prisoners called him Moe. Basically the first day I was in the unit I found out that Greg had been charged with the murder of Jaidyn Leskie. Basically because you are in the same unit you would run into each other and you would say "Hello" to each other.

Greg was always worried because he thought someone would get at him so he tried to develop a lot of friends. Greg used to speak a lot to a prisoner who I also used to speak to a lot, so Greg probably thought it was OK to speak to me.

Basically at first when I spoke to him he denied being involved in Jaidyn's death and throwing the blame at the copper from up there who he says was rooting his ex-missus. At first he was at home with Jaidyn, put Jaidyn in the shower, put him to sleep on the sofa, and Greg played Nintendo games and then went to pick up his girlfriend, missus, whatever she was. He rang up Yvonne's, his ex-missus. Initially he rang and later went around to her house. Searched for the kid. I remember him saying he got pulled over by the local uniform.

Chapter Thirty-two

Basically that was his initial story. Went to the police station and reported it. At that stage I didn't really like him and I made it pretty clear to him that I didn't want him to come to my cell. After a while I started feeling a bit sorry for him because he always came across as a victim. He was always saying that he had been set up by the copper and Yvonne but he never seemed to show any remorse. He was always feeling sorry for himself. He never seemed to say anything about the kid.

He started coming into my cell and talking to me because he knew that I'd been around a bit. He was asking me who was a good barrister, who was a good solicitor. He asked me what I thought of Colin Lovitt.

He was coming up for a committal hearing and he kept asking for my advice. I said to him, if you want my advice, stop telling me shit. He said something like, "What if I told them I was working on the car and I had Jaidyn with me helping me and I broke his arm but it was an accident if the car fell off the ramps?" I said, "If it was an accident, why didn't you take him straight to hospital?" He said, "If I'd done that then people might've thought I'd bashed the kid." I then said to him, "Is that what happened?" He got up and walked out of my cell and went into one of his fits of laughter.

There were other conversations, most of them in bits and pieces.

I remember one day, I remember the exact words. He came into my cell and said, "I couldn't have put Jaidyn in the dam because I can't swim, but me mate's got a dinghy." He looked at me and laughed and smiled. It was like he was trying to tell me something. He got up and walked out. I think at a later stage I asked him about the dinghy and he mentioned something about it being sold or he got rid of it or something.

One day we were sitting down eating dinner. Greg was sitting next to me eating his dinner, which was unusual because he usually ate his dinner in his cell. I was talking to another prisoner, M, and Greg said in a pretty loud voice, "I shouldn't have used that crowbar." M at that time was living in unit xx.

I asked him at one stage when he got pulled over by the police where he'd been and he said at Yvonne's. He said that there were wet clothes on the seat. I'm pretty sure he said the front seat. He said the clothes were wet from when he was working on his car, he was lying on the ground working on the car.

He said to me at one stage, "What if the whole thing that happened to Jaidyn was an accident?" and I said, "It's probably a bit late now" because of the callous way that Jaidyn was disposed of. He said, "But what if the whole thing was an accident?" and I said, "It's up to you if you want to tell the truth or not."

He also mentioned something about the ranger at the Blue Rock Dam living close by and that he had heard from someone that the ranger can't say that it was him at the dam.

I remember Greg was saying once that the front door of the house was locked but how could they have fitted through the hole in the window? I don't know what that was all about.

He also told me that he had thrown some tissues or bandages in the bin in the bathroom with blood on them. I can't remember what exactly it was about but it was something about the tissues and a bin. He said something about how Jaidyn got injured.

He said the crowbar wasn't his crowbar, it was his mate's crowbar, and they were pulling some bricks or foundations up and his mate had left the crowbar there.

Chapter Thirty-two

He was saying that this copper that was going out with Yvonne had put something at his place or on the railway line to set Greg up and make him look guilty. He also mentioned a few times that this copper and Yvonne had killed Jaidyn and disposed of the body.

I asked him about the wet money and he said that everything got wet when he was working on the car. I asked him how did it get wet inside the wallet and he said everything got wet and he changed the subject.

I asked him about the phone call when he rang or she rang from the pub and he said about Jaidyn being burnt. I said, "It's a bit nasty" and he said, "I'm a prankster".

He asked one day if they could tell where blood had come from — whether it was from the head or the leg. I said I didn't know.

He told me one day he had been working on his car and that he had found Jaidyn bleeding, but he didn't know how it happened. He said that he had taken Jaidyn into the bathroom and he was bleeding everywhere, that's when he gave him a shower. He then said, "What have I done?" and left my cell crying. The next day he came into my cell and told me that what he had said yesterday was not true and that Jaidyn had been playing with the dogs and one of them had bitten his lip.

At one stage I think he said to me that he had bandaged Jaidyn's arm up and what would happen if he said that he had done this? I don't remember what happened after this.

I'm not sure what the dates and times are when Greg told me all these things; it was just when we were in the unit together, because in prison one day is just like the other.

M told me that when it came out on the telly that Jaidyn's body had been found that Greg broke down. He was then put into unit xx with M. I don't know whether this was on a full-time basis or not. M was a prisoner, but it was like he was an overseer, someone who helped people out with their problems. M told me that while Greg was with him in unit xx that Greg told him the whole story.

M said that Greg had said that [when] he had been working on his car, he had Jaidyn with him. That something happened at the car which caused Jaidyn's arm to be broken. Greg took Jaidyn inside and bandaged his arm and gave him some sleeping tablets, which put him to sleep. Greg was worried that people would say that he had done it intentionally so his intention was to burn Jaidyn's arm and say to people that Jaidyn had burnt himself and that he had broken his arm when he had pulled him away.

After Greg had given him the tablets he had fallen asleep and he had put him on the couch. Then Greg was playing the Nintendo game and Jaidyn woke up screaming. Greg picked him up and was shaking him. I don't know if it was while he was shaking him, or he threw him, but Jaidyn's head hit the fireplace. M told me this before he had the committal hearing and before I spoke to the police, because I told the police to go and see M because he knew the full story. I didn't tell the police who came and saw me about what M told me because I thought M was going to tell them.

From being in the unit with Greg I know that Greg is a Nintendo freak. He was always trying to get a top score, especially on the car racing. If he was close to a top score and you bumped him or the table he would do his 'nana. He would go right off his head and yell and scream. He was dead-set obsessed by Nintendo.

Chapter Thirty-two

All these conversations that I had with Greg happened between when I got to the unit in February and his committal hearing. Because of what Greg had told me and the fact that he thought he was my friend, I thought that I might be able to get him to confess to murdering Jaidyn.

I told the police that were handling the xxx matter what Greg had told me and that I was prepared to help the police investigating the murder of Jaidyn. I spoke to two of the police who came to the prison. I offered to try to tape Greg confessing to killing Jaidyn. The police didn't offer anything to do this and I didn't ask for anything to do it. At that time I had no matters that had not been dealt with at the courts.

At some time after this one of the prison guards pulled me aside and told me that he knew that I had been talking to homicide [and] that there was a bug in my cell. I know this got back to Greg pretty quick.

At the time of the committal hearing an affidavit was sworn regarding the information F gave about the confession.

Mr Lovitt was again enormously suspicious of the alleged confession, claiming that all of the supposedly damning information could have been gleaned from media reports.

"It is transparent rubbish, isn't it, Mr Sheather? You just wanted to believe it," Mr Lovitt challenged homicide squad Senior Detective Russell Sheather, who had taken the statement.

"Wanted to believe what?" Sheather asked.

"These jailhouse confessions. You know they are not worth two bob, but you wanted to believe them, didn't you?"

"As a result of the investigation we attempted to corroborate those statements via the listening device and did not succeed with that."

Mr Lovitt was deeply suspicious of F's claim that swearing to the confessions was a benevolent act for which he stood to gain nothing. F, Mr Lovitt said, was due to be sentenced just days after making his original statement and the sentence he then received, given his criminal record, was surprisingly low. Low enough to suggest a deal had been struck. F was moved into a housing commission house upon release from prison — one Mr Lovitt claimed was made available to him and his de facto because of the evidence he offered.

Feeding this notion of lenient treatment in exchange for testimony, Sheather had a curious reference in his diary notes which raised the alarm of Colin Lovitt. The notes read: "Get Missus Housing Comm house, poss. Not fair dinkum." Sheather denied this was a reference to police attempting to source a housing commission house for F's wife and maintained that he had not offered any inducement to F to give evidence.

As we are unable to dwell here on F's background and involvement with police due to legal reasons, it is sufficient to state that Mr Lovitt condemned him as an "inveterate liar, a user of the system and a manipulator of police". He had been a career criminal who beat a murder rap while his co-accused went down for the same crime. Mr Lovitt claimed that it was only once there was no further opportunity to profit from offering evidence in the Jaidyn Leskie case that F changed his mind about co-operating with police and then invented the suggestion he was in fear of his life. Mr Lovitt and Enright argued heatedly over F and his evidence. Although legal reasons prohibit us exploring this evidence, it is reasonable to say Enright vehemently defended F's credibility as a witness. While acknowledging him as a criminal Enright asserted that he had always found that what F had said to him was reliable and verifiable.

★ ★ ★

Chapter Thirty-two

M's appearance in court was not dissimilar to F's: brief. If, like F, he was claiming to be fearful of his own safety as well as that of his family's, he was not saying so. In fact, he was not saying much at all.

"In the months before you left the [Melbourne Assessment Prison], did you see him [Greg Domaszewicz] regularly?" asked Jim Kennan, counsel assisting the Coroner.

"I can't recall," M replied.

"Did you have a number of conversations with him?"

"I can't recall."

"Do you recall making a statement to the police in November 1998?"

"No."

"Would you just have a look at that statement? Have you read through it?"

"Yeah."

"Does your signature appear on the bottom of every page?"

"It looks like my signature."

"The statement was written out by a Mr Cripps, is that right? A Detective Senior Constable?"

"I don't remember."

"On the last page there's a line there that says, 'I hereby acknowledge the statement is true and correct'."

"It looks like my signature ... It looks like my signature, but I didn't say it is my signature. I can't remember making the statement. I can't recall having conversations with Domaszewicz, and I can't recall having conversations with anyone else around at that period of time. Unfortunately, that's the way it is."

That statement read in part:

> When I first met Greg [in the protection units at the Melbourne Assessment Prison] I called him Moe and this name seemed to stick. When I first started talking to him

he was just talking shit, saying things like, "I still love Yvonne," and "Brett Leskie's not the father of Jaidyn."

About the third week Greg was in unit xx (he came straight into unit xx) he told me that he was having trouble looking after Jaidyn. He said that he used to call Jaidyn his friend, but sometimes he got out of hand with his screaming and couldn't handle it and didn't know how to cope. After that he didn't say much about Jaidyn, just that he still loved Yvonne and how Bilynda used to throw bones on the floor for Jaidyn to eat.

Not long after that he transferred to unit xx so I didn't get to see him that much.

After that, two or three times a day I would go across to unit xx to see F; sometimes Moe would come into F's cell and talk to us. One day we were talking, I asked Moe why his clothes were wet. He said, "My feet were wet because there was a hole in the floor and the water used to come in." I said, "But your wallet was wet," and he said that was because he was working and [sic] the car and it was raining. That's when he said that Jaidyn was under the car and the car fell off the blocks and he hurt his arm. Moe said that he pulled Jaidyn out. Moe seemed to realise what he was saying. He stopped talking, got up and left the cell.

A couple of days later I walked into F's cell and Moe was sitting there. I overheard him having a conversation with F about Blue Rock Dam. Moe said he couldn't swim but my mate's got a dinghy. He seemed to realise what he said and just shut up. That is all that was said.

The only other thing that I can remember is that on the day that the body was found or the day after I went to see him to see if [he] was OK. Moe said to me, "M, what have I done?"

On the time that we spoke to Moe in F's cell after he left, F and I would talk [about] what he had said.

Chapter Thirty-two

As the prisoners noted, Greg Domaszewicz had achieved a level of celebrity in jail. The publicity of the case imbued him with a prison cache – a modern turn on celebrity. Like Paris Hilton, famous for being famous, Greg was famous for ill-founded reasons. He began to associate with others of a similar public profile. In jail he formed a close relationship with Leslie Camilleri, one of the two men accused, and subsequently convicted, of the sadistic double murder of two schoolgirls in the New South Wales coastal town of Bega. Camilleri and Domaszewicz were close friends in prison, such that they corresponded when Greg was moved during his committal hearing.

Domaszewicz also established friendships inside with figures affiliated with Melbourne's underworld murders – men such as Steve Veniamin, the brother of Andrew "Benji" Veniamin, one of the most vicious and brutal of Melbourne's underworld crime figures. Andrew Veniamin was the right-hand man and confidante of Carl Williams, an underworld serial killer who was subsequently convicted of multiple murders. Andrew Veniamin had also committed several murders before being killed by Carlton identity Mick Gatto during the bloody crime spree in Melbourne through the early part of the new millennium.

During the Coroner's inquest, a tape recording was played of a telephone conversation between Greg and Steve Veniamin, which occurred on 7 April 2004.

"What about when you tormented that kid?" Veniamin asked.

"Yeah, that was different, it was a long time ago," Domaszewicz laughed.

"Well, why was that different?"

"No, that's just a fuckin' stupid thing to even say. I never done nothin'. It's like everything's so –"

"You dropped that car on it, mate."

"No. If – mate, I'm telling you now there's a big difference from that and fuckin' murder, that ... that ... for a start that's accidental death."

"Yeah."

"You know what I mean?"

"Yeah."

"And I'm not stupid, Steve. You know I'm not stupid."

Veniamin declined the Coroner's entreaties to contact him and make a statement about the discussion. Mr Kennan admitted the conversation between Domaszewicz and Veniamin was of very limited value, for although it contained something of an admission it also contradicted itself. It can only be speculated that perhaps it was Greg's new associations with the likes of Veniamin and his friends that might have created the fear and apprehension in the prisoners about testifying in court. In any event Mr Kennan conceded that jailhouse confessions by law were regarded with significant suspicion for the varied motives of those involved, and, in this case, the timing of the confessions during the trial, when there was a large amount of detail about the case in the media, added to that suspicion. However, he still set store by the confession of R, for compared to the other two prisoners he had at least testified to the confession during the "first inquest" and his evidence had "not been undermined by cross-examination".

Colin Lovitt had a vastly different perspective on the confessions, noting that prosecutor Bill Morgan-Payler had had the material made available to him at the trial, but had declined to include it because he saw little evidentiary value in it.

CHAPTER THIRTY-THREE

The word of a prisoner is a fraught basis upon which to establish anyone's guilt. Their rather dubious word therefore needs to be critically considered and scientifically challenged. Consequently Dr Shelley Robertson was asked to make a supplementary report for the Coroner, assessing the scientific validity of the prisoners' statements, testing their claims against the findings of the autopsy.

Jaidyn's injuries, she said, were consistent with at least one of the versions of how the prisoners said Greg told them he had killed Jaidyn. The difficulty of course is they were not specific about quite how he did it, but all mentioned the fact that the car had fallen off the jack and broken Jaidyn's arm. Robertson thought this feasible. "The mechanism described is quite consistent with the observed injury," she said.

Prisoner R had said Greg told him he slipped Jaidyn something to keep him quiet, which was hardly news-breaking given it was well known Jaidyn had been found with drugs in his body. The scientists had already concluded that benzhexol or artane – which Jaidyn was found with in his body – was not a typical pain-relieving drug as it was normally used to treat the symptoms of Parkinson's disease. It would, however, have at least temporarily sedated a small child.

Jaidyn's massive skull fracture could have been caused by any number of blunt instruments, which meant it was scientifically possible that the version presented that Greg put a pillow over Jaidyn's head and hit him with a crowbar was feasible. Of course, no pillow or pillow-case was found to further support this suggestion. Maybe Greg had lost it with Jaidyn's crying and shaken him in anger and frustration? Perhaps he got so wound up he just threw the boy and he hit his head against the fireplace? Maybe.

Forensic expert Sergeant Trevor Evans had taken skin and hair tissue from the heater, so this suggested someone had touched the burning heater at some point, but the tissue and hair had been damaged by the heat and the scientists couldn't get a satisfactory DNA profile from it. In any event, what would that have proved? If it was impossible to determine how long the hair and skin had been on the heater, how could you say it happened when Jaidyn died? It might have occurred six months earlier. What it could do is further build a picture that, yes, this was said to be how he died and, yes, we have found some forensic evidence that could be interpreted to support the claim – but it could also be interpreted as something completely different.

Shelley Robertson reckoned that if Jaidyn had died after being thrown against the heater she would have expected the skin over the fracture to be damaged, which it wasn't. The location of the fracture was also troubling for this theory. The base of the rear of the skull, which is a relatively protected area, is not normally the place of impact from a fall or accident.

Science was of little value for categorically ruling the prisoners' claims in or out. All three prisoners spoke of the car breaking Jaidyn's arm and this was scientifically plausible. They spoke of Greg slipping the boy something to quieten him and benzhexol had obviously been found in the body. And severe impact with the crowbar or the fireplace could have caused the skull fracture. But then these were the only two theories

Chapter Thirty-three

challenged by science. Equally, Dr Robertson was not asked if a baseball bat, rolling pin or falling from a hot air balloon could have caused the fracture.

The decomposition of the body meant it was no longer possible to verify if a dog had bitten Jaidyn's lip or nose as Greg had suggested at one point in his police statement, and as one of the prisoners had mentioned; however, bloody tissues were found at the scene.

The body's decomposition was also a point of contention. How long had Jaidyn been in the water? It was a key issue at trial, for obviously if the boy had only been there three or four months when he was found, then someone else must have been involved and Greg would not have been the one to dispose of the body. Indeed, it opened up the possibility the boy had been alive for longer than the day he disappeared. But the body, the scientists said, looked as one might expect a dead body to look had it been in cold water for six months.

"The level of decomposition I observed in the child was certainly consistent with six months, but it could have been more or it could have been less," Shelley Robertson said somewhat vaguely. How much longer or shorter he had been dead she did not say. Likewise the broken arm occurred anywhere from 24 to 48 hours before death – but could have been as recent as half an hour, she reckoned. And, despite what the movies might have told you, hair does not grow post-mortem.

Feeding this theory that Jaidyn might have been alive for some time after he disappeared was the contention that when his body was found, his hair was longer than it should have been had he died immediately the day he went missing. Bilynda and Katie were troubled by the length of Jaidyn's hair in forensic photos but Lori Leskie, Jaidyn's aunt, who as a hairdresser had cut Jaidyn's hair six weeks or so before he died, told the Coroner the hair in the photos appeared to be about the appropriate length for six weeks' growth after a toddlers' haircut.

The Jaidyn Leskie Murder

Professor David Ranson, pathologist and Deputy Director of the Victorian Institute of Forensic Medicine, compiled a report for the Coroner based on autopsy photographs, x-rays, Dr Robertson's reports, the statements of prisoners F, M and R, the trial transcripts of the evidence of Dr Robertson and Dr Byron Collins, photographs provided by the homicide squad and bloodstained tissues uncovered during the investigation. In short, everything possibly available to assess the forensic pathology of the case. And he agreed with Dr Robertson – Jaidyn probably died of a head injury.

This, to the layman, appeared something like: the side that kicked the most goals won the football match. But it is not always the case. Yes, Jaidyn had a skull fracture sufficient to cause death, but had something else done the trick before the skull fracture? Drugs, for instance? Or a heart attack from the pain and shock of the broken arm? Had the broken arm happened before or after death? Or even months before death? Had Jaidyn died and the head injury occurred in a fit of frustration and rage? Or when the boy was being disposed of? Science, at the very least, was able to point to the obvious.

"It is really a question of saying: what facts have you got?" said Professor Ranson. "What interpretation do those facts lead to? The interpretation of the facts as I have seen them is that the most probable thing would be the head injury, but because of the decomposition you can't unequivocally state that that was so. It is just that the majority of the factual evidence that I see suggests that."

Pathologist Dr Richard Collins witnessed the post-mortem and reviewed the autopsy findings after the prisoners' statements at the request of Greg Domaszewicz's legal team. He doubted the arm could be fractured in the way it was if it was lying flat on the ground when the car landed on it. He also agreed it was reasonable to presume the skull fracture and brain haemorrhage killed Jaidyn, but felt that the decomposition of the body meant

Chapter Thirty-three

it was impossible to rule out other conditions – such as heart or lung disease, epilepsy or asthma.

"Are you saying to me that you couldn't exclude a natural cause process as the cause of death?" Coroner Graeme Johnstone asked.

"I'm saying on clinical grounds one may be able to, but on the pathological grounds one can't. I qualify that by the fact that there is this considerable degree of decomposition."

That is reasonable from a scientific point of view. However, one might also think that given the child was found with his head caved in, with a badly broken arm crudely bandaged, and tied up in a sleeping bag weighed down with a crowbar in a lake, it is equally fair to presume the child had not died suddenly of natural causes.

The broken arm was perplexing to the scientists. Firstly there was the sort of fracture and then the sort of natural repair of the arm and what that meant for the timing of the injury. Radiologist Dr Andrew McLaughlan examined post-mortem x-rays. At Greg's trial Dr McLaughlan said he found evidence of a periosteal reaction – when new bone is being formed to naturally repair a break – in one of the fractures of the arm, which would suggest Jaidyn might have been alive for some time after the injury. However, he said it was also possible that a "post-mortem artefact", or a natural process of decomposing after death, could create a similar appearance. At the trial Dr McLaughlan figured the bone reactions had most likely occurred after death. Now he wasn't so sure.

"The more that I've thought about it and have done some searching on the Web [internet], I suspect that it's probably a periosteal reaction, but I cannot be certain," he said.

The fact the arm had been bandaged added to his view that it was less likely to be caused post-mortem. He also found it hard to explain why one bone in the arm would have a periosteal reaction and not the other. It either indicated that the fractures happened at different times or one bone was healing faster than the other. The importance here attached to how long before death his arm was broken. This amount of natural bone repair would take four to six days, Dr McLaughlan felt, which suggests Jaidyn either suffered the injury in the week before he disappeared — and none of his family or friends have ever claimed this — or he was alive for several days after he went missing. Or the doctor's first inclination was right and what he saw was the reaction of the body after Jaidyn died and was not a sign of the bone healing.

Orthopaedic surgeon Dr David Bainbridge said the unusual manner of the break being to both bones in the forearm meant it was extremely unlikely to have come from a fall, a blow, or from being crushed beneath a car. It looked more like someone had grabbed Jaidyn and snapped his arm, like a twig, between their two hands. The healing broken rib, which had been missed earlier by pathologists, could have occurred up to two weeks before Jaidyn died, Dr McLaughlan said.

"It's your clear view — 90 per cent or more likelihood," asked Colin Lovitt, "that the child was alive for several days, if not longer, before — or the child was alive after sustaining the injuries to the arm and the rib, is that right?"

"Certainly the rib and probably the forearm, yes," Dr McLaughlan said, but when pressed further by the Coroner he could not be conclusive about any scenario.

Benzhexol — commonly sold by the name Artane — had been used in previous decades to treat the symptoms of Parkinson's disease and for people suffering the side effects of anti-psychotic medications. However, it had almost disappeared from use by 1997 as better drugs with fewer side effects had arrived on the market. Recreational drug users, particularly in the Moe area, had misused it for years as it was relatively cheap and it caused euphoria and hallucinations among its side effects.

Chapter Thirty-three

The doctors could not rule out the drug as the cause of death but considered it unlikely. It would probably have knocked the boy out, but not killed him.

The Coroner ruled: "It was during Mr Domaszewicz's period of caring for Jaidyn that he died. The cause of death is most probably from head injuries. Precisely how he died remains a matter of contention and conjecture – whether the circumstances leading to the death occurred by accident, by omission or otherwise. Precisely how he suffered the injuries to the arm also remains largely a matter of conjecture, other than the fact that it occurred shortly prior to death."

CHAPTER THIRTY-FOUR

How Jaidyn was killed was one thing, how he ended up in Blue Rock Dam was another. Was it feasible that one person could dispose of his body in this manner? Could they tie him up in a sleeping bag, lash the bag to a crowbar and launch it into the dam alone? Could one person manage to hurl the whole bundle as far out into the dam as the crowbar was found? This, putting aside the accusation that Greg Domaszewicz did so in the darkness of a cold winter's night.

The inquest quickly discounted the suggestion the body had been disposed of using a boat. Although Domaszewicz had been part-owner of a little aluminium boat, he had sold his share days earlier and it was in Loch Sport at the time. The idea of the use of a boat also overlooks the obvious argument that if the person who disposed of the body used a boat, why would they drop the bundle with the crowbar in the water just metres from the dam wall? If they had gone to the trouble of launching a boat, surely they would motor out to the deepest part of the dam where recovery would be less likely.

Senior Constable Ian Veitch of the Search and Rescue Squad re-enacted for the Coroner how a person acting alone might have thrown the weighed-down body into the lake. His attempt was in daylight, in dry conditions, and with the water level slightly different to that on the night Jaidyn went missing. He

Chapter Thirty-four

used two hams of about the same combined weight as the baby's body – 18 kilograms – and tied them together in the sleeping bag with roughly the same contents as were found in the sleeping bag when it was fished from the dam; then he lashed the lot to a crowbar.

When he threw the bar and bag from the roadway it did not go far out into the water at all. The further down the sloped wall of the dam towards the water he moved, the further out he was obviously able to throw the bundle. When Jaidyn's body was recovered from the dam, police divers found the crowbar and the bag of clothes and other items submerged 12.7 metres down the sloping dam wall. In order to throw the re-enactment bundle that far out, Senior Constable Veitch needed to wade into the water up to his chest and armpits. However, the water level on the day of the re-enactment was almost a metre higher than the day Jaidyn went missing and the day his body was found. The lower water level would have meant the killer would not have had to walk as far out into the water to throw the bar and bag for it to reach the 12.7 metre mark. Presumably he still needed to get wet but perhaps only to his waist. This scientific re-enactment also presupposed a similar level of strength from the policeman as the person disposing of the body. The impact of adrenalin in a person who was nervously trying to rid themselves of the body was another complicating factor.

Colin Lovitt argued that despite the urban myth that when Greg had been stopped by police on the night Jaidyn disappeared that he was sopping wet, this was untrue, and "There is no evidence in the history of this case – leaving aside false rumours and erroneous reportage – there is no evidence whatsoever that Domaszewicz was seen with any moisture on him at all" on the night Jaidyn disappeared.

Sergeant Trevor Evans was recalled to clarify the dampness of Domaszewicz's wallet, which was wet when it was recovered in the foot well of his car by crime scene examiners. He said the

The Jaidyn Leskie Murder

wallet was wet enough to have been in Greg's pocket if he waded into Blue Rock Dam. The wallet had been found in the car along with a wet jacket, while the car's carpets were also wet. Evans said when police searched Greg's house the first time he made a mental note of wet washing in the laundry but believing this unremarkable had not written down the observation.

"At the time we went there we didn't know what was going on. We found unusual things there, blood, a pig's head. I didn't find it unusual to find wet washing in the laundry," he said.

Mr Lovitt again argued that the money found under Greg's bed wasn't in fact wet and Evans had exaggerated. Evans said it was so wet the wallet either had to have been immersed in water or the money had to have been taken out and put in a pocket when someone went in water. It is also curious to think if the notes were not laid out to dry beneath the mattress, why would someone separate the notes under the bed and not just put a bundle there?

Senior Constable Veitch said the surface of the sloped dam wall was rough with a pebble mix concrete render offering some grip. However, his rubber wet-suit and wet-suit booties also meant that he was more buoyant in the water as he waded out and this actually made walking more difficult than had he been in street clothes and runners.

Mr Lovitt contended, as he did at the trial, that the gate to the road the police were using to access the dam wall was locked on the night Jaidyn disappeared. Police did not know if the gate was open or closed but Senior Constable Veitch said it was easy to gain access by foot if the gate was locked, then walk about 400 metres to the dam. Mr Lovitt also told the inquest that evidence from the Ford motor company was that a crowbar would not fit in the back of Greg's model of Ford. It would fit in the back passenger section of the car, but not the boot.

Chapter Thirty-four

Neither the police nor the defence held the proverbial smoking gun. But they did have a crowbar. For the prosecution it was the item that physically connected Jaidyn's disappearance to Greg's house. Which was not to say it meant Greg had committed the murder, but it did link Jaidyn's disappearance to Greg's house on that day. The crowbar, which was owned by Paul "Lizard" Lietzau, had been at Greg's house prior to Jaidyn going missing and, he reckoned, not afterwards. So when it was found in Blue Rock Dam having been used to weigh Jaidyn's body down, it proved one thing – if the crowbar was with Jaidyn when he was found, and had also not been seen the whole time he was missing, it suggested both were thrown in the dam the same day: 15 June 1997.

At the trial the defence seized on a slightly blurry forensic photograph of Greg's backyard to contend that the crowbar was in fact still in the yard after Jaidyn disappeared. A Moe resident Sue Haslam even gave evidence at the inquest stating that weeks after Jaidyn disappeared she saw police walking from Greg's house carrying the crowbar. If the defence could prove the crowbar was in the yard after the alarm had been raised of Jaidyn's disappearance then it must surely put Greg in the clear. No-one would dispute that Greg was under close watch by police, friends, the media, indeed the entire state, in the weeks after Jaidyn disappeared, so his opportunities for disposing of a body after this time would be almost nil.

One of the difficulties in all of this is that crowbars are rarely distinctive or memorable. Any one normally looks like any other so the process of conclusively identifying one from another is problematic.

Photographic experts were once more called to attempt to establish whether the crowbar depicted in the photo was the one fished from the dam. They were not in accord on the evidence in the picture – did the crowbar in the photo protrude half a millimetre above the fence, as one expert contended, or was it more than a foot? Could Pythagoras' theorum deduce the length of the crowbar as 1.63 metres or 1.81 metres? They could not agree. In fact, there was uncertainty as to whether the item in the photograph was even a crowbar. Maybe it was a shovel?

In making his conclusion on the crowbar, the Coroner relied upon this comment from Jim Kennan:

"When taken as a whole, the evidence does not establish whether the object shown in the crime scene photograph was a shovel or a crowbar. It does no more than establish that the crowbar recovered from the Blue Rock Dam may have been the same crowbar that Mr Lietzau left at Mr Domaszewicz's house the day before the deceased disappeared."

Which is to say this: Lizard left a crowbar at Greg's house and when he wanted it back Greg gave two versions of where it might be and it was in neither place. Then a crowbar Lizard instantly thought was his turned up fished from the dam along with Jaidyn. He inspected the crowbar and still reckoned it was his.

As for the crime scene photograph, experts could not agree about whether it was a shovel or a crowbar. Lizard, however, needed no experts to tell him what he already knew – it was his crowbar.

CHAPTER THIRTY-FIVE

Graeme Johnstone woke on the morning of Friday 5 December to learn he had lost control of his own inquest. And worse, he was being misled as part of a major cover-up. At least that was the claim.

When he arrived at court for the ninth day of hearings Mr Johnstone was told world DNA expert Professor Barry Boettcher had claimed in the *Herald Sun* and on morning talkback radio that "serious forces" were trying to prevent him giving evidence at the inquest. He said there were attempts to pervert the course of justice and the Coroner had lost control of the inquest, which was being run by counsel assisting and not the Coroner. It was big news for the paper and the radio stations. It was also news to Mr Johnstone.

Professor Boettcher declared he had become aware of contamination of DNA samples at the state's forensic science laboratory and was frustrated at attempts being made to stop him giving evidence and blowing the whistle on his discovery. The Coroner was unimpressed. A quietly spoken man, he was not about to be misheard or misunderstood when he made a statement at the start of the hearings that day.

"I should say quite clearly, I want to make it clear to everyone concerned, from the outset of this inquiry when the issue of potential for contamination was raised, this matter has been one of the major issues for this investigation. Clearly, the issue of contamination has been at the forefront, one of the major issues, for this particular inquest."

There followed days of tedious, excruciating exploration of the minutiae of scientific testing methods and laboratory procedures.

The issue of the female DNA was yet another turn in the tangled mess that was the saga of the disappearance, murder and investigation of Jaidyn Leskie. Since anonymous DNA had been found on the bib that was with Jaidyn when he was found, it was one of the more confounding and compelling elements of the mystery of what happened to the boy. For some it was the piece of evidence that proved the involvement of others. It allowed fingers to be pointed wildly at women throughout the breadth of the Latrobe Valley. Requests were made to test a range of possible suspects identified by players in the drama. All were tested. All were discounted.

Then, in January 2003, a match was unexpectedly made. Scientists testing the samples of DNA ran the profile through the forensic science data base. The computer shot back the details of a 22-year-old rape victim from Melbourne's west. This was a crucial breakthrough, but it still only answered one element of the puzzle. Now they knew whose DNA was on the bib. What they didn't know was how it got there, or when.

Detectives went immediately to the woman's house and quizzed her. Did she know Jaidyn? Did she know Greg? Bilynda? Brett? Anyone in the Latrobe Valley? Had she ever been to the Valley? Where was she in June and July of 1997? Could anyone vouch for her whereabouts? These questions demanded answers and they were given. The woman didn't know Jaidyn, Bilynda, Brett, Greg, indeed anyone from the Latrobe Valley. In fact, she could scarcely recall ever visiting the area. She knew nothing of the boy's disappearance nor how her DNA had wound up on his bib. It was rapidly apparent something was not

CHAPTER THIRTY-FIVE

right, though it could hardly have come as a surprise to anyone that this case should take an unusual turn.

There were several possibilities for how the woman's DNA had come to be on the bib. Firstly, that it came directly from the woman, known for legal reasons only as P. This was ruled out.

Secondly, that DNA from the samples from P's rape case had become contaminated with Jaidyn's while all items were being tested at the science centre. The condom used in the rape and the clothes P had been wearing at the time of the rape were being tested at the McLeod Forensic Science Centre around the same time as items belonging to Jaidyn. This seemed a likely option.

Thirdly, there was a chance an "adventitious match" had been made between the DNA profile of P and an unknown person whose DNA profile appeared on the bib and the track pants. That is, that P had the same DNA as another unknown female whose DNA was on the bib and pants. This option was initially considered technically possible, though not probable.

There was the possibility the declaration of a match was not correct and that what appeared at first a match between the DNA profile of P and the DNA profile on the bib and pants was incorrect. DNA is tested by means of establishing matches in a range of loci in each of the samples. Some testing regimes test more loci than others. In some parts of the world the testing is of five or seven loci in order for it to be considered a match, while in other countries nine loci are tested. A DNA match in this case was made after five loci were tested. The bib was then tested to seven, 10 and later to 12 loci and matches were still made. The odds of an adventitious match after a test to 10 loci was put at one in 171 billion. It was ruled out.

Regardless, scientists remained insistent that laboratory processes were such that it was inconceivable that items could be even accidentally contaminated. A battery of experts was called, world leaders in their fields. Much time was spent on the issue during the inquest, not only because of the ramifications for the murder of Jaidyn but for the consequences for other trials involving DNA testing in Victoria.

The coincidence of timing of the testing of items from P's rape case and Jaidyn's bib and track pants at the Forensic Science Centre in January and February 1998, and the fact they were both analysed by the same scientist, was a compelling argument for accidental contamination.

Professor William Thompson, an American lawyer and professor in the Department of Criminology, Law & Society at the University of California, who was a member of OJ Simpson's legal defence team in the famous murder trial, was one who sided with accidental contamination of the samples in the lab. Another American, Professor Dan Krane from Ohio, was a leading DNA expert who had given evidence in more than 45 criminal cases around the world. He noted the DNA sample on the bib and track pants had degraded at a similar rate to the DNA from the condom. The likelihood of them both doing so at the same rate was extremely remote. It was also curious to him that none of Jaidyn's own DNA was found on his bib, yet P's DNA was there, which suggested to him that the DNA came to be on the bib and pants after being recovered from the dam.

Jim Kennan hadn't planned on calling Barry Boettcher. But after the professor's stunning accusations he was left with no choice. To deny Professor Boettcher's claims, no matter how easily refutable or absurd, would only fuel his conspiracy theories. Professor Boettcher had claimed evidence was being deliberately withheld from the Coroner by senior public servants. He said the most likely source of contamination was a blood sample P had given in 1997, which was being kept from him and the Coroner. As sensational as the claim was, the professor was spectacularly wrong: P never gave a blood sample in 1997; rather, the accused rapist had.

Chapter Thirty-five

The retired professor got his day in court, even if he soon wished he had not. The former biologist, who had worked in DNA since the early 1960s though never as a forensic scientist, said he had been approached to give evidence by Cecilia O'Brien, the first lawyer for Bilynda Williams. He was provided with information by Ms O'Brien and it was on the basis of this information that he assumed P had given a blood sample in 1997. She, and consequently he, was wrong. No blood sample was taken from P until 1999. Coroner's Office documents had blood samples labelled WBSA and WBSC. So, the professor wondered, where was WBSB? If there was a WBSA and WBSC, logically there must surely be a WBSB.

This assumption was the basis for him making the extravagant claims of cover-ups and conspiracies. Unfortunately for Professor Boettcher, while there was logic to his assumption, it was wrong. The samples were not marked alphabetically but marked to refer to the person providing the samples. Thus, the A in WBSA stood for Accused and the C in WBSC stood for Complainant. As Professor Boettcher conceded at the inquest, there never was and never would be a sample marked WBSB being kept from anyone.

"I was giving consideration to the situation at home on Sunday," said Professor Boettcher, "and I suddenly – it suddenly dawned on me, hey, what happens if that blood sample was not from the rape victim, but somebody else associated with the case? And I basically said to my wife then, 'Uh oh, I might have made a serious error'." Indeed he had.

"So that suggestion ... falls to the ground?" Mr Kennan offered.

"That falls to the ground, yes," Professor Boettcher admitted.

However, the professor wasn't completely retreating from all of his wilder theories. While he may have been mistaken about the cover-up, he didn't resile from the accusation the bib and track pants could have been deliberately contaminated with P's

DNA. No-one else realistically suggested that if contamination had occurred, someone had done so deliberately.

"The possibility of deliberate contamination is something that I have said on the basis of the degree of the staining that we should not discard," he said. He also stood by his claim "powerful forces" were trying to stop him giving evidence. (Though many in court might have wished there were forces that could have successfully intervened.)

Counsel representing the Victorian Forensic Science Centre, Mr Tovey, condemned the professor in a blistering attack.

"Professor Boettcher should be ashamed of himself. This is not just some sloppy scientific work. This is reckless. This is defamatory. It is done in the face of the evidence, which he knows to exist. It is done without him taking the trouble to check at all," he said.

Putting Professor Boettcher's claims aside, it seemed clear from the expert evidence that the previously anonymous DNA had got on the bib accidentally during the testing at the science centre. Which meant the riddle of Jaidyn's murder was not likely to be advanced by the presence of female DNA on his bib.

To Colin Lovitt, the entire issue was academic. It was quickly established that it had little relevance to Jaidyn's case and served only as a distraction. And he was right.

"It is plainly obvious to us what's happened," said Colin Lovitt. "What then results from that is another matter ... I totally agree with Your Worship that that whole issue operates as a complete distraction."

In his finding Graeme Johnstone was similarly succinct. "The match to the bib occurred as a result of *contamination* in the laboratory and was not an *adventitious match*," he concluded.

CHAPTER THIRTY-SIX

For 20 days of hearings the issue hung over the inquest. After his initial hairy-chested enthusiasm for testifying it began to appear increasingly unlikely that Greg Domaszewicz would ever take the stand. Believing the inquest had been designed for the sole purpose of incriminating his client, Colin Lovitt was determined that Domaszewicz should not participate.

"It is becoming more and more apparent to everybody connected with this case that this exercise is nothing more than an exercise in chasing my client around a courtroom with a few gratuitous slurs on Mrs Williams to boot," he said. "It is an exercise where people dissatisfied with an acquittal have decided to have another go, as it were, and the recalling of this witness is a perfect example of a rehashing of old material trying to find an excuse to simply lay this all out in front of the media."

It was day 20 of the inquest and for the first time Mr Lovitt hinted that Greg would be unlikely to take the stand. Three summonses to appear to give evidence had been issued but lapsed through no fault of Domaszewicz, for the dates simply passed before the court was ready to hear from him. Although technically required to by law – if subpoenaed by the Coroner, Domaszewicz would be compelled to give evidence – Mr Lovitt now opened up two avenues for him to avoid the box. First, he flagged a challenge in the Supreme Court to the Coroner's jurisdiction and authority to stage such an inquest, and second, he suggested that Greg might not be well enough to give evidence.

"My client is mentally not exactly well at the moment. He has been the battering ram of certain media organisations for a long time and it has taken its toll on him, and if indeed he was forced to give evidence we would be submitting that that would have to happen with him at another venue; in other words, by video..." he said.

The question of whether Domaszewicz would ultimately testify remained unanswered for the time being as the case went on. It was the elephant in the corner of the court that no-one spoke about. With each passing day the chances of him appearing to give evidence seemed more remote. Outside court Bilynda Williams and her supporters handed out fliers campaigning for 'Justice for Jaidyn', calling for Domaszewicz to testify. Indeed, this very sentiment was at the heart of the legal challenge mounted by Domaszewicz in the Victorian Supreme Court. There it was contended the inquest was a show trial contrived to embarrass and incriminate him. It was argued the State Coroner lacked the jurisdiction to void the first coronial finding and launch the hearings. Domaszewicz's lawyers argued for a permanent stay of the inquest. They had a win and a loss, which ultimately created a speed hump in the process but little more. The Supreme Court agreed that the Coroner had exceeded his powers in voiding the initial finding, but only in so much as he had applied the wrong section of the Coroners Act. The Supreme Court ordered the Coroner to terminate the first inquest but rejected the application for a permanent stay. The Coroner followed the ruling and terminated the first inquest, then began a new inquest under the correct section of the Coroners Act and admitted into evidence all testimony heard in the first inquest.

Chapter Thirty-six

The Supreme Court, in rejecting his application for a permanent stay of the inquest, specifically stated that it was open to Domaszewicz to return to the Supreme Court if he was compelled by the Coroner to give evidence. Colin Lovitt advised the court that were the Coroner to follow this path and subpoena his client, he would not hesitate to return to the Supreme Court to challenge the order. If left to Domaszewicz the question of whether he would testify was an emphatic and unreserved "No". As Mr Lovitt opined, if the proceedings were designed to implicate Domaszewicz and little more, why would his client possibly agree to co-operate? The Coroner had offered Domaszewicz the option of submitting a written statement. He refused. After three weeks of sitting days, and years of anticipation and waiting, the issue could be deferred no more. Jim Kennan as counsel assisting began to equivocate on whether he believed it was truly necessary for Domaszewicz to testify. After all, the lengthy police statement would be tendered so it was not as if nothing would be heard from the witness; and if he were a hostile witness what further information would be likely to be elicited from him? Was it really worth the hassle? Given Colin Lovitt had already indicated the subpoena to testify would be challenged on legal and medical grounds in the Supreme Court, Kennan argued the delay and the consequent cost was simply not worth it. Michael Rafter, acting this day for Domaszewicz, wholeheartedly agreed.

The Coroner wondered if anyone else had any thoughts on the matter. From the recess of the court the small voice of Jaidyn's grandmother Elizabeth Leskie interjected. She agreed with Kennan. It would be a waste of time, so just get on with the rest of the inquest. It was a sign of resignation perhaps that the chief point the families had long championed was conceded – they would not get to cross-examine Greg Domaszewicz, so the better to quickly wrap up this inquest and get on with life.

"I feel that we've spent such a lot of time and effort and money has been taken up with this," said Elizabeth Leskie, "and I think we're continuing to try and get Greg to answer some questions and some of our questions and what we would really like to hear from him, you know, give his viewpoint, and he's never answered questions in court on anything that happened that night. Sure, he has spoken to the police, but I think it's just going to be a continuation of delaying and we're not going to get anywhere by proceeding to try and force him to be in court. I know Brett and Bilynda – especially Bilynda – would desire that, but I don't see that it will get us anywhere to do that."

The Coroner couldn't agree. The inquest had started with the intention of hearing from Domaszewicz. "He is the one who can shed light, or possibly shed light, on the events that occurred to young Jaidyn Leskie. This is a very difficult decision, and I think that on balance I have to decide to issue a subpoena, and I am going to do so because I don't believe the proceedings will be seen to be at an end until I have taken all steps in my power to require Mr Domaszewicz to give evidence," he said.

Whether Greg would be fit to honour the subpoena was another matter. Days later Mr Lovitt arrived in court with two doctors' certificates – the first from his GP, the second from a psychologist – which both suggested Greg had suffered panic attacks, severe anxiety and post-traumatic stress and was therefore unfit to testify. The deterioration in his medical condition had overtaken the previous stated intention to challenge the subpoena in the Supreme Court. Greg had been on anti-depressant and anti-anxiety medication and had been prone to vomiting and diarrhoea.

"It may well be that any consideration of having to attend court would be so dysfunctional for Mr Domaszewicz that he would exhibit serious medical difficulties to the point that he could not go out in any case," psychologist Ian Joblin said. Indeed, when he had had to attend Mr Lovitt's city chambers

Chapter Thirty-six

Greg would dress up in a disguise to avoid being identified. His medical condition was such that his answers could not be relied upon, Joblin said, contending that he was more inclined to get the ordeal over with and ease his stress level than to necessarily be troubled to provide the correct answer. Expedience, not truth was his motivation, said Joblin. Mr Lovitt took up the point, saying that the ongoing media coverage, which created a general feeling that his client had got away with murder, had made Greg's condition even worse.

The Coroner, reluctantly, agreed.

"I'm not proposing to proceed and hear from him if it's likely to affect his mental health and, secondly, I have evidence to suggest that the reliability of the evidence would be in question. But I think, more importantly, it is important for all to recognise that the process should not proceed to completion in a way that detrimentally affects a person's mental health," he said. With that it was put to rest: Greg would not testify.

Without his evidence little more needed to be said. The inquest was rapidly completed.

CHAPTER THIRTY-SEVEN

When the finding arrived, it came by post. On 4 October 2006, after nine years, a trial and three inquests, the State finally decided how the official public record should forever account for Jaidyn Raymond Leskie's death. Following the years of drama and public spectacle it was a sober moment, oddly without fuss. Just a simple letter. Or rather just a simple document that ran to 100 pages. It was the case distilled to its bare facts, with emotion and personalities removed.

It made the impact of what Graeme Johnstone had to say no less powerful: Greg Domaszewicz threw Jaidyn into Blue Rock Dam. He might have killed him, but the Coroner could not be sufficiently certain to say so. But he did dispose of the body. Which of course begged the question: why would Greg dispose of the body if he had not killed Jaidyn?

The Coroner could not be certain, based on the evidence, that Greg had killed Jaidyn, but that did not mean he was not responsible. As the person charged with caring for Jaidyn that day the Coroner said Domaszewicz consequently had to be considered responsible for Jaidyn's death. It happened, as he said, on Greg's watch. Putting aside sundry lesser issues, this was the nub: Greg was looking after Jaidyn and while he was doing so someone killed him. Greg cannot satisfactorily explain his movements and behaviour that day.

Chapter Thirty-seven

The Coroner reckoned the evidence mightn't have allowed him to conclusively determine that Greg killed Jaidyn but it was sufficiently clear to say that, at the very minimum, for whatever panicked reason, Domaszewicz threw Jaidyn in the lake.

Jim Kennan's submission to the Coroner had been clear: Domaszewicz had killed Jaidyn and disposed of his body. He essentially held the line of the Director of Public Prosecutions in believing the police had got it right in charging Domaszewicz with the crime and taking him to trial based on all the evidence before them.

Greg was not the only person condemned for an abrogation of responsibility to Jaidyn. Bilynda, too, as awful as it might be for her to have heard, could not escape blame. She had failed the first basic rule of parenting – caring for your child and putting their concerns first and foremost.

"The role of the parent, in this case Ms Williams, is to act protectively towards the child," the Coroner said. "By leaving Jaidyn in the care of Mr Domaszewicz, who had a previous history of at least one incident of inappropriate care, she did not act protectively towards her son. Also in the late afternoon of 14 June, Ms Williams was concerned to find out where her son was. She could not get a lift to Mr Domaszewicz's house and, in the evening, she unsuccessfully attempted to telephone him on a number of occasions. When she could not connect with Mr Domaszewicz on the telephone, rather than beginning by going to Narracan Drive in an attempt to find her son, she went to a party and from there to a drinking session at the local hotel. Thus, Ms Williams did not act responsibly towards her son, a fact she appears now to have acknowledged."

This was a carefully considered finding, which navigated a path through possible Supreme Court challenges. During the earlier challenge in the Supreme Court to the Coroner's jurisdiction to hold an inquest, the Supreme Court had ruled that while it was open to the Coroner to hold a new inquest under the properly applied section of the Act, the Coroner should make any finding available to affected parties prior to its public release. Those parties would then be given time to consider the finding and challenge it in the Supreme Court if they believed they had grounds.

The logic of this was that it would be so much harder to close the gate after the horse had bolted. If the court was to ultimately find in favour of any appeal against the Coroner's finding, then the better to prevent the publication of that finding in the first place. In the event, no-one appealed so it was publicly released. The finding, as it was, did not trample over the jury's verdict. It did not ridicule the court system with a finding in direct contradiction of the criminal trial. The Coroner incriminated Greg in disposing of Jaidyn's body and spoke further of his broad responsibility for what happened to the boy the day he disappeared, but he did not defy the jury verdict and say that Greg killed Jaidyn.

The Coroner, in his finding, combed over all relevant issues, making comment or a ruling where deemed appropriate. Interestingly, compared to a criminal verdict that concisely announces one way or another only on the accused's guilt, the Coroner's findings are detailed, picking over each issue to make a judgment explaining the reasoning behind his thinking. He outlined the known, uncontested facts of the day leading up to Jaidyn's disappearance, and dwelt on the telephone calls that late afternoon and evening and of Greg's movements in driving to Ryans Hotel. He considered also the fabricated stories Greg gave Bilynda, which appeared to be designed to prepare the ground for the discovery that Jaidyn was missing.

"Over the telephone and after picking up Ms Williams from the hotel, Mr Domaszewicz gave Ms Williams a number

Chapter Thirty-seven

of explanations about how the child was injured and had been taken to the hospital. The last of these explanations given to Ms Williams was in the drive from the hotel to the Narracan Drive house. This final explanation was that Jaidyn was injured and in the hospital. All these explanations were false. They are, however, explanations that could reasonably be construed as having been designed to set the scene for a child that is missing. At this stage, Mr Domaszewicz was not aware of the 'pig's head' incident as it had occurred while he was away for about an hour picking up Ms Williams from the hotel," the Coroner said.

If Greg were to be believed, that he left Jaidyn in the house when he went to collect Bilynda, then his behaviour upon his return, when he discovered the windows of his house smashed and Jaidyn missing, did not tally with regular behaviour. The Coroner touched on the police interview with Domaszewicz and his inability to properly explain his movements in the two-hour period between dropping Bilynda at her house and returning to raise the alarm of Jaidyn's disappearance.

"There are puzzling aspects of Mr Domaszewicz's reactions on his return to his house with Ms Williams on 15 June and later that morning. After discovering the damage to the house (and the pig's head) he did not mention to Ms Williams that Jaidyn was missing. His explanation was (in part) that he did not want to alarm Ms Williams by telling her that the child was missing. Yet, a little earlier, he had been prepared to alarm her by telling her that her son was injured and in hospital. It is noted that at the hotel Ms Williams' concerns about Mr Domaszewicz's comments over the telephone were allayed by her sister (who had also spoken to Mr Domaszewicz over the telephone) when she was advised that he was joking," the Coroner said.

"It is noted that, in his record of interview, Mr Domaszewicz indicated that he noticed Jaidyn was missing when they went inside the house. According to Mr Domaszewicz, Jaidyn was left on the couch when he left for the hotel. He also noted that it was not possible that the child had injured himself while he was away. Also, although Mr Domaszewicz considered Ms Penfold was possibly involved and he had driven past her house (and briefly telephoned her), he only looked through the windows of the house. He did not try to raise her in order to try and find out where Jaidyn was. When he was in his car in the early hours of the morning (between leaving Ms Williams at her residence and allegedly visiting Ms Penfold's house), ostensibly looking for Jaidyn, he did not comment to police who intercepted him that he was looking for a missing child."

Further, the Coroner considered the discovery of Domaszewicz's wallet, the money beneath his mattress, the carpets on the floor of the car and a jacket on the back seat all being wet, and Greg being unable to satisfactorily explain why, as "telling".

"Mr Domaszewicz had both the time and opportunity to dispose of Jaidyn's body between when he left Ms Williams at her house and when he took her to the police in the early hours of the morning of 15 June. Alternatively, there may have been a window of opportunity before Ms Williams was collected from the hotel."

It was one of the factors that drew the Coroner to the conclusion of Greg's involvement in disposing of Jaidyn.

"It was during Mr Domaszewicz's period of caring for Jaidyn that he died. The cause of death is most probably from head injuries. Precisely how he died remains a matter of contention and conjecture – whether the circumstances leading to the death occurred by accident, by omission or otherwise. Precisely how he suffered the injuries to the arm also remains largely a matter of conjecture, other than the fact that it occurred shortly prior to death," the Coroner's key ruling stated.

Chapter Thirty-seven

"However, as a helpless 14-month-old infant, requiring total support, care and protection by an adult, ultimately it was Mr Domaszewicz who failed to provide that adequate and very necessary level of protective supervision, care and support to look after the infant – otherwise he would not have received the injuries from which he died. Whatever happened to result in the injuries that were occasioned to Jaidyn occurred on Mr Domaszewicz's temporary watch, thus he has contributed to the death.

"No satisfactory alternative explanation of the circumstances has been given by Mr Domaszewicz.

"After Jaidyn's death Mr Domaszewicz disposed of his body in nearby Blue Rock Dam. Clearly, he had the opportunity and time to do so. The indicators that lead to this conclusion and comfortable satisfaction are:

(a) The last known person to see Jaidyn alive was Mr Domaszewicz;

(b) After the incident or incidents that eventually resulted in Jaidyn's death, Mr Domaszewicz had time to dispose of the body in the dam either before collecting Ms Williams from the hotel or in the early hours of the morning of 15 June or after leaving her at her home and before they both went to the police to report that the child was missing;

(c) Mr Domaszewicz gave false explanations to Ms Williams about Jaidyn's whereabouts and state of health both before and after she was picked up by him from the hotel;

(d) Ms Williams was not shown Jaidyn when she returned to Mr Domaszewicz's house from the hotel (when Mr Domaszewicz says that he realised the child was missing); and

(e) Mr Domaszewicz's wallet and money were wet (consistent with having entered the water in order to dispose of the body).

"The fact that a decision has been made that Mr Domaszewicz disposed of Jaidyn's body does not enable any conclusion to be reached about precisely how the child died — whether by accident or otherwise."

CHAPTER THIRTY-EIGHT

So that was it. Greg threw Jaidyn's body in the dam, and he was at least in part responsible for his death. But the courts had fallen short of saying he had also killed him. Quite how or why he would dispose of the body but not be involved in the death was a conundrum.

Greg was silent on his thoughts of the Coroner's finding. He did not challenge it in the Supreme Court prior to final publication, nor comment on it once it was released. He had preferred not to co-operate with the inquest throughout, as his lawyers were convinced the inquest had been designed solely to incriminate him. Given this view, one can only presume that the finding did not come as a shock.

Among Jaidyn's extended family there was quiet resignation and almost a sense of relief that now, finally, it should end and hopefully they could be left alone to get on with their lives. No more court cases, no more stories in the media to keep it all dribbling on. Jaidyn was gone, the killer had not been punished, one man was accused of dumping his body, and the courts had finished with the matter.

It had taken nearly 10 years from the moment Jaidyn disappeared for the court system to resolve itself. It took just months short of a decade for the justice system to consider what happened that day, to investigate and prosecute the accused, then manage the fallout and navigate the various inquests before concluding to the best of its ability what had happened. Had he lived, Jaidyn would have been at secondary school by this time.

For a decade the events of that chill Sunday morning in a cold forgotten corner of what had been, until then, just another regular Latrobe Valley town had captivated a nation. People across the breadth of the country had come to know Moe and something of the weird story of the baby, the pig's head and the internecine family relationships and been compelled by every juicy, shocking development. The interest was part genuine murder mystery, part understandable shock and outrage at a child's disappearance and part patronising Jerry Springer-like voyeurism at an unconventional social group.

Having followed the story for such a long period, many people had established – as with the Azaria Chamberlain case – a fixed view of the guilt, either criminally or morally, of those involved. The general coronial conclusion that Greg Domaszewicz had likely been involved in Jaidyn's death in some manner did not surprise many. The talk of the tea room was how and why someone would dispose of a body if they hadn't been involved in the murder. It was another minor oddity in a most unusual case. After 10 years there was a wary acceptance that no-one would ever be properly held to account for the toddler's death and that legally the system could not be satisfied sufficiently to declare who had killed the boy. It seemed most people had a fair idea of who probably did it, but the justice system rightly needs more than that. This was at once disheartening and reassuring.

For Bilynda the intervening years had provided time for introspection and contemplation not only of the facts, but of her own erratic behaviour. Naturally, there was regret. She mourned still for her son, but also for her own lost life. She

Chapter Thirty-eight

regretted not only his death but her lamentable behaviour in the aftermath of his disappearance. Barely more than a teenager she was ill-equipped to cope with the emotional trauma of what occurred. But that did not absolve her of responsibility for the appalling choices she made. In the years since, the move from Moe and a late-developing maturity had drawn her to make difficult, embarrassing admissions about her own behaviour.

Late one evening at the end of the inquest she wrote a long and searching email to Rowland Legg – the detective who had led the investigation into Jaidyn's disappearance and death – to perhaps help purge herself of her own guilt. There was deep resignation in her thoughts – the Coroner's finding would only be a formality for her now. Bilynda knew the case had reached an end and no result could really satisfy her. Bilynda and Rowland Legg agreed to allow us to publish that exchange:

Dear Mr Legg,
I would like to take this opportunity to apologise for everything back in 1997 and although this letter may mean nothing to you I would like you to at least hear me out.

In court, when Kenny gave his evidence I cannot explain why or what he said but whatever it was made me realise that you were right about Greg the whole time.

I have had a lot of time to think these past few years and I realised today that I don't think I wanted you to be right. It was so hard trying to understand why one minute I had a little boy and then he was gone. I had all of you homicide team telling me Greg killed him and the truth was I didn't want to believe he was dead. Even after his body was found I didn't believe you were telling me the truth.

I know this sounds ridiculous but the only thing that kept me going back then was Greg and his letters and his phone calls because he was the only one who spoke of Jaidyn in terms of being alive and not dead.

I think it would have been easier for me to blame the Penfold family for Jaidyn's death because of their hate towards Greg rather than know that the person I chose to leave my son with [was] someone who would kill him.

I want to thank you for all the hours and the effort the police force put into finding my little boy and trying to get him the justice he deserved. My fight for Justice is over now, Greg may never be imprisoned for the death of my son and I know that is what Jaidyn would have wanted but I feel Jaidyn is smiling just knowing that I know the truth.

I am sorry that I dragged it out over so many years but I do hope you understand that I felt a need to know the truth of what really happened on the night Jaidyn died and why he died . . . I guess I will never really know now but at least I know in my heart who was responsible.

Mr Legg, I didn't hate you like Robin Bowles stated in her book [*Justice Denied*], I hated what you told me when you said my son had died.
Bilynda Williams.

[email]
From: Legg, Rowland
To: Williams, Bilynda
Sent: Wednesday November 16, 2005, 7.09 p.m.

Bilynda,
I was on leave when your letter arrived. I've tried to call

Chapter Thirty-eight

you several times but as is the case tonight I've called when you were out.

I imagine it must have been difficult to write such a letter and I appreciate your going to the effort to do so. I can't say you weren't a handicap to the investigation at times but I can assure you in absolute honesty that from the beginning our interest was in finding some justice for Jaidyn and bringing the person responsible to account. It would obviously have been both easier and more rewarding with your support, but that's life. After thirty-two years in this job and fourteen in the Homicide Squad acceptance of many situations is essential for survival and there is little that shocks you.

Despite mixed feelings over the years one aspect I have not been annoyed about for one moment has been your persistence in bringing about an inquest. You were entitled to do so and I hope the ultimate result brings you some peace of mind.

I shall continue to try contacting you by telephone but didn't want more time to pass before acknowledging your letter.
Kind regards,
Rowland P LEGG
Detective Senior Sergeant
Homicide Squad/Violent Crime Investigation Division

[email]
From: Williams, Bilynda
To: Legg, Rowland
Sent: Wednesday 16 November 2005, 22.38

Dear Mr Legg,
Thank you so much for your email.

The Jaidyn Leskie Murder

I cannot begin to tell you how much it meant to me, and you are right, it was a very difficult letter to write, but I know I hurt and frustrated a lot of people and wanted to apologise for the way I did treat people and for the way I acted.

I know I was a handful in 1997, I look back now and I am so sorry not only to the police and the Homicide Squad but to a lot of people that I hurt by believing in Greg and giving up on everything, sadly even my own daughter, because of that belief. My biggest hurt is that you were all telling me Jaidyn was dead and there was no proof, to this day I still haven't received a death certificate. I don't know if one exists.

I fought you all and I wouldn't listen because I didn't want to believe you, I had it in my head that Jaidyn would come home and prove you all wrong.

One thing my mother told me from the start was "the police are usually right, Bilynda, it's not very often they get it wrong".

Even now all these years later it is still extremely hard even trying to come to terms with the fact that he will never come home.

I still hope with my heart that he may walk through the door some day, but I know in my head that he won't. Nobody would let me see him and hold him and that's what upset me the most. Nobody can even tell me what date his death occurred.

I never did get to say goodbye and in a way I still haven't.

Thank you so much, Mr Legg, for what you said about not being annoyed over my persistence in bringing about an inquest. That means a lot as I know many people are angry at me for doing so (especially the Domaszewicz legal team) but I truly believe that I did

Chapter Thirty-eight

the right thing by re-opening the case over and over again because I did this not only for an answer for myself but truthfully I did this for Jaidyn.

His life was taken and I felt that he was forgotten in it all and right through even with all the abuse I copped outside the court rooms, all the nasty letters I received, and all the threatening phone calls to our home, believe me, Mr Legg, there was many a time I wanted to give up and then I would see a picture of Jaidyn and keep going because I knew I couldn't give him anything else.

The biggest issue with Greg was that you all said you had evidence against him but I wasn't shown it, I felt that you all wanted me to believe you but you wouldn't show me anything. I asked and asked and asked to see the police videos from his interviews but was told I would have to get them from him, he kept promising that he didn't have them and that he didn't get a copy. I didn't get a copy of my cassette tape-recorded interview so I gathered he was telling the truth.

I managed to get my hands on a copy of the interview a while back and I can tell you, Mr Legg, if you had shown me that then I would have told you he was lying about a lot of things.

Everything he said to me was backed up by his friends and the media. I felt a lot of anger at the time and in a way I still do because I felt as though the police were not believing anything I said even when I explained what I had given Jaidyn that day. I felt as though I wasn't believed especially when I was asked about Jaidyn's bottle, I just knew it had a mermaid on it. I knew those things but every time I described something I was asked, "Are you 100 per cent positive? Because if you lie you will never find Jaidyn."

In a way I guess I even rebelled against you all because I felt instead of asking the Penfold family questions you were searching a rubbish tip.

I had no reason to lie. I would not have lied for anyone, not even my own family. He was my son.

I can also understand that you were not showing me things in fear I would tell Greg and his legal team and I admit that most times I did, but we can't go back now because if we could I would make sure he would never have walked from that courtroom.

I see now that the truth was in front of me all along, I just didn't want to believe that someone I trusted with my child's life went and took that life and dumped him like he was nothing.

I made a mistake with Jaidyn, I look back now and this is something I have never told anyone but as much as I thought Greg was good to Jaidyn (and from what I saw he was, he really was, I was unaware what was going on when my back was turned) but that day, the day I kissed Jaidyn goodbye I saw it in his eyes and I felt that Jaidyn didn't want to go, I know it sounds silly but my little boy did not want to go with Greg and I have lived with that all these years and just with that thought alone I still struggle to understand why I still believed in his innocence but I did and I cannot change that.

Greg was *the only one* telling me Jaidyn was alive. Greg was *the only one* who promised to find Jaidyn's killer when Jaidyn was found and to be honest, Mr Legg, even though I had half of Australia wanting to support me including my own family and friends *the only one* I believed in was Greg and all that he was telling me.

Even up until Kenny Penfold gave his evidence I still believed that Greg was right in saying that the Penfolds had killed my son.

Chapter Thirty-eight

Everyone thinks it is because I had a lot of people in my head, and thinking back now, I know I did listen to a lot of garbage and I know now that Greg lied to me over and over and over but at the end of the day it was me who made the decisions and it was me who believed in every word that he, Greg, said to me and it is me who should apologise for my actions and when I am wrong I say I am wrong.

I have written Greg many angry letters over the years and I know that I have gone through believing him one week and then not believing him the next and if that was frustrating for all of you then I hope you could understand how frustrating it has been for me.

My biggest fear would be knowing that my son's lifeless body was in the boot of the car when he picked me up from the hotel because that would just kill me.

I don't even remember much about Jaidyn any more because all the good memories have been faded by the bad.

To be honest, Mr Legg, no matter what the Coroner says now, I know it was Greg Domaszewicz who took my Jaidyn away from me, not only in heart now but in my head and the saddest part of all is that after all the years I have fought for the answers Greg basically told me himself on the phone anyway.

In a way I guess it is a little easier to talk about it now, but knowing that my son was murdered and dumped in a dam and I never got to see him again I don't think will ever be easy and I know it is something I will never get over, but I feel I can move on from it now, I feel Jaidyn was the only victim in all of this and it just kills me to know that when whatever Greg did to hurt him he was probably wanting his mummy and I wasn't there.

The Jaidyn Leskie Murder

On the subject of Justice ... well, everyone is telling me to push for the double jeopardy law now and as much as I want that mongrel to live the rest of his life in prison with nothing but a visit from his mother on weekends I believe in a way he is in a prison of his own as it is only him who has to live with the thought of whatever it was he did to my Jaidyn and just those thoughts alone I'm sure would get to anyone in the end. I can only hope ...

Thank you, Mr Legg, for everything,
Bilynda Williams.

About the Author

Michael Gleeson has been a senior sports writer with *The Age* newspaper in Melbourne since 2005. Having covered crime for years with the *Herald Sun* he moved across to the safer sanctuary of sports, where a bad day involves a player's knee injury, not the death of a small child. He has also written three AFL diaries of a season. He is married to Michelle and they have two boys – Joseph and Rafferty.

www.ingramcontent.com/pod-product-compliance
Lightning Source LLC
Chambersburg PA
CBHW022032290426
44109CB00014B/835